The Myth of Superwoman
Women's Bestsellers in France and the United States

Resa L. Dudovitz

Routledge

London and New York

First published 1990
by Routledge
11 New Fetter Lane, London EC4P 4EE

Simultaneously published in the USA and Canada
by Routledge
a division of Routledge, Chapman and Hall, Inc.
29 West 35th Street, New York, NY 10001

Typeset in 10/12 Times by Columns of Reading
Printed in Great Britain by Richard Clay Ltd, Bungay, Suffolk

British Library Cataloguing in Publication Data
Dudovitz, Resa L.
The myth of superwoman: women's bestsellers in France and the United
States.
1. Fiction in English. American women writers. Bestsellers, 1800–1988.
Critical Studies
2. Fiction in French. Women writers. Bestsellers, 1800–1988. Critical
studies
I. Title
813'.009'9287

ISBN 0–415–03186–9
ISBN 0–415–03187–7 pbk

Library of Congress Cataloging in Publication Data
Dudovitz, Resa L.
The myth of superwoman: women's bestsellers in France and the United
States/Resa L. Dudovitz.
p.   cm. Bibliography: p.   .Includes index.
1. Best sellers – France – History. 2. Best sellers – United States –
History. 3. Women – France – Books and reading – History. 4. Women
– United States – Books and reading – History. 5. Popular literature –
History and criticism. 6. American fiction – History and criticism.
7. French fiction – History and criticism. 8. Fiction – Publishing –
History. 9. Women in literature. 10. Myth in literature.
I. Title. Z1033.B3D83 1990 028'.9'088042 – dc20   89–10158

Contents

Contents

Acknowledgements

This book is the result of the participation and help of many people. I am greatly indebted to Janet Smarr of the University of Illinois who provided invaluable critical advice throughout the writing of this book. Her position as an outsider in the field of popular culture frequently forced me to reconsider and refine many of my ideas. A special acknowledgement to Simone Chambon, and Claire Bruyère from the University of Paris VII. Their critical reading of the manuscript in its earlier stages, and our many conversations about bestsellers provided me with many insights. I would also like to thank Janice Price of Routledge for all her encouragement throughout the somewhat arduous process of rewriting and Susan Tapponier for her help in unscrambling some of my awkward prose.

A number of people gave me their time, and I would like to thank Sylvie Messinger of Messinger Publishers, Jean Rosenthal of Stock Publishers, Régine Deforges, Françoise Xenakis, Herbert Lottman, and Elaine Benisti for the interviews and astute comments on French culture they accorded me. I would also like to thank the librarians at the American Library in Paris for their time and help throughout the researching of this book.

I wish to express my very special appreciation to Jane Mohraz and Belden Fields for their moral support and long friendship, and to Cheris Kramerae for having encouraged me to take popular women's novels seriously.

Finally, I must assume all responsibility for the translations from the French unless otherwise noted.

R. Dudovitz
Paris, France

Introduction

Women read fiction. Women need fiction. Men do too but only
the discerning. They read good novels. Women, even those
with brains like razors, never lose that longing for the Big One,
the big emotional high.

Rachel Billington, *Guardian* (1981)

Contemporary women's bestselling fiction has either been
ignored or attacked by both the traditional literary establishment
and women scholars. Despite growing interest in the subject, a
certain amount of hostility still exists among some feminist critics
who attack the novels as ideologically incorrect and supportive of
traditional patriarchal values. Attitudes towards women's popular
fiction have changed from the sort of outright condemnation
voiced by Germaine Greer in *The Female Eunuch* (1971) where
she attacked romance fiction as sanctioning "drudgery, physical
incompetence and prostitution" (188) to a genuine interest in
what kinds of fiction women read and the reasons why they read
the fiction they do.[1] Too many of the existing book-length
studies, however, tend to see Harlequins or romance fiction as
representative of the wide range of women's popular fiction, or
only examine fiction published within the writer's own national
boundaries and overlook the interlapping network of authors
who write for an international audience. Serious consideration of
bestselling women's fiction which falls outside the area of formula
fiction is still quite minimal despite the fact that women's fiction
in all its many forms, in addition to being a multi-million dollar
international business, reaches an enormous number of women
throughout the western world and constitutes a significant portion
of their reading material.

1

This book is therefore a cross-cultural study of the phenomenon of women's bestsellers. The publishing world has long since expanded from the cottage industry which was characteristic until the 1970s, when multi-national financial groups began investing heavily in publishing. Today, popular fiction critics can no longer confine their considerations of publishing trends to only one country. Nor, with the advent of simultaneous releases in different languages is it completely accurate to isolate a bestseller to one country. Judith Krantz's novels are "international bestsellers" because they are published in the United States, England, France, Germany, and Italy. The mini-series of her novels are televised throughout Europe as are those of Colleen McCullough, Shirley Conran, or Barbara Taylor Bradford. Furthermore, next to the American group Simon and Schuster, the German group Bertelsmann and the French group Hachette are the largest publishing concerns worldwide. Critics must extend their cultural analysis of mass-produced culture beyond strict national boundaries if for no other reason than the phenomenal expansion of publishing groups into the international market.

Given, in addition, the mutual fascination readers have for each other's culture, a cross-cultural analysis of the bestseller, and women's fiction, is imperative. Paris, London, and New York provide the setting for an overwhelming number of novels. For the average American or British reader, Paris is synonymous with the ultimate in avant garde, chic, elegance, and dreams. Paris, more than any other European city, represents escape and romance, just as London is the city of an aristocracy which so fascinates Americans bred on democracy. From the other side of the Atlantic, the United States beckons to many French women as the land where so much more is permissible. New York represents the New World where all is possible: ambition, success, advancement.

Popular women's fiction has come under attack for a number of reasons. For one, popular culture specialists raise the issue of the passive consumption by women of mass-culture products which present women with negative role models. Most leisure-time activities are, in fact, passive, and few critics fault male readers with passivity when they read detective novels or westerns. The choice to read a book or to turn on the television implies a certain complicity on the part of the participant, and the ever increasing number of bestsellers with independent, active heroines reflects readers' demand to be presented with more positive female models. The writers and publishers involved in the romance business rightly point out that few women blindly buy by imprint. Rather, they choose their books according to the author and thereby avoid those known to include violence or rape in their novels. Vivian Lee Jennings, editor of *Boy Meets Girl*, a romance newsletter, in a 1983 article pointed out that 1983 would be a good year "for the consumer, due to the wide selection, but it may be a difficult year for publishers because the writing and editing will have to be the best." Publishers, she goes on to say, can no longer assume readers will buy just anything:

> The romance consumer is now more sophisticated; they don't want the same old plots and devices – they want books with fresh surroundings and characters. And they're buying a lot by author now. (Maryles & Symons 1983: 55)

Although Vivian Jennings may not be an authority traditional university critics know of or respect, her role as newsletter editor gives her a closeness to the average reader few critics have. Her point that women are now showing more discrimination in what they read, and that they are refusing to buy books which they find offensive or badly written refutes the view that romances are a heinous plot hoisted upon unaware women: women actively choose what they do and do not want to read. Of course, the actual choice that publishers offer women can be questioned but a good case can be made for the narrow range of books published. The success or failure of certain series and the continued "updating" of the types of books offered, however, not only proves that the readers exercise some control over their reading material, but also situates the reader in a more active role. She either accepts or rejects what booksellers offer.

Donald Lazere, in his introduction to *American Media and Mass Culture*, further criticizes popular culture critics for their failure to question the assumption that popular culture is a mirror which "reflects the values of the people, not the values the producers impose on them." (1987: 3) Lazere's assumption that the consumer passively accepts cultural products which are produced independently of his or her desires overlooks the fact that women's popular fiction in the form of the bestseller, while reflecting the values marketed by producers of popular culture, also embodies the values and beliefs of the women who create and support the market. As one of the most direct expressions of the social mythology of a particular culture, popular fiction and the changes it continuously undergoes in content and subject matter best illustrates the contradictions between the ways women are perceived by the larger society and how they perceive themselves. Moments of social upheaval and feminist activity have historically produced new variations in the fictional representation of women. Called the "new woman" by her contemporaries, variations on today's superwoman appear throughout the corpus of women's fiction. The Industrial Revolutions in the United States and in Europe, the American Civil War, the birth of the French Republic, the two world wars, and moments of changing social conditions have all contributed to the evolution of feminine heroines. In the 1920s, for example, popular women's novels countered the expectation that women should pick up their lives as they were before the radical changes wrought by the First World War. One such "new woman" is Diana Mayo, the heroine of Edith Hull's bestselling *The Sheik* (1921), or, on the other side of the Atlantic, Claude, the heroine of Raymonde Machard's *La Possession* (The Possession) (1921). Throughout Hull's text, the narrator contrasts Diana's "masculine" upbringing by her brother with conventional standards of femininity, which are found to be inadequate for the "new" woman. Diana dresses in trousers, refuses marriage, and defies social conventions. Claude is a surgeon and, like Diana, has had an unconventional upbringing as her doctor-father's "son." Both authors, however, are uneasy with their unconventional heroines and without completely disowning the "new woman," force the young women to relearn what it means to be a woman. In *The Possession*, the greater part of the narrative is devoted to resolving the conflicts which arise between Claude's professional life and her love affair. The fact that both authors stop short of suggesting radical social change, and end their novels with the satisfactory resolution of the heroines' emotional lives, is as much a rhetorical strategy the genre imposes as it is a way of ensuring the cohesion of daily life. The ways in which the text points out how the "new woman" learns to modify her previously radical behavior to conform with socially accepted norms are ultimately more important than whether or not she marries at the end of the novel.

The penetration of the women's movement to different social groups in the late 1960s and early 1970s also saw the emergence of a more active female character in American women's fiction which was translated and read in Europe. "Women-oriented fiction" by such diverse writers as Erica Jong, Marilyn French, Alix Kates Shulman, or Maxine Hong, which, according to Elizabeth Fox-Genovese, wrestled with "the problems raised by the women's movement and by the escalating tensions between the public and the private spheres" reached a large audience in the US and abroad. (1980: 221) But the "liberated woman" found in these novels was by no means the exclusive property of feminist or pseudo-feminist literature. From Jacqueline Susann's *Valley of the Dolls* (1971) and Grace Metalious's *Peyton Place* (1956), to Sue Kaufman's *Diary of a Mad Housewife* (1968) or Alix Kates Shulman's *Memoirs of a Prom Queen* (1972), traditional sexual and social norms were being called in to question. In the wake of the so-called second wave of the women's movement and the large number of women entering the professional world for the first time, a corresponding demand for fiction which foregrounded women's experience took place. Feminist or not, women's bestsellers of the 1970s and onward spoke to the pressing concerns of the moment through a reformulation of the previously dominant social mythologies of woman as wife, as mother, or as passive heterosexual lover. Today, contemporary bestsellers written for, by, and about women continue to recreate the current version of the "new" woman through altered versions of traditional cultural definitions of what it means to be a woman.

The relationship between the social status of women's fiction and the fiction as a mirror of women's position in society, however, is complicated. Since popular fiction is also an integral part of the mass communication apparatus, it maintains social cohesion by producing and reproducing the "consensus, and the collective will which ensure the harmonious functioning of society and the coexistence within it of different groups and classes". (Mattelart n.d.:7) Women's popular fiction may incite rebellion at home, but it will never cause social upheaval because of its emphasis on the personal. Few bestselling authors ever reject the outright traditional female roles because to do so would compromise their novels' appeal on the mass market. As configurations of home, personal identity, and life outside the purely domestic sphere, the novels incorporate radical changes in the economic and professional aspects of women's lives in a basically conservative form. If a novel's content should ever become too radical, the delicate balance between social consensus and discontent of a particular society's various groups is threatened. The critical and social relegation of women's fiction to the domain of "popular" minimizes disruption because neither the critics nor the readers themselves take what they read seriously. I don't intend, by any means, to make this sound like a deliberate plot perpetuated on women by either the academic or publishing world, because that is not the case. Rather, the low social status of women's fiction surfaces throughout the entire history of women's writing. The contempt most (male) critics express *vis-à-vis* popular women's fiction contributes to the devalorization of the fiction so many women read which, in effect, also devalues one of the principal "public" means women have of expressing dissatisfaction with dominant social institutions and conformist ways of behavior. Women's entry *en masse* into the novel-writing profession in the nineteenth century and their appropriation of the romance form as a particular form of women's writing has led to widespread contempt not only for women's fiction, but for romance in general. Critics uninterested in women's fiction in general, and women's popular fiction in particular, dismiss the novels as trivial because they deal with what is pejoratively dubbed "women's concerns."

Women's bestsellers, when placed within the context of the internationalization of the publishing world, more often than not propagate a world and class view incompatible with that of the reader. In a study of cultural production in Latin American countries, Michèle Mattelart points out that whereas the cultural industry

underpins and promotes a consumption-oriented life style . . . so the internationalization of cultural goods promotes the export and expansion of a particular type of economic development. When these cultural goods are internationalized,

they provide publicity for a particular type of development; they advertise it, or consolidate it, and present an attractiveness of it which arouses aspirations and wins support.
(Mattelart n.d.: 10)

The contradictions which often arise between the actual social class or race of the reader and the content of the text not only remain unresolved but even contribute to the fiction's success. Translated into a variety of languages and exported all over the world,[2] American and British bestsellers succeed in a plurality of cultural contexts precisely because of the idealization and desirability of the life style they represent. North American cultural dominance is such that many of the most popular British writers either create American heroines or send their women characters to the United States. Furthermore, the image of the modern American woman who single-handedly manages family life and achieves professional success not only does not shock the average reader but complements the Americanization of French society which has become so pronounced since the mid-seventies. Furthermore, the unlikelihood of the majority of the readers heading their own financial empire does not negate the pseudo-realism of a novel because there is a generalized message which appeals to the imagination of most readers. The rewriting of the race for success in "humanist" terms counterbalances the acquisition of any unsightly masculine traits which might detract from the heroine's femininity as well as the realities of capitalist life. The white upwardly mobile American or British woman who fills the pages of so many of the novels rarely stops to look back during her rapid ascent of the social ladder at those who are left behind or to wonder why. The female capitalist tales of Judith Krantz or British-born Barbara Taylor Bradford exemplify bestsellers which present capitalism not only as the natural way of the world but also as the environment which best nurtures women's aspirations.

Critics also attack the novels on the grounds of their subtle racist message. While not explicitly racist, the greater part of women's bestsellers ignore any questions of race. In most English language women's bestsellers, be they feminist or not

The pervasiveness of white female as the secular icon of

7

femininity in our culture is so strong as to affect even the most well-meaning members of the sisterhood. . .

(O'Neale 1986: 141)

Outside of the novels written by black women writers, bestsellers show a virtually complete absence of black women characters who do not conform to stereotypical images. When present, black women characters are either housekeepers, nannies or mistresses. In the last few years, however, exceptions to this view of the world as exclusively white have begun to appear. British-born Madge Swindells, who was raised in South Africa, writes about racial discrimination in South Africa in her 1983 bestselling novel *Summer Harvest*. The story of Anna van Achtenberg, the daughter of Cape Town's richest landowner, the novel touches on what apartheid means when Anna decides to run as a liberal anti-apartheid candidate in local elections. It comes out however that her daughter is, in reality, the offspring of her husband's rape of a young black girl of fourteen. Anna's fight to protect her daughter and the reactions of the community when they discover Katie is part black draws attention to the destructiveness of South Africa's racial politics. And in Swindell's novel *Shadows on the Snow* (1986), the heroine's assistant is a black woman whose life and problems are an integral part of the narrative. This contrasts with so many other novels in which black women either lack a life other than in relation to the white woman or are shadowy characters. Kate Coscarelli's novel *Living Color* (1987) goes one step further in questioning the presumed preferability of being white. Two sisters discover that they were separated at birth, one going to the black father's family, the other to the white grandmother. Once reunited, Lilah, the sister who was raised as white and lives in an exclusive white Chicago suburb, must come to terms with the implications of having a black mother and being considered black by racist American society. When her husband finds out about her sister he tells her:

I'll admit I was upset for a while. God, what an insidious emotion prejudice is. It eats away one's reason. Then I remembered how beautiful and intelligent and talented you are.   (362)

Muted as the anti-racist message of the novel may be, it none the less forces the reader to consider how race is used to define people and their relationships to one another. Despite the appearance of novels like those by Swindell and Coscarelli which raise questions of race, however, the majority of the bestsellers assume a white world view.

The various considerations I've just enumerated are by no means trivial and provide enough evidence to send all closet romance readers to their nearest garbage bin to rid themselves of such sexist, racist, and classist reading material. What I would propose instead is to reformulate some of the questions we ask when analyzing women's popular fiction and to expand the boundaries of study. Feminists have only just started to grapple with the contradiction between the growth of the women's movement and the continued consumption by millions of women of what are labelled escapist romances. A questioning of the assumption that feminism precludes the reading or writing of women's popular fiction is beginning to emerge from the growing corpus of scholarly material treating the subject. Janice Radway, in her innovative work *Reading the Romance: Women, Patriarchy, and Popular Literature*, while concluding that romance reading deflects social change by

supplying vicariously certain needs that, if presented as demands in the real world, might otherwise lead to the reordering of heterosexual relationships   (Radway 1984: 217)

and that it is impossible to claim that romance fiction functions as

an active agent in the maintenance of the ideological status quo because it ultimately reconciles women to patriarchal society and reintegrates them with its institutions   (217)

refrains from attacking the novels. In *Loving with a Vengeance: Mass-produced Fantasies for Women*, Tania Modleski analyses the content of Harlequins, soap operas and gothic novels from a psychological approach, arguing that "while popular feminine texts provide outlets for women's dissatisfactions with male–female relationships, they never question the primacy of these relationships." (1984: 113) Rosalind Coward treats the subject of women's cultural production from the perspective of desire and pleasure in *Female Desire: Women's Sexuality Today*. Many women's novels, Coward writes, focus "exclusively on the sexual experience" (1984: 183) but this does not necessarily invalidate their attempts to represent the changing position of women. In France, outside of one or two articles published in *Elle* or *Marie-Claire*, there has been little work done on contemporary women's popular literature. A recent study by Michelle Coquillat, *Romans d'amour* (Love Novels) (1988), attacks women's romance fiction for propagating submissive female images. However, Coquillat not only assumes that women exclusively read formula fiction, but she puts all romance fiction written over the last eighty years in one category, thereby denying the possibility of any change in content. The few other articles which exist deal with nineteenth-century women's literature. The historical distance of the literature confers a status not yet extended in France to contemporary popular fiction.

Little work has been done in the specific area of women's bestsellers. Madonne Miner examines five bestselling twentieth-century women's novels in her 1984 study *Insatiable Appetites: Twentieth-Century American Women's Bestsellers*. The novels, she writes, share "narrative motifs and structures characteristic of . . . the gothic," and "partake of gothic structure and motifs as they depict heroines struggling with issues of separation, individuation, and identity construction." (1984: 130) The novels, Miner goes on to say, rather than changing in reaction to social developments, have basically retained the same kinds of characterization. John Sutherland, who devotes two chapters to women's bestsellers in his book *Bestsellers: Popular Fiction of the 1970s* (1981), identifies Colleen McCullough's *The Thorn Birds* (1977) and Erica Jong's *Fear of Flying* (1973) as the only two works by women in the decade's top ten sellers. In his discussion of Jong's novel he concludes that the so-called enlightened women's fiction of the 1970s, of which *Fear of Flying* is the most successful example, came to a dead end. The reason for the disappearance of such fiction, he writes, is that the aspirations of the women's movement were "too articulate, too urgent and too self-important to be contained within the limitations of mere fiction." (84) Although Sutherland speaks of the women's movement's uneasy relationship with fiction, he assumes that all of the bestsellers he refers to – Marilyn French's *The Women's Room* (1977), Lois Gould's *Such Good Friends* (1970) or, for that matter, *Fear of Flying*, can be considered as feminist fiction. The novels address the issues of sexual liberation and a changing way of life, but they rarely suggest ways in which women can radically change their lives. He also overlooks the muted feminist messages which structure more recent women's bestsellers.

I want to avoid falling into the trap a qualitative literary analysis of popular fiction can lead to because this not only tends to attack the reader but also indiscriminately lumps all the books together into one category. It is more useful to look at the way the fiction straddles social realities and the mythic world recreated in its pages. Lillian Robinson reminds us, in her fascinating article on popular women's fiction, that

> to attack the reactionary image of women and the ideology about our nature and roles that such novels present . . . is to mistake the thing on the page for the experience itself. A full feminist reading of women's books must look at women as well as at books, and try to understand how this literature actually functions in society.　　　　　　　　(Robinson 1978: 205)

How then are we to determine the role of women's popular fiction? Does it function merely as escape or as an easy form of education? Why has this kind of fiction managed to have such a grip on the feminine reading public? The accelerated production of feminine bestsellers since the mid-seventies testifies to women's desire to formulate and read about other images of themselves outside the context of either the restrictive romance formulas or the current bestsellers by men which portray women in violent or degrading situations.[3] It is clear, on one level, that the popularity of women's fiction lies in its ability to communicate the awareness and fantasies women have about themselves. The typical bestseller heroine experiences the same day-to-day problems as the reader – the rush to make dinner after a long day's work, do the shopping and laundry, and get the children to bed – but she also succeeds in controlling her life in a way few readers actually manage. One way of understanding the function of popular fiction and the role these novels play is to read them as a compendium of contemporary myths about the modern woman. The realism of the fictional world balances enough negative and positive aspects of the real world to lure the reader into accepting it as reality while it verges, in fact, on the mythical. Myth, as a system of communication, a message, or a mode of signification, according to Roland Barthes (1957) is defined not so much by the object of its message, as by its presentation. In some cases the use of myth is obviously manipulative, as in the case of the literature and images promulgated by the Nazis in Germany or by the racist apartheid government in South Africa; in others, it is what Barthes labels the natural outgrowth of existing ideological systems (237).

In fiction, myth expresses a reality which has been simplified or emptied of its complexity. The repetitive fictional recreation of the social world in book after book produces a reality which, while not absolutely ahistorical, sidesteps many of the vital contradictions inherent to the real world. The popular novel, for example, traditionally avoids the unhappy ending. One way contemporary writers have resolved this dilemma and still remain within the realm of the real, while not violating the conventions of good story-telling, has been to create superwomen characters who confront the problems which touch women's lives but who also emerge victoriously. For myth to function effectively within the text and survive within a particular cultural setting, it must call forth a reality which lies outside the textual experience (Barthes 1957: 237). These contemporary superwomen are frequently feminists, although most authors only hint at what feminism means and, in keeping with the creation of myth, rarely delve into it in any great detail. The texts and discourses of the women's movement, however, provide the extra-textual reference of the image of the independent woman. Frequently authors incorporate feminist texts directly into the novel's dialogue. Yet, because fiction must also maintain a particular social cohesion, a certain deformation and naturalization of the complexities of the discourse occurs. When the transformation from discourse to fiction takes place, "things lose the memory of their fabrication." (Barthes 1957: 230) In other words, the historical and political causes inherent in the feminist struggle fade away and the successful businesswoman who outdoes her male rival becomes, in the fictional context, a feminist because she has proved that as a woman she can succeed in a male world.

One contradiction which immediately becomes evident is the conflict between the very nature of myth-formation which resists rapid change, and the changing value system upon which myths – in this case the myths of feminine independence and superwoman

– are founded. The superwoman found in so many of the current bestselling novels shares certain important characteristics with her male counterpart, Superman, despite her very earth-bound origins. A brief digression to look at the reasons behind the continued success of the Superman myth will help explain the force behind myth-making and its impact on the public. Superman's appeal, according to Umberto Eco, comes from the ease with which the average reader can identify with his human counterpart, Clark Kent:

> through an obvious process of self-identification, any account-ant in any American city secretly feels the hope that one day, from the slough of his actual personality, there can spring forth a superman who is capable of redeeming years of mediocre existence. (Eco 1979: 108)

Kent not only embodies many of the general fears and insecurities the reader experiences but also situates Superman's actions within the realm of the possible. A mythical character's actions must remain within a world which is familiar and plausible to the reader. Once that personage steps outside the realm of the possible and assumes god-like qualities he or she loses their mythic aspect. Superman's double identity fulfills this narrative obligation and prevents the loss of the necessary reader identification.

The mythic character's successful representation also depends on the value of his or her actions. These actions must be beneficial to the larger social group without ever engendering any kind of radical change. The fact that Superman operates within the public sphere and his actions are carried out on behalf of his community makes him a "perfect example of civic consciousness, completely split from political conciousness." (Eco 1979: 123) Superman, by concentrating his energies in the pursuit of criminals who defy the common good of the community, emerges as a pedagogic example for his readers to emulate without threatening the status quo in any way. His actions translate, in ideological terms, into a statement against anyone who menaces the American way of life. Superman neither questions nor attacks the capitalist system of which he has made himself a defender. To question or to attempt to change the system would make Superman a revolutionary, a narrative element which goes contrary to the very basis of popular fiction.

Superwoman, like her male counterpart, also hides behind a double identity: during the day she successfully manages her professional life, commands the respect of her colleagues and, in general, assumes the role of a responsible adult. It is only in the evening when she enters the front door, drops her briefcase, and effortlessly picks up her apron or the baby bottle from where she had dropped it on her way out the door that morning that she must slip back into the role of the less than intelligent creature known as the housewife. The average woman reader, in the majority of cases also a mother and wife, can easily identify with the demands of family and job faced by the bestseller version of superwoman. Her conflicts, like those of superwoman, originate within the domestic sphere. In keeping with this need to create a bond with her reader, the heroine, even when she attains enormous wealth, frequently putters in the kitchen or does her own housework. She is rarely surrounded by servants, and the one or two present are usually portrayed as more friend than servant. The reader can fantasize about superwoman's access to power through the interesting job, charming lover, or well-behaved children she, in actuality, lacks. By identifying with the two roles superwoman assumes, the reader, according to Thomas Andrae, in his study of Superman, can "acknowledge the facts of power in daily life but need not confront the painful necessity of changing his or her situation to achieve that power." (Andrae 1987: 132)

Superwoman shows her readers that women can accede to positions of greater power without radically changing the larger social order. Furthermore, contrary to the messages of alarm which are becoming so current in the press, the family, once it has made the necessary accommodations to superwoman's new status in life, emerges strengthened rather than weakened. If, as frequently happens in so many of the novels, the family breaks down with the departure of the husband who is unable to contend with his wife's professional success or unwilling to change his sexist behavior and alter his traditional assumptions about so-called correct female behavior, a new family forms by the end of the novel with a more understanding and more modern male. Since the survival of her family is, in a vast majority of cases, the motivating force behind superwoman's struggle, she remains consistent with the most traditional things women have been taught. The family is a woman's uppermost consideration. The means for its survival may have changed, but not the reasons for its existence.

Family life, as presented in contemporary women's bestsellers, like the overall economic system, appears natural and immutable. The world vision presented in the text is familiar to the reader and poses a minimum of unresolved contradictions. Furthermore, the problems women face within the fictional world are resolved regardless of the complexities involved. What has changed over the course of the history of women's popular fiction is the expansion of the realm of possible resolutions which are open to the heroines. Whereas previously she was locked into a purely domestic world, today the intermingling of the private and the personal has given her new possibilities. Personal development in the form of increased assertiveness, for example, is encouraged and shown to be one way of competing within a male world.

Love, after the survival of the family, remains the other major concern treated in women's popular fiction. The differing approaches Superman and superwoman take to romance and love affairs also reveal not only the principal priorities of a man's and a woman's life but also the major differences between the two genres, i.e. action novels and women's fiction. In order to fulfill his civic obligations and to sustain narrative tension, Superman has always remained free of any permanent romantic entanglement. True to traditional male roles, he does not mix romance and "work." Superman ignores the advances of Lois Lane, who actively pursues him, and renounces his love for the mermaid Lois Lemaris because, according to Eco, her underwater habitat can only offer him "a paradisiacal exile" which he must refuse because "of his sense of duty and the indispensable nature of his mission." (1979: 115) The myth that a man's duty is to his community or country and a woman's is to her family remains intact in the romantic lives of these contrasting mythical figures. For the superwoman of bestseller fame, such a separation is impossible. By definition she must juggle the private and personal spheres of her life.

Superwoman's entry into the fictional world is not in an iconic form but rather as representative of a specific ideological discourse. Superwoman as found in the bestsellers published in the United States and Great Britain is more than just a media creation. She is intimately tied to the influences of the women's movement. In her aspirations and attempts to acquire power additional to that normally accorded to women, superwoman shares a number of characteristics with the feminists without appropriating the label. An extension of the feminist dialogue of the 1960s and early 1970s, superwoman frequently discredits those aspects of the feminist discourse which call for structural changes to society as being too radical, but she still sets herself off from more traditional and conventional women.

The jacket cover blurb of *Women's Work* by Anna Tolstoi Wallach, a 1981 bestseller, exemplifies the way in which the various and often contradictory discourses of the women's movement merge together and take on mythic overtones in the bestsellers. The struggles of women to attain job equality are collapsed into a simplified and homogenized image of the contemporary woman:

> beautiful and brilliant, a woman who embodies all the drives and desires, conflicts and confusions of talented women everywhere . . . a true heroine of the 80s . . . a novel for every woman who wonders what success costs and what success is worth, and for everyone who wonders what today's women really want.

The implication here is that despite differences of race or class, all women want to emulate this kind of success story. The bestseller heroine despite her handicap of being a woman in a male world emerges at the end as superwoman, the dominant social myth of the eighties. This creation of a new set of mythical female characters resolves the contradiction between the roles women are traditionally expected to play and which are justified in the name of femininity, and their rapidly evolving social position. The message is quite clear: the acquisition of a position of power by women in a patriarchal society becomes possible when women become superwomen. In addition to her traditional roles as wife and mother, she now proves her abilities in the public sphere as well. Lois Lane has exchanged places with Clark Kent, but the means of her transformation remain as mysterious as his. Superman defends an ideology but his extra-terrestrial origins set him apart and prevent the reader from seeing him as representative of that ideology. Such detachment, however, is representative of that ideology. Such detachment, however, is not possible for the earthly superwomen who live fully within the ideology they champion.

This book is organized in such a way as to compare both the cultural systems which produce the bestseller and the texts themselves. In Chapters One and Two, I look at the origins and growth of the bestseller system in France and the United States, the criteria used to define a bestseller, how these differ from one country to another, and how they apply to women's bestsellers. This also includes an examination of the principal strategies of production and marketing used to promote the novels, the increasingly aggressive advertising tactics and the application of marketing approaches to the sale of books, as well as the systematic introduction of new series which presume to speak to the contemporary woman's life and problems.

To understand the role and valorization of women's fiction within the overall literary system, in Chapter Three I situate the activity of writing popular fiction in its historical context and look at the evolution of women's fiction in France and the United States over the last two hundred years. It is in the nineteenth century that women first begin to expand upon the romance form as a particularly feminine form of writing. The evolution of the feminine novel in nineteenth-century France and the United States, identification of the readers and the writers, some of the major themes which were treated, the contrasting critical reception of women's fiction, and the position women's fiction occupied in the overall literary hierarchy will be touched on. I turn to the twentieth century and examine the various forms of the romance novel, and the ways it replicates the form and function of the nineteenth-century feminine novel. From this look at some of the major women writers of the period I then examine the particular case of Harlequin novels and show that rather than continuing in the tradition of the nineteenth-century feminine novel, they are the new product of an industrialization of fiction.

In Chapters Four, Five, and Six I turn to the bestseller texts and examine the political and social context in which they are written, the case of the historical bestseller, and the mythical representation of the contemporary woman as superwoman. Among the many different forms of fiction being offered to women today, I have taken as a point of departure those novels which initially attained bestseller status when issued as hardcover originals. Within this large corpus of bestsellers written by women there are a number of novels which have achieved recognition by the literary establishment as superior literature. I limit my discussion, however, to those novels which tell a woman's story in a conventionalized form. My interest in this study is in identifying and analyzing those novels which conform to bestseller conventions in terms of style and topic matter, in order to show the dynamic nature of popular fiction and the ways in which dominant social myths have undergone transformation to reflect the current situation of women. Furthermore, in view of the frequent overlapping between the various types of fiction, I refer by necessity to romance novels which are also bestsellers.

This final section poses such questions as: in what ways do women determine their social identities through the texts they read and write, and, by extension, what is the identity women gravitate towards through their particular choice of reading material? In what ways do the novels resolve the conflict of independence for the modern woman? How is marriage represented and how do the heroines resolve the conflict of family and career, as well as the tensions this produces in terms of their relationships with the males in their lives? How do the bestselling novels present this mythic figure of a woman who is able to manage her professional, family, and personal life without losing her femininity? In what ways and through what kinds of ideological messages do the novels reflect the concerns and problems articulated by feminists in the last five or ten years?

Notes

1 For further examples of articles about romance fiction see bibliographical entries for Kate Ellis, Minette Marin, Leslie Rabine, Pat Aufderheide, or Catherine Rihoit.

2 In France for example, 13 per cent of the total fiction titles published in 1982 were translations from a foreign language, with the leading language being English (the French distinguish between translations from "American" and from "English.") J. Favero (1984) "Dix ans de traduction littéraire en France," *Livres Hebdo*, 6 February, pp. 88-95.

3 It is interesting to note an increase in the number of bestsellers written by men which attempt to reproduce the same types of popular novels women are writing. And, as I will show in Chapter Four, in France, it is the men who figure quite prominently in the field.

Chapter one

Definitions of the bestseller

Any book not written for the majority – in number and intelligence – is a stupid book.

Baudelaire, *Oeuvres Complètes* (1980)

Critics, publishers, and the general public use and understand the term "bestseller" in a number of varying and often contradictory ways. Today, the label "bestseller" automatically graces the front cover of many newly released books. On the basis of such a recommendation the public is urged to purchase the "latest bestseller by X," or "the latest novel by the bestselling author. . . ." These claims, backed by authoritative-looking lists which allege to represent sales figures from thousands of bookstores and distributors appear weekly in publications all over the western world.

How is this indiscriminate use of the term "bestseller" to be interpreted? Are all these books in fact written by authors whose novels have sold enough copies to secure a place on a national list? Or has "bestseller" come to signify a particular form or genre of literature conceived with a specific audience in mind? And if this is the case, what values, given the overall limitations of the genre, lurk behind the usage of the label? What does it or doesn't it tell the reader about the novel she or he is about to purchase or read? What makes a novel a bestseller, and do these criteria change significantly from one country to another? Does the term "bestseller" signify the same thing when used in different cultural settings? Does bestseller status in one country necessarily ensure the same reception when the novel is translated and exported? Does the situation change when it comes to women's bestsellers? Are women's popular novels treated in the same manner as other bestsellers? Are the same criteria used to judge their success when the novels treat so-called "women's" topics? And, how have women's bestsellers been treated in relation to the overall literary production of a particular culture and the prevalent notions of the literary canon?

Origins of the bestseller system

Bestsellers have existed for as long as books have been printed and distributed in an organized fashion, but, as students of literature learn quite early on, they are usually relegated to that dubious category of literature which critics most pejoratively label "popular." And, as most students of literature are also taught, the commercial success of a book is frequently its strongest indictment against literary quality. Furthermore, the fine line drawn in literary studies between those works worthy of scholarly attention and inclusion in the canon and those assigned to the category of popular literature is often contingent upon the author's sex and choice of genre.[1] Proof for Fiedler's comment that "the struggle of High Art and low has, moreover, been perceived as a battle of sexes," (1982: 93) abounds in any corpus of critical work dealing with a national literature in which the number of women writers is woefully inferior to that of men writers. Nina Baym (1981: 123–124) points out that, as late as 1977 the "American canon did not include any women novelists. . .," yet the most widely read novelist in the nineteenth century was a woman, Mrs E.D.E.N. Southworth. Fiedler, in fact, representative of a critical tradition which has pervaded American literary studies, wrote not so long ago about nineteenth-century women authors as writers of the "flagrantly bad best-sellers" (1982: 93). The situation in France is no different. Béatrice Slama, critic and professor of French literature, writes that

> women, lots of women wrote in the nineteenth century. Of them all, only two show up in school books. The two "great" ones: Madame de Staël and George Sand. (Slama 1980: 213)

This neglect, Slama goes on to point out, extends to the Countess of Segur, the most frequently reprinted eighteenth-century woman writer. The virtual absence of either primary or secondary sources treating popular women writers is in keeping with the generally low position women have occupied and continue to occupy in the French literary world.

Books earn the label "bestseller" precisely because they succeed commercially within a particular culture at a given time. In some cases, they actually survive the test of time and are granted reluctant admittance into the canon. *Uncle Tom's Cabin* (1892) by Harriet Beecher Stowe is a classic case of a bestselling novel dismissed by its contemporaries because of a popularity which, according to Jane Tompkins (1985: 124), is now being re-evaluated. Yet, in spite of posthumous honor bestowed on commercially successful books, there has always been a certain discomfort on the part of the (male) literary establishment with any equation of literary worth and financial remuneration. The nineteenth-century French critic Sainte-Beuve scoffed at the proliferation of bestselling novels and claimed that Literature would be over-run by what he termed "industrial literature" (quoted in Crubellier 1985: 27). Melville expressed a total disdain of financial matters, to the extent of proclaiming, "Dollars damn me . . . all my books are botches." (quoted in Fiedler 1982: 28) Both comments epitomize the views held in intellectual circles that literary talent and commercial success were incompatible. The "true writer" wrote out of vocation and not to fill his pocket. Such attitudes, however, belie the reality of trying to earn one's livelihood by writing. They also refer, if somewhat obliquely, to that part of the writing population which did manage to gain some financial security, that is, to the growing number of women novelists who were acquiring a large public and who posed a threat to the male literary establishment which saw its works largely being ignored by the general public in favor of fiction it scorned and dismissed.

A correlation also exists between the evolution of the reading public and the way in which the term "bestseller" and the object it represents have come to occupy such a disputed place in the world of letters. A novel which sold well in the eighteenth century – and even the most successful book rarely sold more than a few thousand copies – did so within a fairly closed circle of readers, many of whom as writers also participated in deciding the prevailing criteria of literary excellence. It is only towards the end of the eighteenth century, with the emergence of a more broadly based reading public and an expanded publishing apparatus, that the distinction between popular and elite literature assumed a real importance. Throughout the eighteenth and nineteenth centuries the accelerated rate of development of capitalism and urbanization brought about a rise in the general level of literacy in the United States and Europe, as well as producing the technical means necessary to satisfy the new demand for large quantities of reading material. The progressive radicalization of the printing process and the introduction of a succession of innovations in printing techniques – the mechanical steam press, mechanical type-setting, and machine-made paper – dramatically changed the nature of the book market and the books which were available for mass consumption. The immediate success of literature written to appeal to the newly literate group, such as the penny novel in the United States or the feuilleton, a short novel published in pamphlet form in France, indicated to publishers the true extent of the market.

By the mid-nineteenth century cheaper editions and improved access to reading material through subscriptions and, in France, through reading rooms, pushed sales of a popular novel as high as 10,000 copies. Although critics continued to function as the arbiters of taste, the critical elite could no longer claim literature to be their exclusive property.

Once literacy began filtering down to the working classes, the function of reading changed dramatically. The popularly held view in the nineteenth century that books exerted a democratizing influence on the previously uneducated population accelerated the production of a new kind of reading material geared towards this emerging group of readers, namely books believed to have an educative value for the working classes or for women. During this period there was

> spectacular growth in the commercial publication of reading material – newspapers, magazines, novels – dealing with every aspect of family life and individual affection and emotion.
> (Heath 1982: 12-13)

In both France and the United States manuals instructing women on all aspects of daily life, including how to raise their children or how to keep their house, and novels thought to have an uplifting effect, proliferated. However, France's unstable political situation, in the mid part of the nineteenth century slowed down somewhat the spread of popular literature. Projects to open libraries throughout the city of Paris after the Revolution of February 1848 ended with the demise of the Republic and were not really revived until after the 1860s. The creation of public libraries at that time radically expanded not only the reading public in France but the availability of accessible reading materials.

This growth in the potential market of readers also had far-reaching consequences for the critical literary apparatus which included both authors and critics. Until that time, the cultured elite remained the principal participants in "the formation of influential literary opinion," (Escarpit 1966: 23) but as the publishing industry expanded and assumed a greater economic importance and the number of copies printed increased to the thousands, authors lost direct contact with their readers. Writers could no longer depend upon their readers for financial support through subscriptions, nor could they assume the existence of a set of shared assumptions.[2]

The introduction of copyright laws, the payment of authors' royalties, and the emergence of the publisher as an entity distinct from the printer or the bookseller further shifted emphasis away from the literary aspect of a work to its profitability. (Eribon 1984: 60-61) These changes also had an important effect on the way a writer perceived him/herself professionally. For example, in both France and the United States, copyright laws not only ensured writers a certain degree of security against pirated editions, but also guaranteed them a living. Emile Zola, in a 1880 study entitled "Money in Literature," addressed the financial problem of being a writer. Zola praised the recently implemented "innovation" in which an author received a certain percentage of book sales, but also pointed out the grim reality of trying to live on such meager earnings:

> I must also add that unless a book is very popular, it never enriches the author. Also, three or four thousand copies sold is a good sale. (quoted in Brenner 1988: 119)

Zola calculates that after one year of work an author ends up with a modest sum barely adequate to live on. The payment of royalties, however, resulted, according to Raymond Williams, "not only in a new concept of literary property but new, or at least amended social relationships of writers." (Williams 1981: 47) The writer now not only participated in the sales process of his or her writings but had a greater interest in producing a marketable product.

Despite the paucity of the royalties an author received, an assured income encouraged the transition of the activity of writing into a profession as opposed to a strictly creative activity. Most of the major male writers in the United States had professional lives separate from their writing. It was the American women writers, many of whom wrote to provide their families with a steady income, who most profited from this professionalism which took hold in the publishing industry. According to Madeline Stern, women writers in the United States benefited from a close relationship with their publishers who, in a paternal way, took them under their wing and encouraged their production. (Stern 1985) Unlike the male authors of the period the professional approach women took to their work gained them the emotional and financial support of their publishers. This meant that women writers kept to their deadlines and produced the promised number of pages. Stern has pointed out the case of Louisa May Alcott who, having heeded the advice of her publishers and met deadlines, achieved greater financial success than other of her contemporaries.

The institutionalization of book sales already begun in the nineteenth century and the promotion of the literary product on the basis of sales figures followed as the logical consequence of the commercialization of literature and its entry into the market place. Closer attention had to be paid to the potential profit of a book than to its actual literary value. Today, this is truer than ever as more and more publishing firms are either sold or incorporated into multinational conglomerates.[3] The publication of books is now as much a matter of profitability as artistry given that people outside the literary world indirectly determine what is to be published.

Until the massive take-over of the publishing world by huge financial groups, the bestseller was a fairly reliable indication of popular tastes and concerns. The examples are quite obvious: from Harriet Beecher Stowe's *Uncle Tom's Cabin* (1852) to Nevil

Shute's *On The Beach* (1957) to Solzhenitsyn's *Cancer Ward* (1970), bestsellers have been books which address major concerns of a population. Today, the massive industrialization of the book industry has turned the bestseller into a book whose success, despite disclaimers by most publishers, is manipulated and engineered in advance of its release. The pre-publication furor over the discovery of the octagenarian Helen Santmeyer's manuscript *Ladies of the Club* (1984), vaunted by the press as the result of thirty years' work, made the novel an instant bestseller even before its actual release. Everyone I know bought the book, myself included, intrigued by all the stories which had appeared in the press about it, but few people actually managed to read or finish the novel.

Bestsellerdom has traditionally indicated wide-spread public popularity, but today the label is often used before the actual proven success of a book. A first book author may be praised as a sure bestselling writer or a book will be labeled a bestseller in order for it to become a bestseller. What then is a bestseller?

Defined by bestseller lists

Above all, the bestseller is a book which appears on a list most commonly known as the bestseller list. The bestseller list represents the numbers game played by the publishing industry to create interest in a new book. The first use of the term "bestseller" was in 1895 in the United States when the *Bookman* recorded titles in order of their demand. (Sutherland 1981: 12) The oldest systematic listing of bestsellers is that of *Publishers Weekly*, which since 1911 has published a yearly report analyzing the leading sales of the preceding year. Currently *Publishers Weekly* publishes weekly listings of hardcover and paperback fiction and non-fiction books as well as short reviews of newly released books. *Publishers Weekly*, however, is primarily a trade publication. The most important mass circulation listing is that compiled by the *New York Times Book Review*, the primary national source about newly released publications. The lists, meant to impress and influence, regularly inform the reader that his or her choice is based on findings derived from:

> computer-processed sales figures from 2,000 bookstores and from representative wholesalers with more than 40,000 retail

outlets, including newsstands, variety stores, super-markets and bookstores.

The sheer weight of the number of bookstores they profess to represent endows the listings with the respected voice of authority. A book published in the United States which can claim to be a *New York Times* bestseller, or to have lasted six months on the *New York Times Book Review* list, is guaranteed attention because of the prestige the lists have acquired. With a circulation of 63,000 in addition to the 1.5 million readers of the Sunday edition, the *New York Times Book Review* reaches and has the potential of influencing large numbers of readers with its weekly bestseller lists and reviews of current novels. According to Mitchel Levitas, the recently named editor, the book reviewing policy of the *New York Times Book Review* is to review every bestseller: "Even though the *Book Review* is on the whole more literary, we believe our readers want to know about the bestsellers as well." (Reuter 1984: 18) The *New York Times Book Review* lists indicate the fifteen top-selling hardcover fiction and nonfiction books, and paperback mass-market and trade books, as well as their current position and number of weeks the book has appeared on the lists.

Bestseller lists are standard items in most American mass circulation publications and can be found in the weekly magazines like *Time* or *Newsweek*, campus newspapers, local Sunday editions, and women's magazines. When the lists are not direct reproductions of the *New York Times Book Review* lists, the books indicated frequently correspond to local or regional interests. Campus bestseller lists emphasize reading material that might appeal to students, for example, whereas those compiled for use in women's magazines represent books which appeal to the female readership.

The widespread listing of bestselling books in the European press is relatively recent, however, and does not pretend to reach such diverse groups as in the United States. In Britain, the listing of bestsellers only became current in the 1970s with their appearance in the *Sunday Times*. West Germany's *Der Spiegel*, a weekly news magazine, first published paperback lists in 1978. In France bestseller lists, a relatively recent innovation, are not as systematic as in the United States. They tend to be less exhaustive, rarely faithful to one fixed format, and are found, for the most part, in weekly magazines and not the newspapers. And in an attempt to differentiate themselves from the American bestseller mania, most of the publications which contain bestseller lists avoid the use of the English word "bestseller." *L'Express*, the weekly news magazine which was the first to publish bestseller lists in the 1970s initially produced a "Successes of the Week" rubric which was divided into Novels/Stories and Studies/Essays/Documents. Fewer books are listed than in American publications and they are not subdivided according to paperback or hardback. *L'Express* recently changed their list to a color-coded summary of the week's top twenty selling books in which novels, nonfiction essays, practical books and guides, and *bandes dessinées* (cartoon books) are intermingled in one list. *Le Point*, another weekly news magazine, publishes bestseller lists entitled "Books at the Top" which are divided more along the lines of the US lists, with categories for novels, essays, political books, and paperbacks. They also offer their readers the additional advantage of being able to obtain "complete results" on their Minitel although it is not quite clear why the reader would want more comprehensive sales results than those already listed. *Lire*, the literary magazine published by Bernard Pivot, the presenter of *Apostrophes*, a weekly literary television program, prints monthly lists of "expected and unexpected bestsellers." None of the newspapers publish lists as those in the United States do. In part this is explained by the absence of a large Sunday edition, but most of the newspapers produce a weekly literary section which treats new books and special topics. None of these literary sections, however, print bestseller lists.

In addition to a variety of formats, the French bestseller listings differ from those in the USA in that they often reflect the political leanings of the publication in which they are printed, and are based on reports from very different kinds of bookstores. *Le Nouvel Observateur*, for example, which lists only five or six novels, bases its choices on sales reports from the Paris FNAC stores[4] and stores in nine other large cities whereas *Le Point* or *L'Express*, more conservative publications, base their lists on figures from supermarket book section sales. The figures listed in the majority of bestseller lists not only fail to represent broad-based consumption, but are sometimes doctored by publishers who send specially hired employers out to designated stores to buy up their stock of "bestselling" books. Furthermore, as Brendan Murphy points out in a 1987 *Atlantic* article, interestingly enough entitled "A Nation of Readers: The best-seller list in France is a serious affair indeed," the lists are often based on bookstore owners' subjective views of which books are doing well or, as bestseller writer Françoise Xenakis told me, which books should be doing well.

Not surprisingly, given their initial reticence on the categorization of books by their commercial as opposed to literary success, European intellectuals have objected to the publication of bestseller lists since their inception, with the loudest accusations being the "commercialization of literature" and "americanization." In England, according to John Sutherland, the lists are suspected of being

> inherently spurious in their attention to quick, rather than real bestsellers. Their week-to-week attention singles out sensational books of the moment, at the expense of longer-lived titles or groups of books which might eventually have the larger, if less dramatic sales. (Sutherland 1981: 15)

Do the lists create bestsellers, or are they, as some publishers claim, true indicators of popularity? The lists do not function alone, and are only one part of the process of creation of bestsellers. The view that the public can be passively manipulated by the publishing industry can be carried only so far. It is the combined effort of advertising campaigns, bookclub promotions, and bookstore displays which draw the public's attention to a particular book. And, in the end, the public decides which book will become a bestseller. Advance bookstore sales which put a newly released book immediately on the bestseller lists can only be considered as a shove in the right direction; if the book is not picked up by the public after one or two weeks, it either reappears as a paperback or disappears from view. It must also not be forgotten that many women ignore the lists altogether and choose their reading material either through reading clubs, word of mouth, or through newsletters. One French woman with whom I spoke said she never looks at the bestseller lists, but rather buys books which are prominently displayed in a bookstore. Since the displays, however, are tied to the lists, they do have an indirect effect.

Europeans tend to associate the institutionalization of bestsellers through lists with aggressive American publishing practices. However, Pierre Nora, historian, specialist on bestsellers, and editor at the French publishing house Gallimard admitted in an interview in 1985 that although the current system of classifying books according to their selling power has been influenced by the publishing trends in the United States, "it would be an error to see it only as an American import." (Ozouf and Ferney 1985: 66) The cultural apparatus which presently supports the proliferation of mass culture existed in France substantially before the arrival of printed bestseller lists. In the nineteenth century newspaper reviews rather than systematic lists informed the public of the power of certain books to sell a large number of copies. Furthermore, the establishment of train-station book kiosks by Hachette and a widespread book peddling network favored the promotion of well-received books. It is not the lists which are considered so objectionable, but the treatment of literature as a commodity implicated in the process.

Bestseller: Numbers or readership?

Robert Escarpit, a French sociologist of literature, defines a bestseller as much by the book's sales pattern as by the number of copies sold. He distinguishes three types of success:

1) the fastseller: a book which rapidly sells a large enough number of copies to pay for itself and then drifts into oblivion;
2) the steady seller: a book which starts out slowly but sells over a long period of time;
3) the bestseller: the book which combines the two aspects. It begins as a fast seller and ends up as a steady seller. (1966: 116)

Little controversy exists over what Escarpit identifies as the steady seller, or the "functional book which meets a continuing need." (1966: 118) School textbooks, reference books, and cookbooks usually fall into this category. The bestseller pattern, contrary to the fast or steady seller, reaches an initial peak which is then followed by a leveling off of sales: when released the book makes a strong impact and then continues to sell well over an extended period of time. According to this definition, then, a bestseller is rare and represents only 2 or 3 per cent of all books sold. Escarpit's definition of a bestseller as a book which combines the elements of both a fast and a steady seller contradicts the indiscriminate ease with which publishers label a newly released book a bestseller.

Yet, despite what appears to be the mad proliferation of bestsellers, out of an average 40,000 titles published a year, at most only 100 of these actually end up as bestsellers. When faced with the rapidly escalating cost of authors' advances and royalties, publishers are less willing to take chances on unknown authors, who never have an easy time publishing for the first time. Unless their novels are either backed up by spectacular advertising campaigns or adhere to proven patterns, first-time authors have even less of a chance of being published in the United States than they do in France. It is also rare that an unknown author appears and makes an unexpected impressive showing on the lists. Helen Santmeyer or Karleen Koen, former editor of *Houston Home & Garden* magazine whose eighteenth-century romance *Through A Glass Darkly* (1986) was an "instant" bestseller, are the exception rather than the rule. Furthermore, once an author does demonstrate his or her selling power, their successive books are immediately catapulted to a place on the lists, regardless of their quality.

The internationalization of the market, the important percentage of overseas sales and translations, and the increasingly high number of book-to-cinema sales further reduce the possible number of bestsellers because publishers limit their choices to books of which they can be sure of making a profit. Since the average shelf life of a book today is rarely more than one month and, in some cases, only two weeks, a potential bestseller must demonstrate its appeal quickly or it is removed from the shelves and returned to the publisher. However, once it does become a seller, it remains in the store for an extended period. The bestseller, it is true, remains a "fast seller" but because of a vastly expanded readership resulting from modernized distribution techniques, a successful novel may figure on the lists for well over six months and then appear on the paperback lists for another lengthy period. It effectively blocks the shelf space for new novels by unknown authors.

Nora, given the unreliability of the French bestseller list sales figures, uses what boils down to readership as the primary criterion to determine a bestseller. In a move which circumvents identifying the most widely read books as bestsellers, he identifies three different types of bestsellers. First, he names popular literature which encompasses a broad range of fiction and includes such diverse series as the Harlequins, or writers like Barbara Cartland, San-Antonio, an extremely popular French detective writer, or Delly, a turn-of-the-century French romance writing team. Second, there is what he terms the "programmed bestseller," or novel which is written to be a bestseller. But, according to Nora, the true bestseller is the unexpected success:

> Transgression is the rule of the bestseller, a violation of its natural sociological space, its explosion among a public for which it was not intended. The prof at the College of France who is read by simple folks. The book written by a leftist . . . and which, through anti-intellectualism, is fought over by the right.   (Quoted in Ozouf and Ferney 1985: 67)

In other words, the "true" bestseller is that book which reaches an audience other than the one for which the writer was supposedly writing and not necessarily the book which is being read by everyone. Very few actual bestsellers exist, Nora concludes, because only a limited number of books succeed in appealing to an audience other than the one for which they were supposedly written. Nora's qualification of the bestseller as a book which has had an important impact on the public is valuable in that he insists on examining the relationship a book has to the political and social circumstances of the moment. In other words, the commercial success of a book doesn't occur independently of the historical context and the pressing issues of a particular period in time. The examples of such books are obvious. Shute's *On the Beach* (1957) corresponded to a growing fear in the 1950s of atomic holocaust, and Betty Friedan's *The Feminine Mystique* (1963) responded to women's dissatisfaction with their lives. But by limiting his definition to only those books which exceed publishers' expectations, Nora excludes women's bestsellers which he discounts as programmed fiction. Women's fiction published over the last fifteen years, however, also provides a critic with as concise a perspective of the social changes which have occurred in women's lives as any history book. Women's bestsellers, taken individually or as a group, provide insight into the political or social developments which surround women's lives.

Marguerite Duras' *L'amant* (The Lover) (1984) is one example of a novel which did exceed all expectations to the stupefication of the literary world. As its number of weeks on the bestseller list increased, articles began to appear in the press remarking on its "unanticipated" performance. The comments which the book's success elicited indicate most succinctly the ambivalence in France towards the bestseller. Jérome Lindon, Duras' editor, responded to the book's "mysterious" achievements with a parody of Cocteau's famous remark, "nothing is more mysterious than a bestseller which sells very well." (quoted in Assouline 1985: 37) Having categorized the novel as appealing to a limited readership, critics were surprised when the novel was read by a broader audience.

The "unexpected bestseller" and the kind of surprise Duras' book caused occurs to a much lesser degree in the USA for a number of reasons. First, the interest in literary stars and the supporting literary superstructure which flourishes in France exists in the United States to a much lesser degree. Here I must digress slightly to indicate the differing ways in which bestsellers are received in the two countries, since this has an important impact on determining a book's status. If the average French reader is asked what motivates him or her to purchase a particular book, the answer three out of four times will be Pivot and *Apostrophes*. A weekly televised literary discussion, *Apostrophes* regularly attracts an estimated 5 million viewers, making its host, Bernard Pivot, also editor of the literary magazine *Lire*, the current arbiter of literary tastes in France. The ninety-minute talk show aired at prime time on Friday evenings (and re-aired during the week) is incontestably one of the most popular television programs in France. Frank Prial, in a September 1985 *New York Times Book Review* article, calls it "the world's most popular book show." Its fame has also spread to the United States where, according to *Livres Hebdo*, the French trade magazine, an American university cable station has purchased the show and will broadcast it with an introduction and commentary in English.

Pivot's influence on the French publishing industry is wide-ranging. Not only are there increased sales after an author's appearance on the program, but, according to some, there are actually books written specifically to "earn" their authors a much coveted invitation to appear as Pivot's guest. The books of the four or five invited authors appear in bookstores after each airing of the program with advertising which proclaims, "this week on *Apostrophes*." Poirot-Delpech, a guest speaker at Pierre Nora's weekly seminar on the bestseller at the Ecole des Hautes Etudes in March 1985, admitted that writers will actually write what they think will appeal to Pivot, since it is less a question of a book which pleases the public than one which pleases Pivot. It is incontestable that Pivot has the power to manipulate the ascent of a book to an even greater degree than a publication such as the *New York Times Book Review* which can influence only a fraction of the public reached by television. Pivot's success stems from the personality he has created. Whereas in the early years of his program Pivot attacked and provoked his guests, producing lively and often controversial discussions, today, seated in an informal living-room type setting, he plays the role of the well-informed reader who asks the questions that presumably the audience would ask.

This kind of televised mediation of the public's literary tastes does not exist in the United States. Nor does 'literature' receive the same kind of national attention found in France. The relative decentralization of cultural activities in the United States further minimizes the effect programs such as *Apostrophes* could have on that segment of the public which reads popular literature. The only equivalents are the *Phil Donahue* show or the *Today* show, which are both morning television programs broadcast nationally. On the *Today* show current authors are interviewed in a five to seven minute segment, but, according to Hillary S. Kaye, *Today*'s assistant book co-ordinator, bestselling novelists are more likely to be interviewed on a topic pertinent to their novels than the novel itself. The same thing holds true for the *Donahue* show. Furthermore, the fact that *Today* and *Phil Donahue* are broadcast in the morning as opposed to *Apostrophes*'s evening prime-time setting indicates the broader audience which exists in

France. Morning television in the United States is assumed to have a predominantly female audience.

Duras aside, Nora's qualification that the true bestseller reaches a readership other than the one to which it was destined no longer holds true. Although it can be argued that all authors hope that their books will be read by a large audience, writers of original literature do not, for example, necessarily aspire to write the next *Gone with the Wind*. Increasingly today, a book's success is the result of a process of "bestsellerization". Pivot in France, a movie contract, or a successful television mini-series all influence a novel's climb to success. Alice Walker's *The Color Purple* underwent such a transformation. When the film version of the Pulitzer Prize-winning novel appeared on movie-screens, the novel reappeared on the mass market as a bestseller. The starring cast was interviewed on television, and the film/novel became a media event. Cinema and television tie-ins also play a major role in determining the bestseller status of a book. After the release of the movie *Out of Africa* (1985), Dinesen's novel of the same name appeared on the French lists for over four months. And each time the mini-series of *The Thorn Birds* is rebroadcast, the novel reappears on the French lists. In the United States this phenomenon of re-editions is limited to the paperback listings and a novel rarely appears a second time as a hardcover bestseller.

Bestseller: A genre?

The number of copies sold, the audience it reaches, and its impact on the public all determine a book's status as a bestseller. Given the publishing industry's manipulation of so-called "blockbuster" books, the next logical question to ask would be whether or not the bestseller has now become a genre with its own particular structure and characteristics. A literary genre, according to Seymour Chatman, is a "composite of features." (1978: 18) The label "genre" implies an identifiable pattern followed by all the writers in that particular category. The bestseller, even when the discussion is limited to women's bestsellers, defies this definition because the label covers a wide variety of different types of writing ranging from thrillers to detective novels to romances and historical novels. Even if the analysis is further limited to a study of formula, the bestseller exceeds the boundaries set on any one type of writing. Formula literature, according to Radway, relies on "a recipe that dictates the essential ingredients to be included in each version of the formula." (1984: 29) The standardization of the formula literary product not only permits the publisher to control the production of a series of books and facilitates the promotion of the product, but also reassures the reader as to what she is buying. She knows in advance exactly what type of reading experience she has purchased. Several categories of novels qualify as "programed," and although critics view the bestseller as a novel engineered from its inception to succeed it differs from such formula fiction as dime-novels, westerns, or serial romances because of its individual nature.

The bestseller, rather than reproducing a familiar formula adheres to certain conventions. John Cawelti, in his study of formula fiction, writes that although there is "no such thing as a formula for bestselling novels," (1976: 260) a certain type of novel exists which so consistently achieves bestseller status that one can speak of a bestselling formulaic type, which he calls the "social melodrama." The social melodrama formula operates not so much by a "fixed pattern of character and action," as by a literary type which passes for realistic. (261) The fictionalization of the workings of a particular social institution – a hospital, hotel, or airport – or the events of a significant historical period or political movement gives the reader the sense of sharing "deep social significance and truth." (261) Bestselling male authors such as Arthur Hailey, James Michener, or Irving Stone succeed on such a regular basis precisely because the novels, while pretending to expose pressing social issues, draw the reader into the fascinating and intricate machinery of a familiar institution.

Formulaic literature, according to Cawelti, affirms "existing interests and attitudes by presenting an imaginary world that is aligned with these interests and attitudes"; resolves "tensions and ambiguities resulting from the conflicting interests of different groups within the culture or from ambiguous attitudes towards particular values"; explores "the boundary between the permitted and the forbidden and the carefully controlled experience of the possibility of stepping across this boundary"; and assists the "process of assimilating changes to traditional imaginative constructs." (1976: 35–36)

Women's bestsellers resolve tensions resulting from the changing condition of women in a less threatening and less radical fashion than is the case in "real" life. The difficulty, however, with applying Cawelti's formulaic definition to women's bestsellers is two-fold. While women's novels frequently tackle social issues or delve into the mechanics of particular social institutions, they concentrate primarily on issues which interest a female audience. Priorities are reordered in women's bestsellers. Whereas the love-story part of the novels and the overcoming of the barriers which impede the happy resolution of a union clearly constitute a romantic formulaic structure, a less predictable value system underlies the bestsellers. Love, which women have always been told is the ultimate answer to their problem, is shown to be unreliable.

Second, the contemporary women's bestseller is rarely structured according to principles of good and evil in the same way as the current bestselling melodramas written by men. According to Cawelti, the moralistic predictability of the melodrama is derived from the reader's awareness from the start that "good must triumph, [and] the wicked must fail." (1976: 267) The communist or terrorist, commonly found figures in male adventure literature, for example, are clearly identified as the villain or the other because he or she threatens the equilibrium of the entire western world. In popular feminine literature this opposition between good and evil remains less easily identifiable because the novels reduce this struggle to the personal level of the private versus the public. Although it would be misleading to imply that the import of the bestseller's message derives entirely from the fact that the female character surmounts problems posed by the outside world, it is equally false to situate the morality of the texts within the strictly personal. Perhaps that is what poses the greatest problem when dealing with these novels. Women writers tend to place their characters in confrontational situations with the outside world which are then reduced to power struggles between women and their male opponents. Any expansion of the fictional world is thereby prevented and radical issues of change lose some of their problematic aspect.

I return to my original question. What makes a bestseller? And how does it differ from other forms of women's fiction? For one, the bestseller's insistence upon its singularity immediately sets it off from other forms of fiction. Yet, frequently, this claim to originality is misleading. Once a novel does succeed publishers look for similar types of texts which can then be promoted as, for example, the new *Gone With The Wind*. The recent quite spectacular sale of the rights to the as yet unwritten "sequel" to *Gone With The Wind*, raises further questions about the generic nature of women's bestsellers and publishers' manipulation to produce a bestseller before the actual book exists. Warner Books in the USA has paid $5 million, Belfond in Paris, $1 million, and Shinchoscha of Tokyo $1 million to the estate of Margaret Mitchell for the rights to the sequel. It is not only the financial aspect of a bestseller which is implicated. The issue of the bestseller as a book which succeeds because it touches upon topics important to the reader must also be taken into consideration. The political project of *Gone With The Wind* consisted, in part, of using the period of Reconstruction as "the great unifying and consolidating historical crisis for southern whites." (Taylor 1986: 125) Scarlett was also representative of the changing roles of women in the 1930s. The novel's ambiguous ending was in keeping with its white supremacy politics as a whole and the general racism of the period. The current wave of women's bestsellers, and the family sagas in particular, in fact take up where *Gone With The Wind* leaves off. In other words, many different sequels to *Gone With The Wind* have in effect been written without direct reference ever being made to the specific characters of Mitchell's novel.

The "remake" of a popular film which has become common-place in the cinema equally occurs in fiction. It is not at all unusual to find close renditions of proven successes; be it *Gone With The Wind* or other stories: Cathy Cash Spellman's *So Many Partings* (1984) retells the same tale of a young Irishman's rise to success as did Taylor Caldwell's bestselling 1972 novel *Kings and Captains*. The French writer Régine Deforges, upon the sugges-tion of Jean Paul Ramsay, her publisher at the time, embarked upon a remake of *Gone With the Wind*. The result, *The Blue Bicycle* (1983), followed Mitchell's novel to such an extent that Margaret Mitchell's estate instituted a copyright infringement suit against the French author which she won on the grounds that the novels are two separate and distinct works. When I asked Ms Deforges about the similarity between her novel and *Gone With The Wind*, she admitted that hers is a remake of Mitchell's but that after the first hundred pages, she left Mitchell's novel to write a completely different story. Neither Mitchell's novel nor her characters, she told me, fit with the story she wanted to tell. (Interview 8 February 1989, Paris) Deforges, like Spellman, has altered her novel to reflect the different readership: *The Blue Bicycle* takes place during the Second World War in France, whereas Spellman changes the heir apparent to the father's throne from a young man to a young woman. Deforges's book, a spectacular bestseller in France, flopped in the United States because of its too close resemblance to Mitchell's novel. To be a bestseller, even if it is a remake as was case with Spellman's novel, a novel must be sufficiently different from the original to give the reader the impression that it is unique.

The physical aspects of the bestseller play an equally important role and a bestseller is immediately recognized by its public presentation.[5] Many of them appear on the bookstand only after a carefully orchestrated publicity campaign. Sylvie Messinger of Messinger Books attributes the success in 1971 of Jacqueline Susann's *The Love Machine* (1969) to the mass postering she did in Paris of a suggestive art exhibit type poster. The novel which came out in May had already sold 25,000 copies by the time the first review appeared in July. (Interview 8 February, 1989, Paris) Formula romances never appear on any bestseller lists despite their overwhelming sales figures for the simple reason that they are not written to be singled out from the other books in the series. The category fiction publisher produces nearly identical texts in terms of content and cover presentation which the reader continues to buy because she knows exactly what kind of book she is about to read. And, unlike the larger, more diversified publishers who promote their bestsellers largely on the basis of author recognition, romance publishers publicize their books by series or trade name. Advertising campaigns for Harlequins, for example, promote the Harlequin name along with the series name. Neither author nor novel title ever appears.

Its location in the bookstore further differentiates the bestseller from serial or literary fiction. In the United States, bookstores shelve books on separate racks labeled either "romance," "fiction," or "literature." Bestsellers occupy a prominent location, usually in the front of the store, so that they are the first books the client sees upon entering. Given that most bookstores in the United States belong to a chain, the physical layout is similar throughout the country and thereby always familiar to the buyer. In France, there is a wider variety of types of bookstores, and consequently no one set layout as in the United States, although a limited number of bestsellers are prominently displayed in the window or, if there is enough space, on a table near the entrance. Depending upon the literary pretensions of the bookstore, women's fiction is either shelved according to its genre or intermingled with the other bestsellers. The location of the translations of American bestsellers depends upon the type of store; they do not have one consistent place in the store to which the reader might immediately gravitate. This difference in the placement of the books between French and American bookstores is one further indication of the lesser value given to the books and their readers in France.

The book jacket or cover design is a reader's first contact with a book and provides an essential means of identification. Formulaic romance book covers, although varying from series to series, adhere to one consistent style because the success of the formula romance depends upon its being instantly recognized as such. The romance covers, depending upon the category, range from the simple photograph of a couple favored by Harlequin to the more threatening image of a young girl in front of a dark castle on a deserted moor associated with the gothic novels. In France, the Harlequin-type romance covers follow the same pattern as in the United States with an embracing couple. The so-called modern non-series romance has also evolved an identifiable cover which differentiates it from the series books. In contrast to the embracing couple popularized by the Harlequin novels, the covers feature a highly stylized image of a woman, usually alone, provocatively dressed. She tells the reader that the novel is not "only" a love story but is also about the life of the modern woman. The absence of a man towering over her re-emphasizes that the story the reader is about to read is that of the heroine's struggle for self-identity or success.

In contrast, the bestseller jacket covers are more artistic, less suggestive sexually, and generally simpler in design. Janet

Dailey's *Silver Wings, Santiago Blue* (1984) showed a pair of silver air pilot wings floating against a background of blue sky; and Danielle Steel's novels simply feature her name and the title in bold script. Since the assumption is that the reader buys the book because of the author there is less need to emphasize the romance content. Paperback editions of bestsellers generally follow the same rules. The cover of Judith Rossner's *August* (1983), for example, in keeping with the theme of the novel, simply shows a psychiatrist's sofa.

French publishers have also begun to imitate the American publishers' use of identifying slipcovers on bestsellers. Gallimard or Grasset, both prestigious French publishers who have consistently denied favoritism of one author over another through the use of the same simple cover used for all their books, are now turning to more suggestive or romantic dust covers. Gallimard brought out William Styron's *Sophie's Choice* (1979) in France with an illustrated paper jacket and the cover of Catherine Hermay-Vieille's bestseller *L'infidèle* (1985), for example, showed a drawing of a woman's head with only her hair penned in detail, with the author's name and the title in flowing script. Under the color slipcover is the traditional Gallimard cover showing only the author's name and the book title. When I questioned Jean Rosenthal of Editions Stock about this change of approach to book covers in France, he told me that the cover gives the impression that the book can reach a wider audience and that maybe it's an easier book to read. (Interview 9 February 1989, Paris)

The French book covers are, on the whole, more artistic than those found on American publications and paintings are frequently used. The cover of Nina Moati's *Les Belles de Tunis* (The Beauties of Tunis) (1983) reproduces J.F. Lewis's painting *Life in a Harem*. Another strategy is that used by Belfond. The jacket covers of the women's books he publishes are frequently photos of nature scenes with the overall impression being quite pastoral. Barbara Wood's novel, *Domina* (1983), whose title when translated into French became "And the dawn comes after night" shows a sunset on a field and wheat stalks illuminated by the red light of the sun. One of Belfond's art designers told me that his objective in designing book covers is "to make the simple folks dream."

Besides the differences in the novels' physical presentation, bestsellerdom not only implies greater prestige for the author than is the case for writers of formula romances but also maintains the barrier between creator and consumer. The ongoing need of category fiction publishers for new titles and the fiction's strict adherence to formulaic structures encourages the entry of inexperienced writers. The romance writer, for example, profits from a certain complicity with her readers; the ranks of romance writers are filled with ex-readers who are inspired to write themselves or think they can improve on the current offerings. And, in fact, experienced writers help readers who want to try their hand at writing through romance writer conventions and a growing number of "how to write a romance" books which effectively demystify the process of writing and publication. Mary Wibberley, a Mills and Boon writer who has sold over 80 million copies of her books over the last thirteen years, assures her fans and potential fellow writers that anyone with stamina can write and publish romances. In the case of the bestseller, its position as a unique literary experience precludes its repetition by the inexperienced writer.

In further keeping with the anonymity of the formula novel's presentation, it is not uncommon for the romance writer to use several pseudonyms depending on the type of romance being written, the sex of the author, or the publisher of the series. Janet Louise Roberts, a romance writer who publishes under the names of Louisa Bronte, Rebecca Danton and Janette Radcliffe, explains that she began using pseudonyms "to avoid embarrassing her father, a missionary in a rather conservative church". (Lodge 1979: 12) Bestselling authors have no need to hide behind pseudonyms and, unlike romance writers, their photographs appear on the jacket cover. Even the demand in the last few years by the romance readership to know something about the authors has not changed the basic marketing approach to the formula romance which goes by series rather than author. Although the number of men writing in the genre who now write under their own names appears to be increasing, those who have been publishing for a period of time have done so under female pseudonyms. Tom Huff, the author of several extremely successful erotic historical romances, publishes under the name of Jennifer Wilde.

Whereas the American and British romance writers take a certain pride in their work, the French formula novel writer is frequently ashamed to admit authorship. Catherine Rihoit, a journalist for the women's magazine *Marie-Claire*, speculates that snobbism prevents French women authors from achieving the same kind of success American and British women have. The American or British writer considers her writing as

> a real profession which requires particular qualities and apparently talented French writers don't want to "lower themselves" fabricating this type of text.   (Rihoit 1983: 24)

"Jessica Rampling," one of the French authors Rihoit interviewed, makes her condemnation of the genre in which she participates quite clear:

> If you are sane you can not write that sort of book seriously! I didn't want to be too ashamed. I wanted to be able to show it to my friends. . . .   (Rihoit 1983: 31)

Catherine Plasait, director of the Harlequin series in France, writes,

> The Americans don't have this problem at all: the sentimental novel in the United States has its stars and revered writers.
> (quoted in Rosset 1986: 20)

Romance writers who move on to write bestsellers, however, pride themselves on no longer being romance writers – a category which they find to be less respectable – and are quick to point out the greater "realism" of their novels. Shirley Conran, in an interview given for the British edition of *Elle*, expressed anger at being described as someone who "cold-bloodedly" set out to write a bestseller. When asked if she considered what she wrote to be literature, she responded:

> "What do you think I'm writing?"
> "I think you're writing international bestsellers."
> "And what are those? What is literature? I write books to be read. . . . The last thing *successful* writers bother about is the contemptuous way in which their writing is described."
> (quoted in Bennett 1987: 40)

Bestselling writer June Flaum Singer, author of *The Debutantes*

(1981) and *The Movie Set* (1984), in an interview for *Publishers Weekly* is quite clear about what she writes. She claims her novels are "contemporary women's" fiction and not romance. The difference, she clarifies is that romances are

> about bodice-ripping and girls trying to protect their virtue while getting raped. That's not what life is about. Oh, I believe in romance. I believe in heroes and heroines. . . . But I write about the human condition and the real problems of women. Everyone's life is a potboiler. Fine literature is not what you say, but *how* you tell a story.   (quoted in See 1984: 84)

For Singer and the other writers, the issue is not the inclusion in their novels of romance elements, which are assumed to be an integral part of women's fiction, but the realism of the world presented. Singer's insistence that her novels touch upon the "real problems" of women typifies the bestselling author's desire to set herself off from the less respected romance genres.

Danielle Steel, author of over twenty-two bestsellers, also maintains that her novels are neither written by formula nor romances:

> I think of romance novels as kind of bodice-rippers. The publisher pushed them as that, and it worked. I like to think of them as contemporary novels.
>   (quoted in Noffsinger 1982: B15)

Whereas Steel's early novels reproduced the identical story in the style of category romances, in the last few years she has become more daring in her choice of topics and treats subjects not commonly found in the formula romances such as divorce, abortion, rape, or widowhood. Her heroines, usually intelligent and privileged women who overcome their obstacles in a gracious and elegant manner, embody the new woman found in the bestseller. Sabrina Thurston, of Steel's 1983 bestseller *Thurston House*, singlehandedly runs her father's quicksilver mine at a time when women were considered bad luck around mines, loses a fortune, and then makes a second one through a winery. But, like all of Steel's heroines, she is incredibly feminine:

She knew more than most boys about mines and horses and coaches. And yet, her femininity had remained intact, as though hundreds of years of Southern ladylike traditions were bred into her so deep that they would always be a part of her. She was female to the very tips of her toes, but in all the gentle, loving ways that her mother wasn't. (206)

Female characters in Steel's novels are acceptable role models for the reader because, although they move into male positions of power, they never completely deviate from the norm of expected female behavior. According to Elizabeth Janeway, women who depart from the traditional female roles and take on another remain comprehensible to their milieu and, in this case, the reader as long as the alternative role is not an exclusively masculine one. (1971: 122) In the case of Sabrina Thurston, it is made quite clear from early childhood that she will remain, like Steel's other female characters, unthreatening. Janeway goes on to say:

The role-breaker threatens the order of the universe not just by his own challenge to it, but by disturbing the accustomed connection with this order which is felt by other people. (125)

Steel's emphasis on the character's femininity, and the same thing holds true for other bestselling women writers, reassures the reader that the order of the universe remains unthreatened. The fact, then, that an increasing number of her novels no longer end with the marriage of the heroines is of little actual import when one questions the politics of female representation. More crucial than the question of marriage is the heroine's relationship to her own femininity and the way she is perceived by those around her. Insofar as the fictional portrait emphasizes characteristics traditionally perceived as feminine, the author undercuts any possibility of a progressive message. The heroine, forever an "other" in the eyes of the male world, fails to challenge significantly the position of women.

Despite publishers' claims not all novels written for women automatically become bestsellers, and frequently even the best advertising campaign fails to keep a novel on the lists. In addition to aggressive marketing strategies, a bestseller must also tell a good story if it is to attract and maintain a large audience. Critics, none the less, attack the novels for failing to accomplish something they have no intention of doing. Clive James, in his review of Judith Krantz's 1980 *Princess Daisy*, writes:

> To be a really lousy writer takes energy. The average novelist remains unread not because he [sic] is bad but because he is flat. On the evidence of *Princess Daisy*, Judith Krantz deserves her place on the best-seller lists. . . . As a work of art it has the same status as a long conversation between two not very bright drunks, but as best-sellers go it argues for a reassuringly robust connection between fiction and the reading public. If cheap dreams get no worse than this, there will not be much for the cultural analyst to complain about. *Princess Daisy* is a terrible book only in the sense that it is almost totally inept.
>
> (James 1980: 39)

An appropriate response to a review of this kind was sent by Helen Gurley Brown to the *New York Times Book Review* letters to the editor section. Brown writes apropos another equally negative review of a Krantz novel,

> Couldn't a review just once acknowledge the excellence of a certain kind of book because you can't put it down – well, thousands of us can't put it down, anyway – that you just read and read and read until your eyes drop out because it engages you, entertains you, satisfies you and brings so much pleasure?
>
> (Brown 1986)

Agree as I may with James' assessment of Krantz's lamentable lack of writing ability, I also find Brown's annoyance with such reviewers equally valid. All too frequently critics attack the novels for what they judge as poor writing, and overlook the objective of the novels, which is to entertain their readers and to provide them with escapist reading.

Since a novel's success depends in large part on the facility the reader has in extracting the meaning from the text, an unambiguous plot line remains one of the principal narrative strategies in these novels. The bestseller author usually has an ideal reader in mind and can anticipate potential problems of interpretation. It is not the issues which are treated in the text that distinguishes the bestseller from a literary work but, as Eco contends, the maze-like structure of the text. You cannot use the text as you want, but only as the text wants you to use it. An open text, however "open" it be, cannot afford whatever interpretation. (Eco 1979: 9)

Contrary to the openness of the literary text, as a closed text the bestseller does not involve the reader in the production of meaning. Through the force of repetition and the use of easily understood images and language, the interpretation of the text is given to the reader. Innovation in terms of a slightly different angle to a story counts for more than aesthetic considerations. Style and mastery of language therefore rarely constitute important criteria when judging the current bestsellers, and some of the most poorly written novels succeed commercially because they draw their readers into the text through the narrative. Judith Krantz is a good example. Her *Princess Daisy* is, as Clive James writes, a horribly written book. But, like so many bestsellers, the novel succeeded because it combined a story of glamour and intrigue.

Language, in both the case of bestselling fiction and mass-produced romances, rather than assuming an aesthetic function exists primarily as a vehicle to tell the story and, as a result, is reduced to a transparent simplicity. The vocabulary, the rhetorical figures and the linguistic conventions used in the bestsellers appeal in general to a more highly educated audience than do those of the romances. The romance text, while dominated by simple noun–verb sentence constructions, achieves a pseudo-literary quality through the use of subordinate clause constructions, elaborate similes and rhetorical flourishes. (Radway 1982: 408) The bestsellers tend to avoid some of the elaborate similes found in the romances although the usage of such rhetorical figures is greater in those novels which are more closely patterned after the romances.

Danielle Steel's *Family Album* (1985) and Alice Adams' *Superior Women* (1984) are examples of the wide stylistic range found in the bestsellers. Compare the description of Faye Price, the heroine of *Family Album*, with that of Megan Greene in Adams' *Superior Women*. Faye Price, actress and mother, standing on a stage in Guadalcanal in 1943,

was beautiful, striking, and so damn good at what she did. She had a voice that ranged from molten lava to melted gold, hair that shimmered like a golden sunset, green eyes like emeralds in an ivory face . . . it was the warmth that lit her from within, the brillance that exploded in her eyes. . . . She was a woman, in the best and purest meaning of the word. She was someone men wanted to cling to, women wanted to stare at, children loved to look up to. She was the stuff of which dream princesses were made. *(Family Album:* 11)

Through hyperboles, inflated similes, and easy to understand yet highly descriptive language Steel creates an imaginary world in which women are enchanting and princesses. The fact that Faye, the ideal woman, remains an object, however, is lost under the onslaught of metaphors. In Steel's world, complex emotions such as anger or unhappiness are expressed through an abundance of "rage," "fury," and "streaming tears," and the reader is always told exactly how the heroine feels and why she reacts in the way she does without really coming to understand the psychology of the character.

Megan, in contrast, is described in straightforward, everyday language, devoid of the flourishes of Steel's text:

Megan herself is medium tall and plump, heavy-breasted, with shapely legs. Brown hair and dark blue eyes, a pretty, smooth-skinned face, very serious. Her mouth is sweet and eager, her whole expression is eager, needful. *(Superior Women:* 1-2)

The almost prosaic language Adams uses is as deliberate a choice as is that of Steel. Rather than creating a fantasy world through the use of highly illusory language which propels the reader into an exotic and unfamiliar world, Adams bridges the gap between the world of her heroine and that of her readers by prompting the reader to identify with Megan. Both texts however remain highly accessible to any reader through the absence of any ambiguity of meaning or reference.

The narrative strategy is twofold: on the one hand, if the text is to speak to current issues, the novelist must create a world the reader recognizes. On the other, the escapist nature of the fiction demands a certain degree of fantasy. Simplicity of language, reliance on stereotypical and trite images, the absence of psychological subtlety, and readily identifiable characters permit the reader easy access to the imaginative world because the values these characters represent are obvious and well known to the reader. According to Jane Tompkins, the nineteenth-century sentimental novel moved its audience for exactly the same reason as the contemporary bestseller. In both cases the novel's success depended

> upon the audience's being in possession of the conceptual categories that constitute character and event. That storehouse of assumptions includes attitudes toward the family and toward social institutions; a definition of power and its relations to individual human feelings; notions of political and social equality. . . . (Tompkins 1985: 126-127)

The syntax of the bestseller, while considerably more complex than that of the average formulaic romance or sentimental novel which relies primarily on repetitive linguistic patterns, still ensures comprehension on the part of the average reader through its reference to the "storehouse of assumptions."

Whereas at one time the expression "bestseller" designated a book which stood out from all others either because of its social significance or its literary appeal, today it is used as either an advertising ploy on the part of the publisher or an inflated indication of a book's selling power, and the label has lost much of its specificity. Author recogition, manipulation by the book industry, or, as is sometimes the case, pure chance and good timing rather than impact or actual literary value determine a book's status. There is no question that a bestseller is a book which sells a sufficiently high number of copies to register for a considerable length of time on a national list such as the *New York Times Book Review* and *Publishers Weekly* in the United States and *Livres Hebdo* or *Le Nouvel Observateur* in France. But numbers are frequently misleading, however, and overly dependent upon the publications' literary policies and sources; the reporting of women's fiction, for example, differs significantly on this account in the two countries. Nor is the fiction reducible to one type or category, and I hesitate to apply the label "genre" to the entity of women's bestsellers. But it is also undeniable that bestsellers, and bestsellers written by women in particular, share narrative structures and motifs. The bestseller as we have come to know it today refers to a certain type of novel which, by its adherence to particular fictional conventions such as the appearance of realism and an overtly moralistic message, indicates that it is written for a mass audience and is promoted with the objective of achieving bestseller status. Yet, despite the inflated use of the label the bestseller still remains an indication of what people want to read and of the issues that most concern them.

Notes

Unless otherwise noted in the Bibliography all translations from the French into English are those of the author, who takes full responsibility for any errors.

1. See Nina Baym's article, "Melodramas of Beset Manhood," *American Quarterly* 33, Summer, 1981, for an interesting analysis of American critical theory and the ways in which women's fiction has systematically been excluded from the mainstream of American literary criticism

2. This contact, as will be seen in the section on the romance, has been re-established between the romance writer and reader. Today, the romance writer actively seeks the advice of her readers, and aids the reader in becoming a writer through romance newsletters and annual conventions which bring together writers and readers.

3. The number of publishers who control the paperback market, for example, continues to be reduced: in the United States, 80% of the market is controlled by eight publishers, and in France, ten publishers control 90%. According to Sutherland in 1981 the biggest publishers world-wide are American and many had been bought up by multi-national corporations: "Random House, Ballatine and Knopf are affiliates of RCA; Simon & Schuster and Pocket Books of Gulf & Western, Putnams of MCA; Holt Rinehart & Winston, Popular Library and Fawcett of CBS. Bantam, the biggest paperback publisher in the world is attached to the German multinational Bertelsmann." (1981: 22) Since the publication of Sutherland's book even further consolidation has occurred. Doubleday, Dellacorte and Dell Imprints now also belong to Bertelsmann. Macmillan Inc is a part of Maxwell Communication Corp, and Harper & Row has been absorbed into the Murdoch empire.

A similar situation exists in France, where Hachette controls a substantial number of houses in France and has recently begun buying book and magazine publishers in the United States. One obvious effect of this kind of domination and the tie-ins with other media is the re-ordering of priorities, for example the decision to publish certain kinds of books based primarily upon their potential profitability as a film.

4 FNAC stands for National Buyers Federation and was originally

created in 1953 in order to provide lower prices on stereo and photographic materials. They turned to books in 1973 and today it has significantly expanded its services, and in the area of books the group of Paris FNAC stores is considered to be the largest bookstore in France. 5 Many of the distinctions I will list pertain primarily to novels originally published in the United States; similar novels published by French women authors have not yet come to assume an importance in the overall production of bestsellers in France. Their absence in France, however, is significant in that American novels dealing with typically American subjects have now come to occupy a position in the world of popular fiction which was once filled by French authors. These novels also provide a model which some authors are trying to copy.

Chapter two

The institutional and cultural network of the bestseller system

There is nothing as sad as a bestseller which doesn't sell.

Cocteau, quoted in *Lire* (1985)

The institutional and cultural network in which women's bestsellers are situated equally affect both the types of books which are written and the place they occupy in the overall literary world. The reception, production, marketing, and distribution of a bestseller all contribute to its social status within the larger literary superstructure. Furthermore, given the international market, the bestseller no longer implicates only a single book. The Frankfurt Book Fair, since its inception after the Second World War, and in particular after its expansion toward the end of the 1960s, has become the annual meeting place of publishers from all over the world. Frankfurt is important not only as a meeting place, but as a testing ground for newly released publications. At the Frankfurt Book Fair a single editor can now sell the foreign rights to six or eight countries before the book has even come out in bookstores. Today, the Frankfurt Book Fair, the American Booksellers Association meeting, and the Salon du Livre in Paris have furthered the internationalization of the book market to such an extent that it is impossible to speak of publishing trends in one single country.

French reception of the bestseller

The commercial bestseller as it is known in the United States is a relatively recent phenomenon in France, dating only from the post Second World War industrial boom. Bestsellers have existed as long as books have been printed, but prior to the industrialization of the publishing world, traditional values ruled the French literary world; writers and academics, rather than publishers, deliberated upon the candidates worthy of critical attention. Admission to France's highest seat of learning, the Académie Française, or the winning of the Prix Goncourt, one of the country's most prestigious literary prizes named after Edmond and Jules Goncourt, held greater weight in the reading public's eye than the number of copies sold. Literary prizes in both countries have always exerted an important impact on the number of books sold because the media attention focused on a particular book generates public interest. In the United States Alice Walker's Pulitzer prize winner *The Color Purple* (1982) or Ann Tyler's novel *The Accidental Tourist* (1985), winner of the Critics Circle award for the most distinguished work of fiction, were both bestsellers. In France, however, publishers and the media promote the winners as stars. Raphaële Billetdoux, the winner of the 1985 Renadout prize for her lyrical novel *Mes nuits sont plus belles que vos jours* (1985), for example, frequently models designer clothing in the women's press. A recent advertisement showing Billetdoux wearing Georges Rech clothes equates her skill as a writer with her choice of a certain designer.

The prize system has come under attack by both the reading public and publishers, who feel slighted or underrepresented at the moment the winners are announced. Despite the criticism, though, the number of literary prizes has been steadily growing since the 1920s and before the 1965 guide of all the existing prizes in France gave way to a computer printout, it contained over a thousand pages listing the various prizes to be won. It is the major prizes, however, the Goncourt, the Femina and Renadout which receive the lion's share of the public's attention. To give an idea of their importance, Philippe Schuwer estimates that a badly written Goncourt can reach as many as 250 thousand copies, whereas a "good" one will sell over a million. (Schuwer 1987: 164) Pierre Belfond, head of the Belfond publishing house, and Robert Laffont have fought against what they call "the gang of three" and have accused the more prestigious publishers such as Gallimard, Grasset, and Seuil of controlling the jury's decisions. Laffont and Belfond criticize the fact that jury members are chosen from these three houses, in contrast to the practice in the

USA or England, where jury members change each year and writers not connected to publishing houses are chosen as members. In an attempt to counterbalance what he considers an unequal distribution of prizes Belfond has tried to initiate another prize, which would favor his own books. When I asked Jean Rosenthal about the prize system in France, he laughed and said, "Well everyone knows it's not totally honest, it's arranged within the publishing houses." When the choice of books is good, he went on to say, the system works, but when a publishing house which is in the position to influence the jury doesn't have a good book but definitely wants a prize then bad books are given prizes. If too many bad books win prizes the system will die by itself (Interview 9 February 1989, Paris). The influence of the prizes seems to be somewhat on the decline. Some readers with whom I've spoken told me that they have stopped automatically buying prize winners because so many of them are just not good books.

If October and November are consecrated to the prize winners, it is the period between June and the beginning of September which is the peak bestseller publishing months. As the vacation approaches publishers furiously compete for the summer reader's pocketbook. Since Robert Laffont published Leon Uris' *Exodus* as part of his "Bestseller" series in 1958, France has known the new trend of "hoped for bestsellers" geared to the summer holiday reader. In the USA, the *New York Times Book Review* devotes pages to the choice summer offerings. In France however, books and what people read is newsworthy information. Spates of articles on the bestseller appear in a wide variety of French publications and, more surprisingly, reports devoted to the summer literary offerings have been shown on the evening news. Journalists vie with one another to come up with witty definitions of the bestseller. *Le Monde*'s literary section "La Semaine des Livres", *Le Nouvel Observateur*, or *Lire*, as well as certain of the feminine press, *Marie-Claire*, *Marie-France*, or *Elle*, for example, yearly debate what constitutes a bestseller. Journalist Hervé Prudon of *Le Nouvel Observateur* pejoratively labels the book read during the summer vacation as a bestseller:

In France, a mild climate country, we ski in the winter and read in the summer. . . . Well chosen a single large book can

last the entire summer. OK, the bestseller has a bad reputation: it reeks of trickery, a scheme, large budget film. But . . . *Papillon* has never stolen a reader from Modiano.
(Prudon 1984: 60)

Prudon's slightly sarcastic tone is not uncommon in the discussions about the bestseller which take place in the French capital. By situating the bestseller within the context of summer reading the immediate implication is that such literature is not to be taken seriously. Rather than discrediting outright those books which succeed, critics treat them with mild condescension and place them outside the realm of serious or so-called "legitimate" literature.

The accelerated listings of bestsellers which have appeared in a wide variety of French publications since the 1970s reflect fears brought about by the financial squeeze publishers felt at the time of the oil crisis and the sudden rise in the cost of paper which made publishers even more cautious in their choice of books. This has also brought about the forcible but still problematic recognition of a previously all but ignored category of literature. Contrary to its nominal acceptance in the United States as a literary form, the bestseller in France neither properly belongs to that area which critics and literary scholars fiercely defend as "literature," nor to what they dismiss as "romans à l'eau de rose" (literally, rosewater novels), or "romans de gare" (i.e., romances available at train station kiosks and generally assumed to be escapist reading). The recent bestseller type of novel in France – many of the novels promoted as bestsellers appear only infrequently on any of the lists published by *Le Nouvel Observateur* or *Lire* – falls between the two categories.

Attitudes in France towards the growing importance of the bestseller system remain, at best, ambivalent. Forced to accept its existence because of rapidly changing economic factors and closer international financial arrangements, the French, and in particular French intellectual circles, still regard any book which becomes a bestseller with horror and fascination. Françoise Xenakis, author of thirteen non-bestsellers, told me that she was highly respected in literary circles for her earlier books. But once she decided to write in a more accessible and more popular style, Xenakis, who was Cultural Editor of the newspaper *Le Matin* for twelve years, found that the critics were ignoring her books; lots of publicity in the media but not one literary review. She pointed out that her novel *La vie exemplaire de Rita Capuchon* (1988) which sold over 200,000 copies, was virtually ignored by the critics. In the US, she told me, bestsellers are admired, but in France they are scorned. (Interview 4 February 1989, Paris) Other writers with whom I spoke echoed the same sentiments. According to Régine Deforges, in France, if a book sells more than 3,000 copies, that means it's popular, an equally despised category.

This disdain of the bestseller, curiously enough, is not only limited to French intellectual circles. François de Closets, a contemporary bestselling journalist author whose book *Toujours plus!* (Always More!) sold more than a million copies in 1982, illustrates the public's distrust of the quality of the bestseller in the following anecdote on how people around him react to his bestseller status. He recounts how, to his amazement, a local shopkeeper reprimanded him for writing a bestseller:

"This is not a reproach, but you write mainly bestsellers." Coming from the mouth of an intellectual of the VIe arrondissement this reflection would have scarcely surprised me. In this small seaside resort, it left me flabbergasted.

(de Closets 1985: 77-94)

In the eyes of the shopkeeper, and the public in general, a book which becomes a bestseller represents not so much an original work of creativity as a product whose fabrication is controlled by the application of a few well known formulas. Although de Closets denies that his books follow a particular pattern, the accusation that a significant number of bestsellers do so, and this includes non-fiction as well as fiction, is quite common. The paradox is, of course, the fact that the reading public which suspects the bestseller discredit their own reading choices.

More ill at ease with the equation of the book as product than their American counterparts, French publishers and editors take great care to defend the production of bestsellers on the grounds that they are indispensible to the financial health of their enterprises and support the house's literary selections. Olivier Orban or Robert Laffont, for example, both heads of houses which publish a substantial number of bestsellers, justify their publishing of potential bestsellers as an economical necessity, and deny the harmful effect of the over-production of such a type of literature. The obvious problem with this approach is that the books they consider to be literary, despite their disclaimers, are overlooked in favor of the "bestseller type" of novel. Olivier Orban, a relatively young publisher whose lists contain a high number of bestsellers, insists that in order for a publisher to survive financially, he must publish several bestsellers a year:

> Each year I must find two books likely to become bestsellers which sell at least 70,000 copies. Under these conditions, I can then permit myself to publish first novels or certain essays with a limited audience.   (quoted in Blanc 1984: 78)

Orban is not the only publisher to justify or explain their policy of publishing bestsellers. Alain Carrière, commercial director at Laffont, comments along the same lines,

> Don't ever forget that twenty successes permit a publishing house like ours to publish more than two hundred and fifty books per year and continue supporting the difficult collections.   (quoted in Poirot-Delpech 1985: 18)

Statements of this kind, of course, refer to the realities of the publishing world, but they also reveal the uncomfortable position the bestseller occupies within the larger literary world in France. At the same time that the bestseller is reviled, it is, according to some publishers, the only way in which a publisher can permit himself to publish so-called worthwhile texts.

Women's bestsellers suffer from the double disadvantage of being bestsellers and written by women. On the one hand, everyone connected with the publishing world recognizes the important role women readers play in the success of a book. When I questioned Bertrand Favreul, director at Laffont, on the importance of feminine fiction, he remarked that to be a publisher is to be in a feminine world (Interview April 1988, Paris). In other words, and his comments are representative of most publishers in France as well as in the United States, women readers constitute a vital part of the book market. On the other hand, the literary world devalorizes and marginalizes bestsellers written by women. In an article in the women's magazine *Marie-France* in which she discusses the current selection of books offered for summer reading, Henriette Bichonnier poses the problem of the bestseller somewhat differently from Prudon in *Le Nouvel Observateur*. How, she asks, should the books she is about to recommend be labelled?

> Bestsellers? I hardly dare to say the word because despite their enormous success and their large public, these works suffer from a strange lack of consideration in literary circles and their authors are referred to perjoratively. (Bichonnier 1985: 18-21)

The cynical attitude on the part of the established literary world contrasts with Bichonnier's attempt to reconcile traditional notions of literature with the growing demands of a female public for quality light reading. The critics, Bichonnier goes on to say, attack these novels precisely because they appeal more to the reader's imagination than to the intellect, the assumption being that bestseller status by definition encompasses only those novels which permit the reader to dream, in other words, escapist literature. But above all, she goes on to say, critics object to the authors because:

> they are ladies, their public is feminine and, to top it all, their works don't require any effort (to read at least). (21)

It is true that the novels frequently require little effort on the part of the reader, but that is also one of their primary characteristics. Furthermore, the critique against such literature is not exclusively levelled at women's books; certain French male writers of bestseller novels are also attacked on the grounds that their books demand the minimum of their readers. According to Françoise Xenakis (Interview 9 February 1989) it is the popular novel and not the sex of the author which provokes the greatest disdain from the critics. This is true only to a certain extent and despite the absence of attention from literary circles, male writers of what can be considered women's fiction do not suffer from the same sort of discrimination. Despite a scandal in 1987 as to the authorship of his books, Paul-Loup Sulitzer received the National Order of Merit. In presenting the honor, the then Minister of Culture, François Léotard, rendered homage to "the Alexandre Dumas of the twentieth century."

Production, sale, and distribution of bestsellers

Patterns of production, distribution, and sales of books naturally affect both the composition of the readership and the general attitude of readers towards the books they read. The proliferation of inexpensive paperback editions, the expansion of distribution networks and increased advertising budgets have not only increased the production of titles and books, but expanded the number of readers.

Most bestsellers in the USA and England which succeed in a hardcover edition are reissued in paperback, and in some cases a book will go from hardcover to a slightly less expensive large-format trade edition, and then finally will come out in paperback thereby expanding the circle of possible readers and increasing its visibility. The bestseller's continued success also depends upon its reissue in paperback. The paperback bestseller list in the *New York Times Book Review*, a relatively recent addition to the listing of bestsellers, also adds to the potential pool of sales by attracting attention to those novels which are issued in paperback editions without having first come out in hardcover. In addition to the hardcover bestseller, the ever growing romance market has contributed to the creation of the paperback bestseller, novels which are original paperback editions. Paperback bestsellers, although not the subject of this book, are important to any discussion of women's popular fiction, and, as will be seen, paperbacks have also significantly widened the circle of readers.

Robert de Graff, founder of Pocket Books, is credited with having brought out the first profitable paperback edition in the United States in 1939. Contrary to previous attempts at publishing softcover books, de Graff's genius was in the idea of selling books as if they were magazines, that is, at newsstands, drugstores, and cigar stores as well as at bookstores.[1] Low production costs, affordable prices, and high print runs coupled with expanded distribution networks were soon the rule in the publishing world as other publishers all rushed out to start their own paperback collections.

It took the French almost fifteen years to follow the American move towards paperback book production. The introduction of cheap editions in France, however, is not unique to the twentieth century. Between 1848 and 1859 over 60 million copies of "romans à quatre sous" or penny novels were published, and in the years 1850-55 Henri Charpentier set up an imprint publishing over 400 inexpensive volumes. But as a result of the two world wars and the resulting high cost of paper, inexpensive books were no longer the norm in post-war France. Inspired by its phenomenal success in the United States and England, Henri Filipacchi, with the authorization of Hachette, France's largest publishing group and the third largest worldwide, published his first collection of inexpensive paperbacks in 1953 under the name "Livre de Poche," which by 1961 was producing fourteen million volumes. (Alliot 1984: 17)

In addition to the obvious expansion of the number of affordable books available to the public, the paperback revolution was also said to have "democratized" reading habits. Despite the different moments of the growth of the paperback system in the two countries, defenders in both France and the United States were quick to point out this positive aspect of the emergence of the inexpensive book form. Ray Walters, in a 1960 "Paperback Talk" article in the *New York Times Book Review*, reprinted in 1982, comments on the effects the so-called "paperback revolution" has had on the lives of readers:

> The Paperback Revolution has put books on sale in some 85,000 other retail outlets. They have accustomed incalculable millions of Americans who never owned a book in their lives to acquire personal copies of what they read. (Walters 1982: 12)

French critics also frequently allude to the democratizing effect the paperback has had in France. Frédéric Ditis, former president of the paperback publishing house J'ai Lu, attributes the growth of the reading public to the introduction of the paperback book in France. It was Ditis who, when J'ai Lu first brought out their paperback collection in 1958, turned to the large supermarkets as an outlet for their paperback books:

> The paperback has made books familiar, reassuring. . . . People who because of cultural shyness won't dare cross a bookstore's doorstep have found books at a cheap price, within arm's reach in their immediate environment. Their "dignity" has been respected. (quoted in Alliot 1984: 18)

The availability of a greater number of books offered to the general reading public at lower prices and in areas often outside traditional bookstores resulted in the creation of a new public. Today, in France there are approximately 300 paperback imprints. In 1987 out of an annual production of 360,000 volumes, one out of every three books produced was a paperback and one out of four books sold was a paperback.

The paperback edition in France, however, has remained limited to reissues of books previously published books in hardback and has not attained the importance it has in the United States where a printing of 1–2 million copies of a paperback only edition is not uncommon. In France the printing of most paperbacks rarely exceeds 200,000 copies. Furthermore, outside of the series romances or the "how to" books, paperback originals or trade books do not exist. Prices for paperback books have also remained relatively stable. In the United States, however, the high costs of original paperbacks, and the even higher advance prices – in 1979 Bantam paid over three million dollars for the reprint rights to Judith Krantz's *Princess Daisy* (Walters 1985: 260) – have driven up the costs of what was once an inexpensive edition.

The publishing trend in France has been towards a production system similar to that of the United States, that is, with greater emphasis on the prepublication presentation of the book, television appearances, and accelerated advertising, and a higher number of copies initially printed. This shift in marketing strategies, Herbert Lottman told me in an interview in 1985, began during the early 1960s when French publishers discovered the extent of the mass market and the effectiveness of mass distribution techniques. French publishers, in spite of earlier reticence on their part, also began investing more money in advertising campaigns. The proposed marriage of literature and business in the form of advertising had previously provoked disdain and ridicule: "to advertise books is to place them on the same level as peas." (Julien 1979a: 68) In other words, it was unthinkable to treat food and literature, the two great French institutions, in the same manner. But the successful launching of the Harlequin series in France demonstrated the positive results that organized advertising campaigns could have. Contrary to the average advertising budget of 2 to 3 per cent of the total budget that French publishers traditionally spent on a book, Harlequin devoted 12 to 18 per cent of their budget to advertising, a strategy which has, as will be seen in my discussion of Harlequin Publications, paid off.

Bookstore versus supermarket sales

The high female readership of original hardcover and paperback bestsellers is as much linked to the high number of suburban book outlets in the United States as it is to radical changes in reading and buying patterns. Effective packaging and advertising, rather than "the actual changes in readers' beliefs or in the surrounding culture" (Radway 1984: 20) has led to a rapid growth in the production of feminine literature. It is not so much the number of bookstores which is important, but their location and management. Compared with France, the number of bookstores – and by bookstore I mean a business which primarily although not exclusively sells books – in the United States is considerably less. A 1986 University of Paris-Sorbonne study identified 2,500 stores in France whose principal activity was the sale of books. (Charat 1988: 73) As early as 1974, 75 per cent of American cities lacked bookstores, and outside the major urban areas, books were purchased in supermarkets, drugstores, or shopping centers. (Géniès 1984: 19) Since 1966, when B. Dalton opened its first store, the systematic implantation of bookstore chains has taken place in most regions of the United States. In 1985 Dalton's had 732 outlets. Waldenbooks, the nation's largest chain bookstore, opened sixty-five new stores in 1985 and now operates a total of 932 stores throughout the United States. Crown Books, a newcomer to the field, specialist in discounting bestsellers, has grown to 158 in the last ten years.

This kind of systematic opening of well stocked bookstores in suburban shopping malls has significantly improved accessibility for women who live outside large urban areas. Richard Synder, Simon & Schuster's president, emphasizes the changed nature of the bookmarket:

> The elitism of the book market doesn't exist anymore. . . . The minute you get into the suburbs, where ninety percent of the chain stores are located, you serve the customers, mainly

women, the way you would serve them in a drugstore or a
supermarket.   (quoted in Radway 1984: 37-38)

Neither the growth of suburban bookstores nor the targeting of
women customers has occurred in France. In fact, the equation of
books sales with supermarket or drugstore products has met with
fierce resistance. Rather than praise the supermarket approach to
book sales which have grown at a phenomenal rate over the last
ten years, French critics blame the diminished sale of literary
books on the disappearance of the friendly bookseller who has
been made obsolete by this kind of "chain store" approach to
bookselling. In 1966, considerably before either the chain or
supermarket book sales could influence the market, Escarpit
noted that communication between the producer and the
consumer of books was the special feature of the traditional
bookstore. (Escarpit 1966: 137) The absence of the "let me
recommend this book" voice of the bookseller has, according to
critics, contributed to a decline in the quality of books published.
Jeannette Seaver, in an article discussing the plight of French
books in the United States, points out that the absorption of the
traditional bookstore by the chain bookstores has resulted in the
neglect of the less well known author:

> So called popular literature dominates bookstore sales. Buyers
> are no longer interested in first novels, poetry collections or
> philosophy. Result: literature is faced with a real problem of
> survival.   (Seaver 1984: 56-57)

Certainly, unadvised book buyers are left at the mercy of the
displays which attract their immediate attention, but I wonder if
Seaver is not lamenting something which never existed. The
chains, it is true, promote the bestsellers over less popular
literature, but they also provide a wide selection of books and
reading material to people who might otherwise not enter a
bookstore at all or who, in spite of their desire to buy books,
have no practical access to a bookstore. Monthly publications
produced by the bookstore to promote new books or suburban
romance newsletters, written by women booksellers to inform
their clients of books they recommend or dislike, compensate in
part for the absence of the bookseller's advice. Although this is
not exactly what Seaver is looking for, it indicates women

customers' recognition of the need for someone to advise them on their book purchases.

Traditionally the French, depending in part on their educational level or their monthly consumption of books, buy books in either small literary bookstores or from their neighborhood newspaper shop along with stationery goods or tobacco. Other than the France Loisirs stores, the retail outlet for the bookclub of the same name, chain bookstores do not yet exist in France, and it is unlikely that they will in the near future. For one thing, neighborhood people remain loyal to the local bookstore where a small but varied selection can be had or ordered. Furthermore, new books cannot, according to the law of 10 August 1981, (better known as the Lang law, after Jack Lang, the Socialist Minister of Culture) be released at a discount price. In an attempt to protect the traditional bookstore, the law prohibits discounting a book until nine months after its original publication. An attempt was made to by-pass this regulation by having books printed in Belgium and then imported into France, but the courts ruled this manœuvre illegal. The law thus controls book prices and prevents the proliferation of discount bookstores such as the Crown book-chain in the United States, which discounts newly released books as well as publishing its own editions.

The "grande surface," whose equivalent in the United States would be a large self-contained shopping area such as K-Mart which offers food and other items, is one attempt on the part of French retailers to sell books under the list price. Despite such measures as the Lang law to curb the discounting of books and protect the bookstore, booksales in the FNAC and supermarkets which offer a general discount of 5 per cent are gaining. Today, the two Paris FNAC stores are the largest bookstores in France with a stock of 150,000 titles. The clientele of the FNAC stores is, on the whole, an educated one which is unintimidated by either the size or the organization of the stock. The physical layout of the store is according to subject matter or publisher and is designed for the buyer who knows what he or she is looking for. It is a far cry from the small neighborhood store where the reader can browse for something interesting. According to one employee I spoke to, the FNAC bookstores carry very few romance type novels because the romance reader is more likely to go to her neighborhood store. Although I found that this is not completely true, there is only a small choice offered and it is not immediately visible to the casual looker.

In contrast to the FNAC stores, the "grande surface" book areas are frequented by working-class people and those who are intimidated by the pseudo-sacred atmosphere of bookstores. The shopping center bookracks permit book purchases in a less threatening and often more convenient environment. Demographic factors also play an important role in favoring the working-class "grande surface" equation. In the Paris area many of the "grande surface" stores are located just outside the city limits in suburbs or near housing developments, where the average income is lower than in the center of the city. Nicole Robine, in a study of reading practices among workers, concludes that a young worker feels more at ease and is more likely to purchase a book from the shelves of a "grande surface" than from a traditional bookstore. (Robine 1982: 5-57) A 1981 Ministry of Culture survey confirms her findings: whereas 50 per cent of the working-class people questioned affirmed that they had within a twelve-month period purchased at least one non-academic book, only 10 per cent had done so in a bookstore. This comares with 93 per cent white collar workers who had purchased books, of whom 62 per cent had done so in a bookstore. (Thiesse 1984: 31)

Michel-Edouard Leclerc, founder of the Leclerc stores, one of the largest chains of "grande surface" stores in France, defended his discount approach to bookselling at a conference held in the newly refurbished book center of the Leclerc center in Tarbes, a city of 58,000 inhabitants in the southwest of France: "There are not, on the one hand, good bookstores, and on the other, bad hypermarkets. Let us not forget that we are the second largest bookstore in France after the FNAC." (quoted in Brasey 1982: 114)

Pierre Descomps, president of the French Association for the Professional Training and Perfection of Bookstore and Stationery Personnel (Asfodelp), who defends book sales in the "grande surface" on the basis of their increased accessibility, also maintains that such sales are in keeping with traditional buying habits:

Certainly, people who oppose the irruption of books in popular

areas forget that popular book distribution networks already
existed in the 19th century. . . . In spite of everything, such
books are not sold at Felix Potin's.   (Descomps 1984: 83-85)

The wide selection of books available contributes to the forming
of

the tastes of those who initially buy a book as a tool. They
improve their daily life and open it to a certain aesthetic sense
of nature, and to certain knowledge of history and the arts.
(83)

An additional value of such an approach to book selling,
Descomps further argues, is the diverse collections of good
quality often found: "The reality is that the 'grande surface'
possesses a diversified assortment and even serious literature."
(83) Descomps' arguments echo those of his nineteenth-century
counterparts who also brought their books to people who would
not dare enter bookstores. Book buying outside bookstores is not
new, although the form has changed. Nineteenth-century
publishers sent salesmen outside Paris to sell books, and a system
of book peddling became quite important by the middle of the
century. The first actual rerouting of the public from bookstores
occurred in 1853 when Louis Hachette, copying the model set by
W.H. Smith in England, opened his first bookstalls in train
stations to provide additional access outside the traditional
bookstore environment. Working-class women, according to
Anne-Marie Thiesse (1984) in her study of reading habits at the
turn of the century, rather than buying books in bookstores
preferred to purchase them at the same time as they bought their
household products from peddlers who came to them in their
own neighborhoods.

A 1982 French Institute of Self-Service study estimated that 10
per cent of the book market has been won by the "grande
surface" stores (Blanc 1982: 87-89), a figure reiterated in a study
by the National Publishing Union (Syndicat Nationale de
L'édition 1986). Poirot-Delpech confirmed this trend in remarks
he made to a seminar of Pierre Nora (1984): since 1984, one out
of every two books now sold in France is bought in a large
shopping center such as Leclerc or Carrefour. Other Ministry of
Culture studies, however, contest the view that the "grande
surface" bookstore clientele is the most important. A May 1984

survey listed only 13.5 per cent of the reading population as having purchased their reading materials at a "grande surface."

Descomps' willingness to accept book sales in the "grande surface," where they are given separate racks, does not, however, mean that he approves of the system in the United States where books are sold in a much wider variety of places. He objects to the placement of books, for example, in grocery stores. Unlike the practice in the United States, where books occupy a prominent position at the check-out counter, printed material is not for sale in French food stores, which maintain a relatively strict separation of items. In addition to the paperback racks in grocery stores, the check-out counter in American supermarkets has come to occupy a crucial place in the distribution network. Although more expensive than placement in the store's book racks, check-out space with its display of women's fiction and bestsellers is designed to appeal to the shopper not necessarily shopping for a book.

US publishers do not release sales figures distinguishing between bookstore or grocery store book sales, but the increasing number of chain bookstores opened since the early seventies attest to their popularity. (Radway 1984: 38) The high number of bookstores located in suburban shopping malls makes it clear that American women also prefer buying books in the areas they frequent on a daily basis. Unlike the situation in France, however, class differences in the United States play a less decisive role in the location where a book is procured. The wider range of books offered in the American chain bookstores and the more heterogeneous class make-up of their clients contrast with the "grande surface" clientele, which is largely working-class. The one exception in France, however, is the heavy reader who is defined as someone who reads between two to four books a month. Heavy readers will buy their books in a wide variety of places, and will go to either a "grande surface," the FNAC, or their local bookstore.

It is incontestable that the "grande surface" in France and the US chain stores encourage the sale and production of the bestseller. A new book destined to become a bestseller is the first book a buyer sees when he or she enters the store or area because it is the most prominently displayed. Someone in a hurry or confronted with shelves of similar looking books will gravitate towards the open displays.

Bookclubs

Bookclubs, another vital link of the book distribution network in the United States and Europe, also encourage and promote the bestseller system. The release and promotion of new books, a finely orchestrated operation, function simultaneously with the interests of the bookclubs. Advertisements for bookclub membership assure the reader of a constant supply of the latest and bestselling books. The books which figure in the introductory offer are frequently advertised in or actually appear on the bestseller lists of the same publication, as is often the case in the *New York Times Book Review*. Book-of-the-Month Club now runs a two-page advertisement which reads "Judge our books by these covers," and shows book covers next to front page pictures of *New York Times Book Review* reviews. At the same time, full page advertisements by publishers trumpet the book's status as a bookclub selection as an endorsement of the book's quality.

This kind of full-scale promotional campaign occurs to a lesser degree in French publications: it is rare to find an advertisement for a bookclub in women's magazines such as *Elle* or *Marie-France*, which target young professional women. But, in spite of the absence of visible publicity, bookclubs in France still command a significant part of the market and, in view of their steady growth, have come to assume a special importance since the 1970s. Originally inspired by the American Book-of-the-Month Club, the major clubs in France include France Loisirs, a joint venture of Presses de la Cité and the West German publishing house Bertelsmann; Club pour Vous–Hachette; and Grand Livre du Mois.

France Loisirs, the most important of the French clubs, claims 4 million active members and comprises 8 per cent of the total French language book market, which includes Quebec, Switzerland, and Belgium. In addition to its correspondence sales the club maintains 184 retail outlets all over France and offers its readers a monthly list of 420 active titles, of which 20 to 25 per cent are translations. (Lottman 1984: 22-40) Translations from

English make up a substantial proportion of the fiction listed in the catalogue and available for sale in the stores.

The French view of reading being only part of a person's leisure-time activities further distinguishes French bookclubs from those in the USA. Books comprise an important but not exclusive part of the benefits France Loisirs – in English "French Leisure" – offers to their members. This is also true for the other clubs. Grand Livre du Mois (the French equivalent of Book-of-the-Month), for example, offers advantageous wine sales to its members.

The reasons and conditions for the phenomenal growth of the bookclubs, however, remain basically the same in the two countries. Three major factors which have contributed to the growth of the book clubs include:

1) the ready availability of reading material without having to venture into a bookstore, an important concern when one considers that women make up 70 per cent of the clubs' membership;

2) the attractive hardcover editions produced by the bookclub at a less expensive price (France Loisirs produces their own hardcover edition of a book);

3) the discount factor, although this is of less importance since the Lang Law controls book prices. When the book does qualify for a discount, the reduction averages 10 to 20 per cent off the list price.

Critiques leveled against the bookclubs in France echo those made against supermarket booksales. Not only does the need to enter a bookstore and engage in a dialogue with the bookseller disappear, but through their monthly selections the clubs effectively control their readers' choice of books. This is particularly significant for people who depend upon the clubs for the majority of their reading material. The counterargument that bookclubs provide reading material to those readers who may not otherwise be reached has validity, however, and cannot be dismissed. A high percentage of working-class women and men depend upon bookclubs for the books they read, and it can be assumed that without the clubs their level of book consumption would be considerably less. None the less, the close relationship between the bookclub selections and the bestsellers advertised manipulates the reader's choice as well as valorizing certain literary forms over others. Furthermore, the fact that the bookclubs are owned by publishers also further reduces the number of possible publications.

Politics of translations

Any discussion of the international market of women's bestsellers must also take into account the politics of translations. In general, the flow of bestsellers has essentially been one way: from the English language countries to Europe. This trend began after the Liberation of France, when French publishers started to reprint English and American books which had been prohibited under the Nazis. And since the mid-seventies the number of translations of American publications brought out in France has increased significantly.[2] By 1982, 10 per cent of the titles published in the literature category were translations from American. (Favero 1984: 99-95) It would also appear from the wide range of novels that are now being translated from English, that American bookclub selections which are not necessarily bestsellers are being automatically translated.

French novels which fall outside the realm of classical literature are translated into English on a considerably more modest scale, and despite expensive advertising campaigns few French popular novels attain bestseller status in the United States. Of the bestselling women writers, the only two French women to achieve bestseller status in the United States are Françoise Sagan with *Bonjour Tristesse* in 1955 and *A Certain Smile* in 1956, and Simone de Beauvoir with *The Mandarins* in 1956. The *Angelique* series by the husband and wife team Serge and Anne Golan are translated but never achieve the success in English language editions that they do in France. Régine Deforges' *The Blue Bicycle* (1983) and Simone Signoret's *Adieu Volodia* (1985), both promoted as bestsellers, failed to appear on the lists despite expensive advertising campaigns and full page advertisements in the *New York Times Book Review*. The failure of the books to sell may be due in part to their French topics, but it is not only French novels that the American market resists. The bestseller list responds, on the whole, weakly to novels by writers not American or British.

English language women's bestsellers have fared well in

Europe as a whole, and in France in particular. Frequently the French translation appears simultaneously with the United States publication. Erica Jong's *Parachutes and Kisses* (1984) was one such case. Gail Godwin, Rona Jaffe, Belva Plain, Jean Auel, Janet Dailey, and Judith Krantz, to name only a few, are some of the bestselling American authors who have been translated into French and who are promoted as bestsellers. Krantz, whose books are consistent bestsellers, is a frequent guest on *Apostrophes*. Barbara Taylor Bradford's *A Woman of Substance* (1983) sold over 300,000 copies in France and Bette Bao Lord's *Spring Moon* (1981) was one of 1984's top bestselling novels. Sometimes the reverse occurs, and a novel which did only fairly well in the United States will do exceptionally well in Europe. Marion Zimmer Bradley's *The Mists of Avalon*, a short run US bestseller in 1983, appeared on the French lists in March 1986 and continued to sell well through into 1987.

The French success of English language women's fiction, however, is a change from the recent past and indicative of the present trends of French publishing. Jacqueline Susann's *The Love Machine* (1969), one of the top ten bestsellers in the United States in the 1960s, failed to sell in France at that time but did very well when it was relaunched in 1971 by Sylvie Messinger for Belfond with aggressive advertising tactics. Pierre Belfond, appearing as a guest on *Apostrophes*, on 28 July 1984, to discuss the program's theme "Summer Bestsellers," stated that he devotes a significant percentage of his list to novels written for women, which, he claims, are his most successful.

The number of American or British women authors who actually become bestsellers in France is not, however, always in keeping with the percentages of translations, and few of the American or British bestseller writers achieve recognized bestseller status in France. This probably has more to do with the reporting system, the limited number of books listed, and the elitist nature of the lists than with the actual number of readers. Views as to the success of such novels in France are divided. According to Michelle Collin, a sales representative for Belfond, one reason for the limited number of successful American translations is the nature of the French readership. In a discussion I had with her and other members of the Belfond staff at the 1988 Salon du Livre, Ms Collin reluctantly admitted that the readership of these novels is primarily women between 50 and 60 years old, and this is a very "puritanical public." Many of the novels are considered too erotic.

Why then, despite Ms Collin's comments, are so many of the English language women's bestsellers translated and apparently successful in Europe? One reason, according to Herbert Lottman, author and foreign correspondent for *Publishers Weekly*, is the nature of the book market in the United States. In an interview I had with Lottman in March 1985, he said that the heterogeneous nature of the American domestic market guarantees any author capable of entering into it world-wide appeal. Furthermore, American authors, according to Lottman, and this was affirmed in interviews I had with other people in the book business, take their readers seriously. It is not uncommon for a bestselling author to invest several years of research in a novel. The end result, like a well designed automobile, is made to sell. Eliane Benisti, a Paris-based literary agent who handles the sale of American authors in France, agrees with this view. She told me that the American and British novels written by women for a female audience do well because they are

> novels of entertainment and dream, novels which turn towards the reader. We don't have these novels. People need to dream.
>
> (Interview 18 February 1985, Paris)

Henriette Bichonnier, along similar lines, complains that French writers are no longer able to tell a good story,

> Our literature has specialized for years in works which "have something to say," give a lesson, make a judgement, transmit a vision of something. In short, everything which is intelligent, except a story. (Bichonnier 1985: 18)

Although I question her premise that women's popular novels do not have something "to say" and are purely escapist reading, I heard similar comments from other writers and publishers. During the 1988 Salon du Livre, I couldn't help but notice the important presence of the Anglo-American women writers. The most successful, according to the various publishers I questioned, are the historical and family saga novels. The most frequently chosen novels for translation combine a romantic storyline with a serious content that demonstrates some respect for the woman reader: well-researched novels which presume other role models than those traditionally found. Contrary to the romance novels translated and sold so widely in Europe, the American bestsellers present the French reader with an image of the contemporary woman which challenges the notion that the story of the life of a woman is not a fit subject for literature.

Despite the differences between the distribution systems in France and the United States, the distance which once existed between the publishing tendencies in the two countries continues to narrow with the reduction of the number of publishing houses, the increased take-overs by multi-nationals, and the growth of the bookclubs. Women's fiction, however, is still held in disdain by the literary establishment which still controls, to a certain extent, the critical apparatus and the growing readership. French women writers, unlike the American or British writers, are caught between the low social status accorded to fiction and the general dismissal of any literary product which pretends to deal with topics of concern to women. This lowly position is not a recent development, nor is it strictly connected to the generally low view of romance fiction, but rather has its roots in French literary history. In the next chapter I will look at the historical development of women's fiction in France and the United States for an understanding of the current position women writers occupy in the two countries.

Notes

1. See Ray Walters *The Paperback Revolution*, 1985 for his many observations on the history and development of the paperback industry in the United States.
2. The French attempt to distinguish between translations from North American and British authors, but there are frequently errors, and it's not uncommon to see "Translated from the American" on the title page when in fact the author is British. Often, this error comes from the original place of publication. Most of the authors I will be referring to are from the United States, and when I refer to writers of other nationalities I will specify.

Chapter three

The sentimental novel: A history of popular women writers in the United States and France

We must begin by making women purely aesthetic rather than working beings. It's the surest element of progress.

Jules Laforgue, *Mélanges posthumes* (1887)

I am a writer of romance novels, which is to say I am a pitiable creature, disdained by writers of "serious" books, ignored by reviewers and reviled by TV show hosts – especially those of the male persuasion.

Margaret Chittenden, *Publishers Weekly* (1984)

The internationalization of the publishing world and the movement of translated English language bestsellers across the ocean began significantly before the 1970s. Harriet Beecher Stowe, Miss Braddon, Maria Susanna Cummins and Mrs Henry Wood, to cite a few of the better known British and American writers, were available in French public libraries and reading rooms at the time of their publication in the nineteenth century. Emile Faguet, critic, professor of French literature and member of the French Academy, when asked about the startling appearance of so many women writers in France attributed the swelling of their ranks to the influence of the American and English writers: "English and American women writers have for a long time now set a good example for French writers." (Anon 1907: 159) The extent of the feminine reading public, the class background and number of women writers, and their relative status within the literary world are all factors which distinguish nineteenth-century France from the United States. Yet, despite important political and economic differences – the frontier mentality versus a country in the throes of rejecting a monarchy – noteworthy similarities emerge in the content of the novels being written and the impact the books had on their readers. Novels written by women, be they the sentimental novel, the novel of manners, or the domestic novel, flourished in both the United States and the industrialized cities in France. Bonnie Smith, in her study of middle-class women in northern France, writes that "the sum of women's experience found its voice in the sentimental novel. . . ." Women used the sentimental novel, Smith goes on to say, "to give an ideological expression to domestic life in its fullness." (Smith 1981: 17)

For both the French and American nineteenth-century women writers the novel became a unique form of communication with other women about crucial values in their lives. In fact, when one reads and compares the corpus of women's fiction in the two countries a set of common concerns emerge:

> Well beyond the surface simple . . . fiction written for women over the last two and a half centuries has communicated to its readers a set of common images and values relatively unaffected by the passage of time. (Weibel 1977: 6-7)

I do not want to imply, however, that the experiences of French and American women were the same, or that the corpus of nineteenth-century fiction can be reduced to one type of literature. On the contrary, the literature reflects the different cultural and political climate in France and the United States. In France, the slower rate of female literacy, the preponderance of male sentimental novelists, and most importantly the differences in attitudes towards women in a Catholic and a Protestant country not only retarded the development of feminine fiction in France but also shaped the narrative structure of many of the novels. But in spite of the different social position of women, and their varying relationships to cultural production, the function of their works remains similar: women writers in the nineteenth century as in the twentieth, be they French or American, are preoccupied with presenting their readers with new role models and the means of acquiring power within existing social structures.

The close alignment of nineteenth-century women writers in the United States with the church and local Protestant ministers also afforded American authors more respect than their French contemporaries. Attitudes towards women in France remained shaped by a history which raised Joan of Arc to sainthood. The myth of the virgin who came to the rescue of her country has indelibly stamped the position of women in French society. Identification of the salvation of a country with a virgin has not only valorized the image of the pure woman but has also caused a definite split of the feminine into the messianic virgin and the woman in love.

Contrasting approaches in the two countries towards cultural production and its participants also played a crucial role in public recognition of women writers. Michèle Sarde, in her provocative historical survey of the position of French women in French society writes that whereas American society accorded women an important place in the field of cultural production, a corresponding devalorization of cultural activity occurred; the contrary, according to Sarde, took place in France. French society, and, in particular, nineteenth-century France, "valorized culture and forbad it to their women." (Sarde 1983: 22) Nineteenth-century France is well known for the literary contributions made by male writers, some of whom, Balzac for example, originally published their works in serial form. Yet when it came to women novelists male writers and critics condemned the novel for being taken over by women; Ernest Goudeau wrote in 1889 that the novel appeared to be "in the guardianship of women." (quoted in Angenot 1984: 95) This contradiction between the so-called domination of the novel by women and their relegation to the lowest rung of the literary hierarchy reappears throughout the literary histories dealing with the period.

In the United States, contrary to the situation in France, the absence of a longstanding cultural tradition facilitated the entry of women into the field of writing. American women writers were not faced with the imbred prejudices which existed in France against taking women writers seriously. In France, the rigid distinction between high and low culture, and the historical weight of French culture in general, further prevented the active recognition of women and their talents. Nineteenth-century women writers in France who wanted to display their talents publicly did so within the privacy of their home through literary salons.

Nineteenth-century women writers in the United States and France

Bestsellerdom in nineteenth-century America was synonymous with women writers: "one-third of the books produced by American authors between 1779 and 1829 were written by women," (Papashvily 1956: 24) and twelve women novelists achieved bestseller status between 1820 and 1850. (Rosenberg 1984: 16) Women writers dominated the literary market until after the Civil War: "from 1850 until well after the Civil War (some would say until the 1920s) the novel was chiefly a form of literary communication among women." (Baym 1978: 32) Likewise, in France the nineteenth century

> witnessed the explosion of an unlimited number of women writers whose memory has been lost in literary history books or publishers' catalogues. Of them all, only a few names have been retained. (Sarde 1983: 539)

Sophie Cottin, a bestselling writer at the beginning of the nineteenth century wrote that "the novel has always been the domain of women." (quoted in Slama 1980: 225) And in 1868 Armand de Pontmartin, a journalist for the magazine *Le Correspondant*, wrote that the novel had become inseparable from the female reader: "to tear the novel from the influence of women, to conceal women from the appeal of the novel. . . . It is impossible to imagine one without the other." (quoted in Sauvy 1985: 448)

Figures on the actual number of nineteenth-century French women writers are contradictory and confusing because of the profusion of pseudonyms assumed by women. Research is further hindered by the frequent absence of reliable material. Many of the novels, originally published in inexpensive editions, were discarded because of their relative lack of worth, and the majority of the writers have simply disappeared from critical sight. An idea of the confusion faced by a student of French women writers can be had from the differing accounts of the number of active women writers. Anne Sauvy, in the only article devoted to women writers in the over one thousand page volume concerned with French publishing in the nineteenth century, lists over thirty nineteenth-century women writers. Most of the work of these women, she writes, has been completely lost. She cites the example of the writer M. Maryan: out of a corpus of ninety-four published novels, the Bibliothèque Nationale has in its possession only three of her novels. According to another writer, 17 per cent of the so-called male writers of the period were actually women (Thiesse 1984: 183), although I suspect the actual percentage was higher. I compiled a list of fifty-seven writers from a variety of sources, including a 1920 library catalogue, and found that sixteen of the authors used male pseudonyms, and five signed their works with only family names which give no indication of the author's sex, and which would lead one to assume that they were females. Jean Larnac in his 1929 history of feminine literature in France identifies a total of 535 female members of the Société des gens de lettres, the major French literary society. Larnac goes on to cite Jean de Bonnefon who in 1908 found 738 women writers listed in library holdings. (Larnac 1929: 223) Contrary to Larnac's rather conservative figures, Slama cites O. Uzanne, who speaks of 1,219 women members of the Société. (1980: 214) To add further to the confusion, an unidentified author makes the extravagant claim in the 1907 *Je sais tout* article (Anon 1907) that out of 25,000 professional writers over 5,000 were women. This author, who appears to be a woman author writing in defense of her co-authors, implies that women were an integral part of the French literary scene at the end of the nineteenth century.

Despite such overwhelming evidence in support of the significance of the women writers, they have not only been forgotten along with their works, but have completely disappeared from literary history. Other than Larnac's 1929 history, there are few works in French on popular women's fiction. Michel Mercier's 1977 history of the feminine novel treats the whole of women's fiction in 247 pages. And in his anthology of nineteenth-century popular literature, Michel Nathan (1985) includes only eight women writers out of fifty three.

The fate of women writers in the United States has been less drastic, but they have also suffered from the reordering of literary standards by academics. Fred Lewis Pattee in his 1915 *A History of American Literature since 1870* includes a chapter on women writers after the Civil War. As the members of the New England School which had dominated American letters died out,

Pattee writes, the real succession was feminine. (1940: 220) In subsequent histories written by Pattee, however, such chapters on women writers have completely disappeared. It is thanks to the pioneering works of such American studies scholars as Jane Tompkins and Nina Baym not only that the American literature canon has come to include popular women writers but that a counter-canon has come into existence. Furthermore, an increasing number of nineteenth-century American women writers are now being re-edited and taught in women's studies classes.

In addition to a general disregard for popular women writers, French researchers have also virtually ignored any feminine literary production which was neither feminist nor political. Anne Sauvy points out how feminist writer Evelyne Sullerot, in her study of the nineteenth-century feminine press (1966), ignores any periodicals which were not explicitly feminist, thereby reducing the corpus substantially. (Sauvy 1985: 449) Detailed information on the lives and works of the French female sentimental writers depends upon the political background and perspective of the researcher. Feminist writers tend to ignore completely the existence of the sentimental novelists, whom they dismiss because of their writers' so-called non-feminist writings. For example, Anne-Marie Dardigna, author of a book on the feminine press and another on eroticism, argues, contrary to the above cited figures, that the number of women novelists writing for a female audience declined dramatically after the eighteenth century. Whereas women such as Marie de France or Christine de Pisan had previously occupied the literary space of the novelist, by the eighteenth century male authors had reappropriated what had previously been considered "the prerogative of women." Dardigna attributes women's loss of status within the literary community to the changing class structure of French society. The demand for equal rights which accompanied the rise of the middle class did not extend to the inclusion of women:

> When women's demands for equality were joined to a more general project of social change, they inevitably provoked, it seems, a very strong masculine fear.   (Dardigna 1980: 38)

According to Dardigna, the exclusion of women from the literary world paralleled the rise of the novel as an important and recognized form of cultural expression of the public sphere. As literature became a prestigious profession suitable for men, and the publishing world was increasingly commercialized, women, despite their earlier participation, were suddenly deemed incapable of writing serious fiction. Other than George Sand, who despite her prodigious output – sixty novels, twenty-five plays and innumerable essays and articles – has gone down in literary history as a writer of romantic novels, women lost the status that earlier writers such as Christine de Pisan and Marie de France had. They did not, however, vanish from the literary scene as Dardigna would have us believe. It is also important to note that in France the exclusion of women from the professional and, by extension, the cultural world had already begun at the time of the Renaissance and continued until the downfall of the Ancien Régime. (Sarde 1983: 323) Nineteenth- century bourgeois France continued this exclusion of women from professional life. If they wanted to be loved, women were expected to renounce their creative lives and careers: "Glory or happiness, it was in these terms that Mme de Staël had already formulated the conflict in *Corinne*." (Slama 233)

What accounted for the high number of women writers in the United States and France, and their wide-spread popularity? First, the world of middle-class women was in the process of drastic economic and social change as a result of rapid industrialization. In the United States, the Industrial Revolution of the first part of the nineteenth century and the advent of a market economy transformed the role of women within the household into a less active one as commercial enterprises outside the domestic sphere assumed traditional female tasks. Furthermore, the introduction of mechanical time-savers into the home turned the life of the mid-nineteenth-century American middle-class woman into one of enforced idleness and close confinement to the private sphere of daily life.

By mid century, both French and American middle-class women suddenly found themselves with more leisure time. In the United States, parallel to the growth of the moneyed classes, women's position in the home became more and more ornamental and symbolic of their husbands' newly acquired social standing. And in France oppressive legislation enacted under the Napoleonic code forbad the middle-class woman access to work possibilities, consequently barring her from active public participation and restricting her to the home. In addition, the increased number of men in the United States who either went outside the home to find work or were gone for extended periods of time on business ventures left women to busy themselves with cultural concerns of an exclusively feminine nature. As her sphere of possible activities narrowed, the American middle-class woman, no longer economically productive and turned into a consumer rather than a producer of the items she used on a daily basis, occupied herself with fashion and with reading and writing, both activities being manifestations of the emerging consumerism which also becomes a favorite theme of many of writers of the period.

In addition to the women who had leisure time to fill a substantial number of women turned to writing for economic reasons. In the United States the profession of authorship became inseparable from and constituted by women. Unlike most male authors, who had full-time employment and considered their writing as a creative non-lucrative activity, many of the women writing at the time did so with the conscious intent of earning money. The absence of a male provider through death, desertion, or financial failure forced many women to provide the primary financial support for their families. Given the limited range of possibilities open to a middle-class woman who had to earn her own living, many women chose, rather than go into domestic service or teach, to write, a profession which offered better money and a more influential social position. A new generation of women emerged who, through the sale of their work, moved into the public sphere and managed to become financially autonomous, a fact which enabled them to exert greater control over their lives and to influence those of other women. Women writers in both countries played such an important role in the lives of their readers because they provided women with intellectual enjoyment as well as advising them on their homes and children. Sally McNall in her study of women's fiction in America comments that the novels were so influential

not only because the fiction itself was a powerful carrier of the ideology of domesticity, but because many of the women who wrote the stories also wrote stories for children, or manuals for child-rearing or for housekeeping in general. (McNall 1981: 34)

French women writers, similar to their American counterparts who turned to their pens to support their families, also considered their writing as a career. In the first half of the nineteenth century, however, unlike the middle-class orientation in England and the United States, the major French women writers came from the upper class and were read by educated women of their own class. Mmes de Genlis, Cottin, and de Riccoboni wrote novels for public reading room consumption ("romans pour cabinets de lecture") and enjoyed immense success in France and the rest of Europe until the end of the century. It is not until nearly the end of the nineteenth century, when the novel "slips in the hierarchy of genres" (Thiesse 1984: 176), that women writers who did not belong to the aristocracy assume a more visible position in the production of fiction. But by that time, as part of the group of sentimental writers, they already occupied a low position within the hierarchy of cultural production. Most of the sentimental novelists – male and female – were of humble origins and came from the provinces rather than from Paris, which put them at a further disadvantage. The centralization of literary salons and publishers in Paris contributed to the Parisian establishment's scorn for these provincials. Despite the sentimental novel's domination of the literary market in terms of numbers of titles and copies printed, the French female author was doubly disadvantaged. She was not only confronted with the sexist biases against creative women, but also had to contend with this general contempt for the sentimental novel.

French feminine literature became a vital part of the book world around 1860 when, among other factors, the first lending library opened in Paris. With new laws enacted after 1850 requiring the compulsory education of girls, the female reading population grew significantly larger and expanded beyond the upper classes. According to reader records of the Bibliothèque des Amis de l'Instruction du IIIe Arrondissement, one of the first lending libraries in Paris, the number of women readers steadily increased from the time the library first opened in 1862, when only 10 per cent of the members were women, to 70 per cent in 1898. Also at this time the proliferation of newspapers and magazines contributed to the increasing number of women writers who published their stories in serial form.

After 1860, women from different social classes began to write professionally and their ranks roughly corresponded to the groups of women who were writing in the United States. The two main categories of French women writers were either the religiously inspired who wrote for the service of the Catholic Church (in the case of the USA, it was the Protestant Church) or the lay writers who contributed to the serialized novels published by the popular press. Unlike the situation of American women writers, many of whom as the wives or daughters of ministers were respectable members of their communities, French women writers issued from a variety of social and economic backgrounds. However, all the French authors shared the need to assume male pseudonyms because of the strong feelings against women's participation in cultural activities. Since a literary career for French women was not viewed, as it was in the USA, as a viable alternative to teaching or domestic service many writers used pseudonyms while others exploited their scandalous life style to further their literary ambitions. Some did both. Aurore Dudevant, who wrote under the name of George Sand, Marie d'Agoult who became Daniel Stern, or Marguerite Eimery Rachilde who simply went under the name of Rachilde, were all women who had broken with their families and lived lives "more novelistic than the novels." (Slama 217)

Critical reception of women writers

In France, controversy raged around the issue of women's reading habits: the supporters lauded the educative value of novel reading for women. One writer, in the first issue of the women's magazine *Journal des Demoiselles*, 15 February 1833, praised the effects of reading:

> Reading is the most important area of a young girl's education; it is through reading that her intelligence grows and that feeling develops. It is therefore necessary that a woman reads a lot.
>
> (Sauvy 1985: 448)

With the growth of women's fiction and the flood of women authors on the market, critics began to view the pastime less kindly. Ernest Renan, in an 1889 article, berated novel reading for the negative effects such activity could have on female sensibility: the novel, he writes, "has become a true cause of women's self-abasement." (quoted in Angenot 1984: 83–103) In part, this attitude derived from the general ideological approach taken to education. The current view of female education was that it should prepare a woman to become a better wife and housekeeper, and should further only the kind of reading which would aid her in this purpose. Already, 200 years earlier, Molière had made this quite clear in his *L'Ecole des femmes* (The School of Women) in which his hero Arnolphe states that he wants a wife who is able to read the book he gives her, namely, *Les Maxims du mariage ou les devoirs de la femme mariée* (Maxims of marriage or the duties of a married woman). The women writers themselves rarely disagreed with this position, and as will be seen, their novels also prepare women to become better wives. Contrary to the advice given by Molière's hero, the novelists also sought to instruct men on how to become better husbands.

Furthermore, because of the large feminine audience that novel production represented, French and American male writers alike accused feminine literature of exerting a negative effect on the genre in general. François Coppée, a member of the French Academy, ignoring the changing nature of the market and the growing ranks of new readers, equates the decline in the quality of literary production with women's participation:

> Literature which was once an art has become an occupation – a bad occupation – and it is perhaps only for this reason that I am surprised to see women, generally more practical, devote themselves to it. (Coppée quoted in Anon 1907: 160)

Writers in the United States felt that in order to compete they had to produce fiction geared towards a feminine audience. Hawthorne's consternation at the influence women writers were exerting on the tastes of the reading public, in his oft-cited letter to his publisher, expressed a commonly held sentiment among the male authors:

> America is now wholly given over to a d****d mob of scribbling women, and I should have no chance of success

while the public taste is occupied with their trash – and should be ashamed of myself if I did succeed. What is the mystery of these innumerable editions of *The Lamplighter* and other books neither better nor worse? Worse they could not be, and better they need not be, when they sell by the hundred thousand. (quoted in Pattee 1940: 110)

In France, women writers were attacked as renegades and unfeminine: Jules Barbey d'Aurevilly claimed that when women began to write they were no longer women, "they are men – at least by pretension – and failures!" (quoted in Slama 1980: 222) He goes so far in his attack as to accuse them of threatening the family and posing a threat, in general, to society. These are women, he writes, who want to be the husbands of their husbands. The unidentified *Je sais tout* writer, well aware of such slander, counters the misogynous view of Barbey d'Aurevilly and others that once a woman takes up a pen she becomes a man: "In our days a woman writer is honored to be a woman. . . . Let us abandon the legend that the woman writer is a monster." (Anon 1907: 160) The arguments of Barbey d'Aurevilly and even the unidentified journalist, who is ostensibly defending women writers, point out the precarious position French women writers occupied and that their desire to write was ultimately viewed as an aberration from expected female behavior.

Ironically enough however, throughout the nineteenth century women were singled out as being particularly suited for novel writing. If women are the greatest consumers of fiction, critics noted, they are also the largest producers of novels. This, according to Lucien Auger in 1827, could be linked to feminine nature:

They have proven since a long time their particular aptitude for this type of work, which requires more feeling than thought, more passion than reason, more delicacy than force.
(quoted in Larnac 1929: 277)

Larnac, in his history of the feminine novel, also bases his analysis on feminine nature, which he, contrary to Barbey d'Aurevilly, sees as particularly suited to novel writing:

Whereas men desperately try to earn money women use their leisure to cultivate their minds. Because of this women provide the world with the enlightened amateurs, the writers, artists, "beacons" it needs. (Larnac 1929: 278)

And Emile Faguet, who might imagine he was praising women writers, says:

> If we assume that the novel – except, of course, the novel of important social or philosophical significance – is unworthy of man whose intelligence is reserved for other work, I find it logical and good that women devoted themselves to it.
> (Anon 1907: 159)

Women, Faguet admits, may rarely have genius, but they are frequently talented.

The highly visible division in France between high and low literature and the hierarchization of the various literary forms exerted pressure on women authors to avoid the realm of so-called feminine topics. Throughout the nineteenth century, as is still often the case, critics reproached female writers for writing about women and their concerns, a topic considered to be of interest only to women. Joséphine Maldague, for example, who published her first novel in 1884 as Georges Maldague, touched upon problems in the social position of women and was chastized for this interest. When she applied for entry into the Société des gens de lettres[1] in 1890, jury members criticized her for writing about women:

> A preoccupation seems to dominate (her work) as is natural in novels coming from a feminine pen: the author is obsessed with the consequences of fate – natural and artificial – as well as the indifference of the law on the lives of contemporary women.
> (quoted in Thiesse 1984: 188)

Discouraged by the novel's lack of critical success Maldague abandoned serious writing and turned to popular novels.

The devalorization of women writers and the novels they wrote was so acute that women also participated in attacking their female contemporaries. Daniel Lesueur in the novel *Gilles de Claircoeur* (1912) mocked the female novelist in this playful description of the average women writer:

> She was of that age when Parisians, and especially women of letters, shone in their full bloom. Thirty-eight to forty years

old. . . . Then she dressed so badly with too much pretty fabric, this poor Gilles de Clairecoeur – her real name being Gilberte Claireux. "Gilberte" – due to the romantic tastes of her mother, a Bovary of Angoûmois to whom she owes her imagination. (7)

Daniel Lesueur, in actuality Jeanne Loiseau, satirizes in this portrait her fellow female novelists, and draws upon both the popular image of the stereotyped author who comes from the provinces and attempts to succeed in Paris and the view of the woman writer as an aberration.

The nineteenth-century French woman was considered by her male contemporaries as occupying a privileged position in society, and any demands for liberation were thought of as outrageous. The myth of the middle-class woman as lady, a myth which gained forced in the United States with the growth of industrialization and which underlies the cult of domesticity in the United States, surfaced in French society in a more extreme form. The nineteenth-century Frenchman adored women but, rather than acquiesce to demands for equality, either elevated them to the level of a goddess without any rights or portrayed them as seductresses or coquettes. Michelet, Stendhal, or Hugo all idolized woman in their writings but remained consistently hostile to feminist demands for change. Stendhal, in *De l'amour* (On Love), published in 1829, argues that society has formed women to become coquettes because it is their unique weapon within a male society. Marie d'Agoult, the mistress of Franz Liszt and a contemporary of George Sand, justified the coquette as the only female role which accorded women any power in society,

In civilized society, coquetry has become for women a science as profound as any science or politics. Inactive, they have easily learned to take advantage of the desires of the masculine sex in order to enslave him for a short while, and all their sharpness, all their intelligence, all their powers of observation and calculation are applied to this single goal: inspire love without sharing it, excite passion without satisfying it.

(quoted in Desanti 1980: 57)

Coquetry has always played a vital role in French culture. Bestselling author Marcelle Tinayre, in *La Femme et son secret* (Woman and her Secret) (1933), writes in a chapter on childhood that coquetry is a desire for power. The future woman learns the art of seduction, not because she is content with being pretty but because the admiration of others makes her feel her power. This tradition persists in contemporary French culture, and the quite un-American image of the coquette has appeared in a number of recent French bestsellers. *Modern Style* by Irène Frain (1984) tells the story of two young women who, during the twenties, survive as coquettes, and in Nicole Avril's *Jeanne* (1984), the heroine, a modern-day Don Juan, puts into practice Stern's advice to women to profit from love without giving in to passion. In both novels the female protagonists gain what power they have through seduction. But whether they just survive or truly acquire power is questionable. Soyeuse, the heroine of *Modern Style*, disappears at the end of the novel and Jeanne of Avril's novel falls to her death when she is accidentally pushed down a flight of stairs by her god-daughter, who holds Jeanne responsible for the suicide of her boyfriend who had been seduced and then rejected by Jeanne.

The entrenched patriarchal biases against women's participation in cultural activity in France become most obvious when one considers the writers who do succeed. A glance at the various bestseller lists published in the French press today reveals that things have not changed all that much. Although the need to assume male pseudonyms is a thing of the past, many of the women whose novels attain bestseller status in France are already public figures. Bestselling authors Marie-France Pisier or Simone Signoret are well known actresses and politically vocal, Régine Deforges is a publisher and writer, and Nicole Avril is primarily known as the wife of a well known television celebrity. It is only in the last few years that women writers have been acclaimed on the basis of their writing and not because of their famous or notorious backgrounds, although these cases are still relatively infrequent. It was only in 1980 that the Académie Française accepted its first female member, Marguerite Yourcenar.

The United States: The domestic novel or the cult of domesticity

The "domestic" novel, one of the most popular forms of feminine literature in the United States, dominated the literary market from 1840 through 1880, and continued to attract readers and writers until after the Civil War. A popularizer of the cult of domesticity, the domestic novel evoked the dominant social myth of the period: the middle-class woman as a lady within the family home, her particular arena. Although scholars at one time viewed the novels as a glorification of the domestic situation of American women, recent feminists have challenged this interpretation. Mary Kelley, on the one hand, points out that the female figure found in the novels was

> a strong, commanding, central figure in the home; a supportive and guiding redeemer for husband; a model and teacher of rectitude for children; and a reformer of and servant to an American society judged to be in dire need of regeneration.
> (Kelley 1979: 436)

Yet, on the other hand, an undercurrent of despair runs throughout the novels which question the possibility of women's autonomy and individuality.

Helen Waite Papashvily sees the corpus of fiction as being much more radical in its intent than does Kelley. She argues in response to the domesticity theory of some critics that the novels cannot be dismissed as simple stories of contented middle-class ladies but must be situated within the historical context of the burgeoning women's movement and the increasingly vocal demands being made by women for change. The distance between those women present at the July 1848 Women's Rights Convention held at Seneca Falls, New York, and the readers of popular novels is not as great as may be imagined. Rather, in view of the frequent appearance of unhappy wives and mothers and the high number of desertions and broken homes which filled the novels, Papashvily argues that they should more accurately can be seen as

> handbooks of feminine revolt . . . these pretty tales reflected and encouraged a pattern of feminine behavior so quietly ruthless, so subtly vicious that by comparison the ladies at Seneca appear angels of innocence.   (Papashvily 1956: xvii)

Although the comparison with the feminists of the period who were publishing radical journals analyzing the causes of the desertions and broken homes seems exaggerated, some of the titles of the novels popular at the time confirm the desperate nature of the texts: *The Discarded Daughter*, *The Deserted Wife*, *The Forsaken Wife*, or *Nameless* are only a few examples of the unhappy subjects treated in the novels. The plot, which varied little from novel to novel, narrated the plight of a young girl deprived of her male protection through death, persecution, or neglect. Forced by her drastic situation to fend for herself – which she frequently did quite well – either she was rewarded with a worthy mate who, having come to realize her worth gave up his unacceptable behavior, or she found the man of her dreams already formed in a way she could love and he helps her out of her dilemma.

Mrs E.D.E.N. Southworth and Susan Warner, two popular and prolific writers of the mid-nineteenth century, wrote novels typical of American women's fiction of the period. Mrs Emma Dorothy Eliza Nevitte Southworth who, according to Frank Luther Mott, was one of the greatest publishing successes of the nineteenth century, began writing in 1849 to supplement her inadequate teacher's salary. She wrote over eighteen novels in an eleven-year period and probably published at least fifty throughout her long career. Southworth's favorite narrative situations were, according to Nina Baym,

> daughters disinherited by jealous or materialistic fathers; hasty, secret, and disastrous marriages into which inexperienced girls are forced by importunate suitors; misunderstood wives abused, harassed, or abandoned by self-righteous but deluded husbands. (Baym 1978: 115)

Her heroines sought to secure a place where they could control their lives, which, in the context of the nineteenth century, was the family home. But in order for this to occur the man had to change his behavior and reverse his previous conviction of the inferiority of women. Although in the majority of her novels the men are the cause of the heroine's unhappy situation, in some cases it is an unscrupulous woman who is at the root of the heroine's misery.

In *The Bride of Llewellyn* (1866), Southworth's narrator proposes the rare story of an exceptionally evil woman. The novel tells of a young woman, Gladys, who loses first her mother and then her loving father. The heiress to an immense fortune, Gladys is left in the care of Mrs Jay, her aunt who had insinuated herself into the heart of her father before his mysterious death (caused by foul play on the part of Mrs. Jay). Separated from Arthur, her childhood companion and the man her father had promised to her as husband, Gladys undergoes an incredible number of adventures until she is finally reunited with Arthur. Gladys, however, proves herself to be resourceful and able to survive on her own: she escapes from her aunt despite being drugged, is left undaunted by the loss of $1,500, is recaptured, and so on. But despite her ability to rely on her own resources she willingly puts herself in the power of her husband. The obvious contradiction between her own abilities to survive and her willingness to yield to a husband's authority is pointed out to her by Arthur:

> Why even I, your husband, have no power here that is not derived from you. The terms of your father's will secure every thing to his daughter, as is right.   (520)

But Gladys, ignoring her own capacities, replies "do you think I want any power here that does not come directly from you?" (520) Once safely settled on her family estate, Gladys not only forgives her wicked aunt the money she has stolen, she sends off a wagon full of clothing, food, and money to the three old women who had come to her aid. They in turn share their bounty with those poorer than themselves in their community. Order is restored at the end and the reader is left with the impression that Arthur and Gladys live happily ever after. Although hardly an ending feminists would approve of, Gladys still shows her women readers that women need not passively submit to the will of others. Gladys may end up as a wife, but she has chosen to be there.

Susan Warner, another major bestselling nineteenth-century author, like Southworth and other novelists of the period came from a well-to-do bourgeois family which had fallen upon hard times. Warner first began writing novels in 1847 to help her family's financial situation. She published, either on her own or with her sister, twenty-one novels. Because of her family's increasing debts Warner never achieved the financial independence Southworth managed to obtain. The powerlessness of women in a male society dominates her first novel *The Wide, Wide World* (1852) which sold over a million copies. The first edition sold out in four months, went on to numerous re-editions, and was translated into French, German, Swedish, and Italian. It is the story of an invalid woman and her 10-year-old daughter who, when she is orphaned, is left in the care of unsympathetic relatives. The novel follows the child Ellen through a series of homes and trials until the end when she finds the family setting and man with whom she can be happy. The difficulties in life which first her mother and then Ellen experience result from male desertions and injustices.

For the nineteenth-century writer the family home was the one area in which women could exert some control; yet the home life initially depicted in these novels is overwhelmingly unhappy. Those novels which do open on scenes of domestic tranquility inevitably veer towards tragedy. Or, the unhappiness of the family situation is made immediately apparent. Marriage and courtship, despite the negative descriptions of domestic life, remain the major goal in the heroine's life. The heroine's eventual marriage, as is the case in Southworth's novels, was her way of acquiring a different way of life,

> the means of establishing a family that is not a biological unit but a community of loving adults assembled under one roof.
>
> (Baym 1978: 149)

Behind the cover of religious piety which fills many of the novels and the dependence of the texts on sentimental stereotypes, the popular nineteenth-century domestic novel represented, according to Jane Tompkins, an effort to re-organize society from the woman's point of view. *Uncle Tom's Cabin* (1852), a major example of the sentimental novel is, Tompkins writes, "expressive of and responsible for the values of its time." (1985: 125) Through the sentimental novel, American women writers "elaborated a myth that gave women the central position of power and authority in the culture." (Tompkins 1985: 125) This mythic representation of the power structure remains central to women's fiction long after the demise of the sentimental novel and can be found in many of the contemporary women's bestsellers of the 1980s.

The domestic novel gave way to other forms of feminine fiction after the Civil War and despite Nina Baym's contention that female audiences in the United States turned to "a more androgynous literature" (1978: 298) large numbers of women continued to read and write fiction geared to specifically female audiences, either in the form of novels or magazine stories. Louisa May Alcott's *Little Women* (1868), Elizabeth Stuart Phelps's *The Gates Ajar* (1868), Sarah Orne Jewett's *Deephaven* (1877), and Helen Hunt Jackson's *Ramona* (1884), are some of the more notable New England novels of the time immediately after the Civil War. The market for women's fiction became more diversified at this time, but it would be misleading to assume that the phenomenon of the domestic novel is limited to the nineteenth century. As the economic situation of the American woman changed and more women left their homes to pursue professional careers, women's choice of reading material changed too, as did the ways in which women were and continue to be represented.[2] After the First World War women's novels begin to show female characters in situations outside the domestic sphere; women are employed and frequently engage in meaningful careers. The entire gamut of women's fiction, in fact, from the 1920s up until the 1980s, which unfortunately is out of the immediate sphere of this study,[3] continues to reflect the changes in women's lives. It is not until the 1980s, however, and the appearance of superwoman that any possibility of power outside the domestic sphere is hinted at within the context of popular fiction written for women.

The sentimental novel in France

It is important to stress that the history of the popular novel in France, unlike that of the United States, is not exclusively one of women writing. Male writers, in particular Eugène Sue and Alexandre Dumas, dominated the market and were read by both men and women. For these writers the ideal woman presented in their novels is either the *femme fatale* who acquires her power through seduction, an image which dominates French literature up through Zola, or the angelic passive woman who remains at home and is completely absent from the public domain.

Women, be they seductresses or not, exert a greater power over the men with whom they are involved in the novels written by women than they do in those of the male writers. Defined by the effect her emotions and feelings have over others rather than by any kind of concrete action, she succeeds, like the American heroines do, in converting the male character and changing his initially questionable behavior to one with which she can live. Unlike the female characters in the male-authored novels, she does not passively await her destiny with the "traditional weakness of her sex." (Follain 1971: 37) Women, in the novels of Sophie Cottin, a popular writer at the beginning of the nineteenth century, although fragile and persecuted win out over their lovers through the force of their intelligence, passion, and energy. Cottin's novels, influenced by Ann Radcliff and Monk Lewis, not only borrow from the English formula "boy meets girl – boy loses girl – boy gets girl" but also synthesize themes commonly found in the *roman noir* of the period: women who were unhappily married or imprisoned in their homes by their husbands, or lovers driven to solitary existences through despair. (Olivier-Martin 1980: 15). Love, however, remains the overriding priority for women, Sophie Cottin writes, and is "the story of their lives whereas it is scarcely an episode in that of men." (quoted in Slama 1980: 231) As the one story a woman can tell, love also becomes the vehicle for a critique of the unequal world in which women live, as well as serving as a means of self-identity. This formula is not dissimilar to that found in the American novels in which women, deprived of any meaningful occupation or influence on the outside world, can only hope to acquire some degree of power or reign in her own domestic space. The French heroines are strong, passionate women who are faced with the mediocrity of the men they love. In the novels of Virginie Ancelot, a mid-century writer, for example, the heroines are usually dominant, beautiful women who reign over much weaker men.

The home, as Proudhon remarked in the mid-nineteenth century, was indeed a female domain and the only area in which women had any power: "Women only aspire to marry in order to become rulers of a small Country they call their House." (quoted in Martin-Fugier 1980: 120) Marriage, however, despite its seemingly positive aspect for the nineteenth-century woman, remained, overall, a duty to which women had to submit. And as such, love, marriage, and the education of young women dominated nineteenth-century French women's fiction. The rare exceptions of women characters who overtly express their revolt against the institution of marriage are found in the novels of George Sand and Daniel Stern, the Countess of Agoult. *Indiana* (1832), George Sand's first novel, underscores what women in unhappy marriages suffer. Sand, in the novel *Consuelo* (1842), calls marriage "une prostitution jurée" (legal prostitution) (quoted in Larnac 1929: 187) and with *Lélia* (1833), one of her better known novels, she was accused of being "the anti-Matrimonial Novelist." When in April 1848 Sand discovered her name to be on the list of candidates for election to the National Assembly, she refused the honor and explained the reasons for her refusal in a letter she adddressed to the members of the Central Committee. Women, according to Sand, cannot particip-ate in political affairs until they have broken away from the dependence upon a man marriage implies. Emancipation for women, she writes, consists "simply in giving back to the woman all the civil rights which marriage alone takes from her, and which she may preserve only by remaining unmarried." (quoted in Miles 1987: 53) In Stern's novels *Valentia* (1845) and *Nélida* (1846), young women looking for love experience repulsion at their conjugal duty and revolt against their unhappiness at having a husband they can not accept. Both Stern's and Sand's strong feminist positions filter down through the novels of the senti-mental novelists of the period.

Henry Gréville (Alice Durand)'s 1877 novel *Suzanne Normis: A Father's Novel* questions a woman's right to choose her own husband and to divorce him if she finds him to be incompatible. Raised by her father after the death of her mother, Suzanne, unlike the other girls of her generation, is lively, curious, and independent. Exceptionally loyal to her father, she marries a man she doesn't really love to please her father who believes himself to be on the point of dying. His selfishness, however, causes her to revolt:

I'm married yet I don't have a husband, I distrust and hate him to whom I am tied for life; – what a strange marriage that is! And why am I condemned to bear the name of a man not worthy of me? And why am I, who have never done any wrong exiled from my dear country while he who has tortured me since the first day is happy and well thought of in his country?
(202)

Suzanne's words echo those of George Sand thirty years earlier. Suzanne, like Sand, condemns neither marriage nor the family, rather she distinguishes between the husband who married her uniquely for her fortune and a union made for the reason of true affection. At the sight of a seemingly happy couple she compares their happiness to her own situation:

> That was a family, she said, the father looked at his children with goodness in his eye, the mother looked happy, and when the couple looked at each other I saw that they loved one another. . . . Yes, that is how one should be loved, I understand that's how you loved my mother! Your two lives only one. . . . And me! me . . . who will never be loved, who will never be a mother! (205)

Suzanne's goodness triumphs in the end, when her greedy husband falls down a cliff to his death. Freed from her unhappy marriage, she marries the young man who had helped her and her father during their exile. The novel's happy ending implies that the happy marriage Suzanne had wistfully observed is indeed possible if the partners are equally matched and considerate of each other's needs.

Sonia, published the same year as *Suzanne*, also presents those ingredients necessary for a happy marriage. The novel, about the kind of woman it takes to make a good wife, is from the point of view of a young Russian, Boris, who works as a tutor for a middle-class family. Boris falls in and then out of love with Lydia, the older daughter of the family, because of her superficiality. Upon his return to Moscow after a two-year absence abroad, Boris learns of Lydia's unfaithfulness. Comforted by his friend Armianof, Boris realizes Lydia is incapable of loving anyone because

> by nature she's a coquette and frivolous, in love with luxury and herself, and therefore completely inaccessible to higher sentiments . . . given her natural disposition and the milieu in which she has lived she can not be any thing else but what she is. . . (245)

Gradually, as Boris recovers from his affair with Lydia he realizes that he is, in fact, in love with Sonia, the young orphan he had rescued from the cruel hands of Lydia's family. Having been trained first by Boris's mother and then by himself as his personal servant, Sonia, a simple yet sincere and loving woman, has all the qualities Boris most desires in a wife. Sonia's devotion to Boris and her unrelenting desire to please him make her the ideal companion. The ideal wife then, within the novel's context, is the woman who devotes herself wholeheartedly to her man.

In the 1882 novel of Maryan, *Un Mariage de convenance* (A Marriage of Convenience) the ideal relationship is impossible without a radical transformation on the part of the male character. The young heroine, Geneviève, is advised by her friend Amélie on the way to regain her husband's affection: "Give without counting . . . do not make excuses for your errors by pointing to those of another . . . it's a woman's role." (73) Geneviève attempts to follow Amélie's advice but finds that she is unable to fit into this subservient role without her husband also making an effort. At the end of the novel, when Geneviève is thought to be dying after having given birth, her husband returns to her side and admits to his love and folly. Having learned her value, he can now change his ways and become a good husband. Geneviève, also now reformed, having recovered from the difficult childbirth can devote her energies to being a good wife and mother.

Gyp (the Countess of Martel de Janville), one of the few French women who were actual bestselling authors of the latter half of the nineteenth century, published at least a hundred novels. Her novels, which span a career of fifty years, present a panorama of Parisian life from 1885 to 1933. Gyp's originality, according to her friend and biographer Michel Missoffe, was in her ability to "shake off both the yoke of fashion, caste and clan, and to have escaped the influence of her milieu." (1932: x) Unlike many of the other women novelists of the period, Gyp's novels were controversial and often politically motivated. Focused on the aristocracy her fiction contained biting criticism of her milieu and the upper classes. Gyp, Michel Mercier writes, "denounced through caricature fashionable society and the middle-class of her time by launching a new type of very young girl." (195) Her heroines are either the young independent "tomboy" or elegant creatures who, even when the author disapproves of their behavior, stand out of the ordinary. In *Le monde à côté* (A World Apart) (1933), society is a world in which love relationships boil down to dishonest relationships between men and women. Josette, the heroine, stands apart from the rest of her milieu because of her outspoken dislike of mediocre people. *Le Mariage de Chiffon* (The Marriage of Chiffon) (1894), one of Gyp's better known novels of which a film version was made, presents the rebel who revolts against the prescribed social code. Chiffon, as the young heroine Corsye is affectionately called by her family, refuses to participate in the hypocritical behavior she perceives in the people she lives with. As the novel's title indicates, the story centers around her eventual marriage. Although she never questions the inevitability of her marrying, Chiffon attacks the hypocrisy of a society which equates money with happiness, through caricatures of the clergy and provincial bourgeoisie. A lively, humorous character, Chiffon refuses a highly regarded marital prospect because, as she puts it, she is not in love with him; she aids her socialist uncle in his political campaign, and rarely hesitates to mock those she with whom she disagrees. At the end of the novel, when Chiffon reassures her uncle Marc that, despite their age differences, she is in love with him, she is rewarded for her straightforwardness with the marriage she desires.

In contrast to the frank Chiffon is the other type of woman found in Gyp's novels: the flirt. *Bijou* (Jewel) (1900), *La Fée* (Fairy) (1902), and *Maman* (Mama) (1905) provide an ambivalent portrait of a woman who plays with the emotions of the men surrounding her. Denyse de Courtaix, the young heroine of the three novels, differs from the other women of her social milieu because of her childlike guilelessness and striking beauty: "She was not a woman, she was a fairy." (*La Fée*: 7) Denyse, courted by and then married to a man thirty years her senior as well as childless, was considered by her family to be outside the norm of society because she has refused to lead the expected life of a woman of her age and social class which according to her grandmother is "to have a husband, a husband your own age, and children." (36)

The narrative alternates between tales of Denyse's effect on the unfortunate men who fall in love with her – there are at least three suicides on her account – and admiration for her simplicity. Château-Landon, the young man through whose eyes Denyse's character is revealed in the second novel, decides at one point that she is not a coquette but rather a woman who needs to be admired. The disapproval of Denyse's character, however, becomes quite clear by the end of the third novel. Whereas *Bijou* ends with the announcement of her marriage to de Clagny, and *La Fée* with her pregnancy, the reader discovers in *Maman* that the child who lacks the aristocratic grace of either his mother or his presumed father is not the offspring of Denyse's husband, but rather is the result of Denyse's having been raped by the estate farmer who had been in love with her for years. Château-Landon learns of the circumstances of the incident through a friend, who reveals that Denyse's cousin – the mother of one of the unfortunate suicides – had witnessed the rape and allowed it to occur: "I wanted to enter . . . but my aunt held me back . . . she said to me: – It's justice!. . ." (*Maman*: 115) Denyse, who causes men to suffer and refuses to live the life expected of a woman of her class, is punished by having a child who is a replica of his peasant father.

In addition to her social satires, Gyp also wrote what can be interpreted as political novels. A good friend of Maurice Barrès, one of the leaders of the extreme right, Gyp, while staunchly supporting the military's case against French army officer Alfred Dreyfus, was also capable of attacking the ultra-right-wing Action Française. Virulently anti-semitic, Gyp's novels are filled with fat, uncouth Jewish bankers and their wives who are equally uncouth. *Israel* (1898), a novel especially known for its anti-Jewish portraits, however, was perfectly in keeping with the mood of France after the Dreyfus Affair. *Le Chambard: Roman d'aujourd'hui* (The Upheaval: A Contemporary Novel) (1931) and *Le Coup du Lapin* (Whiplash) (1931), depict the stress that Action Française brought to upper-class French families divided in their loyalties. Portrayed as stupid and incompetent, the followers of Action Française rarely seem to understand the cause they are advocating. The message of these novels, despite their attack on the anti-semitic right-wing group, is far from progressive. Gyp, an artistocrat and royalist, views modernity, and this is especially true in relation to women's behavior and dress, as a regrettable departure from the traditional values which ruled French society before the First World War. Gyp's novels, spanning as they do a period of great change in French history, document a resistance to middle-class values. She emphasizes independence, sensitivity, and Christian charity in opposition to the market mentality she sees invading French society at the beginning of the twentieth century. Throughout her novels an image of a benevolent aristocracy which has been corrupted but which is none the less the only hope for the future of France appears as the unique solution.

Delly, a sister-brother team, also occupies a crucial place in this history and marks the end of the sentimental novel in France. Marie and Frédéric Petitjean de la Rosière published under the single name of Delly during the early part of the twentieth century. Between 1907 and 1941, the team published over a hundred novels which continue to sell prodigiously even today although virtually ignored by the academic community. In 1966 a 15,000-copy reprinting of one of their novels sold out in one day. (Olivier-Martin 1980: 239) A 1973 *France-Soir* article sums up their success: "A dream bestseller which has worked for fifty years." (quoted in Olivier-Martin 1980: 239)

The Delly novels, similar to the formula romances which follow in the form of Harlequins, remained faithful to the well known formula of the orphaned young girl who finds her true love at the end of the novel. The Delly heroine succeeds because she refuses to be deterred from her principles. In *Les Ombres* (The Shadows) (1925),[4] the narrative contrasts Madel, the traditional young woman from the countryside, profoundly Christian and family-oriented, with the "new woman" who ruthlessly ignores her family obligations for career ambition. Florine, the "new woman" of the novel, leaves her father to fend for himself and goes to Paris in an attempt to make a career for herself in the theater. The sympathies of the author, conveyed through the character of Madel, are quite clear: Madel's marriage and the happiness it promises her are deemed superior to the career aspirations of someone like Florine. Unlike the attempts made in a novel like Hull's *The Sheik* to reconcile changing life-styles, *Les Ombres* leaves no doubt as to what is expected from a woman. The final scene between Madel and her husband, much more than a rhetorical ending, reinforces the very traditional life-style endangered by changing morals after the First World War.

You are now my home. It is at your side that I find my duty, my happiness and my household. And all the principles that I have learned from my dear grandparents, the traditional French and Catholic atmosphere in which I have lived I will find them in you, my friend, my dear Bernard who believes as I do and who is a true French man.   (185)

Similar to the novels written by Gyp towards the end of her career, the Delly novels express not only a profound disapproval of modern French society but also of the demands of women to lead less protected lives.

The number of popular women writers continued to be significant well into the twentieth century but the only popular woman writer who has survived to some degree is Gyp. A reviewer for *The Bookman* commenting in 1906 on the state of the bestseller in France remarked that the circulation of 20-25,000 copies which Gyp's books enjoyed was unusual for a woman writer in France "seeing that there is only one other who can claim as large a circulation." (Hager 1906: 30-32) The author he refers to, Marcelle Tinayre, could only claim 10–25,000 copies.

According to critics, the popular woman's novel disappeared from the literary scene in France around the time of the Second World War. Again, it is hard to judge. The difficulty of finding many of the novels hinders an accurate assessment of the female participation in the period between the two wars. It would seem likely that women writers who moved in less exalted social circles than someone like Gyp have simply disappeared from view. The post World War II revivals of English to French translations has, however, once more made popular women's fiction a visible force in publishing circles. According to the Paris based literary agent Eliane Benisti, the French popular novel such as existed at the beginning of the century no longer exists, and today the French market is saturated with American books. (Interview 18 February 1985, Paris) This is not quite true. The *Angelique* novels by Serge and Anne Golan, although not romances in the sense of the Delly novels or the satirical stories Gyp wrote, were an integral part of the book market. Male writers who have always constituted a segment of the popular novel scene in France continue to do so well into the twentieth century. Maurice Denuzière and Paul-Loup Sulitzer, two very successful male writers, consistently produce bestsellers which are read by a large female audience both in France and abroad. Denuzière's *Louisiana* adheres to the romantic historical model and follows many of the romance conventions found in the American historical novels. Sulitzer writes novels which follow the pattern of American superwoman novels. *Hannah* (1985) and its sequel, *L'Imperatrice* (The Empress) (1986), are a fictional account of the life of Helena Rubinstein. *La Femme Pressé* (A Woman in a Hurry) (1987) and its sequel *Kate* (1988) center around the life of a female in the newspaper world. Despite, or perhaps because of the scandal surrounding Sulitzer as to who actually writes his books – he is reputed to have a group of ghost writers who do the actual writing – he is one of the top bestselling authors in France. None the less, the writing of popular fiction by and for women has basically ceased in France and the books have had largely to be imported from abroad.

Sulitzer aside, although the feminine novel came later in France than in the United States, they share comparable narrative structures. A similar treatment of women's concerns can be found in the novels of the two countries during the nineteenth and early twentieth centuries. Both the French and the American novelists are preoccupied with the acquisition of power within the domestic space and ways in which women gain control of their restricted arena. Marriage, although viewed with suspicion and even reviled in some cases, remains the principal channel open to women. Society and manners, however, play a more important role in the French novels than in those of the United States, and the many French novels which feature the coquette mark an important difference between them and the American novels. Without the puritan heritage of the United States and the strong influence religion had on the writers and their fiction, the French novelists feature a more open portrayal of sexuality and the quest for love even outside the confines of marriage.

Notes

1. Membership of the Société des gens de lettres, founded in 1838 in the interest of protecting authors' legal and economic rights, also implied a certain amount of prestige and recognition by a writer's contemporaries. The membership of the Société, although mixed, with writers of

different genres, was predominately male. Ironically enough the founder of the Society was a woman.

2. See Chapter Four in McNall (1981) for a discussion of some of the popular American women writers at the beginning of the twentieth century.

3. I do not intend to go into any in-depth analysis of these novels, other than to point out some of the changes which have occurred in the content. For a more detailed analysis see Chapter One of Modleski's *Loving with a Vengeance* (1984), or Kay Mussell, *Fantasy and Reconciliation* (1984). A number of excellent books exist on American and British women writers by, among others, Jane Spencer, Rosalind Miles, and Jean Radford. The purpose of this chapter has been to present the context out of which contemporary women's fiction has emerged. Because of the relative absence of critical work on popular French women writers, and the total absence of studies other than that of Bonnie Smith in English, I will go into more detail in presenting the French novels.

4. The edition of this novel that I found, interestingly enough, was published in 1983 with no indication of the original date of publication. The cover shows a young woman at the opera or theater with a dark-haired and a blond man on each side. The three are dressed in clothing contemporary to the 1980s, thereby again giving the reader no indication of the actual period in which the novel takes place.

Chapter four

The boundary between the romance and the bestseller: Harlequins, historical novels, and family sagas

> He didn't like books in which dull, cranky writers describe humdrum events in the very humdrum lives of humdrum people. Reality gave him enough of that kind of thing, why should he read about it?
>
> Michael Ende, *The Neverending Story* (1984)

Romance fiction written for women, despite its long tradition, has always taken a backseat to mainstream literature. A stroll through any bookstore will show the careful segregation of romances from what is considered to be authentic literature. The forms romance fiction has taken vary from period to period and depend upon the social and economic status of the reader. For example the *photoroman* and newspaper serials were once exclusively geared towards a working-class readership, and the hardcover bestsellers towards the more educated reader. This remains the case in France, where the series romances such as the Harlequins are not only targeted at a working-class readership but are also assumed to be their primary choice of reading material.

The image of the romance novel written for women, unlike that of mass-produced fiction written for men, remains almost always negative, and frequently functions in more serious texts as symbolic of a heroine's lack of intelligence. Novels abound with feminine characters whose frivolous natures are described through reference to their reading habits. Flaubert, to give a classical example, lays part of the blame for Emma Bovary's downfall on her poor choice of adolescent reading material. If, Flaubert seems to imply, she hadn't had her head filled with unrealistic ideas of a Prince Charming as a young girl she may well have been content to live out her life as it was destined. When a narrator wishes to indicate that a female character is wasting her time, or not being intellectual enough, the most indolent feminine activity she could be engaged in is reading romances. In a contemporary French novel by journalist Katherine Pancol, *La Barbare* (The Barbarian) (1981), the narrator laments her culturally impoverished childhood: "Nothing more than school culture which did not extend beyond the Larousse and novels taken from my mother's bookshelves: Cronin, Maurois, Troyat, Delly. . . ." (13) The same equation of women and romance reading holds equally true for American novels: in Gay Courter's *The Midwife* (1982), when Hannah recites some lines of poetry she especially likes, her husband expresses surprise at her familiarity with serious literature:

> "So," Lazar said, tilting back in his chair and sighing with pleasure. "I thought you only read romantic Yiddish novels. Modern poetry might put ideas into your head!"
> "What do you mean by that?" Hannah asked abruptly, angered by the insinuation that she would be expected to read only the simplest form of literature and embarrassed because the truth was she enjoyed novels the most. (103)

The embarrassment Hannah feels at Lazar's unkind words is common to what many female characters experience when faced with a similar accusation. It is rare, on the other hand, to find a fictional male character accused of or caught in the act of reading escapist literature.

A counterpoint to the fictional character caught in the act of reading romances is the heroine as romance writer. In cinema and fiction, the romance writer living the life of her fictional counterpart has become a popular topic. In the 1984 film *Romancing the Stone*, or in a wide range of novels by such diverse authors as Margaret Atwood, Gail Godwin, Anita Brookner, Barbara Taylor Bradford, or Pat Booth, the principal female characters participate as popular novelists in the production of female fantasy. They write historical novels, bestsellers or general fiction. Atwood's *Lady Oracle* (1976) is one of the few novels, however, which attempts a serious examination of the genre. Joan, the novel's secret romance writer moves between the pages of the gothic novels she pens in secret and her own life in order to free herself from what Elizabeth Fox-Genovese calls "that dangerous patriarchal domestic legacy." (1980: 212) Joan is caught as both a producer and a participant in "the literary culture that most poignantly embodies the fantasies of women who lack even her tenuous means of escape." (212) In the end, Joan, unlike her readers, appears to free herself from the romantic tyranny when she decides to give up writing gothic novels. Other than in Atwood's book, the act of writing women's fiction is a glamour occupation which adds to the heroine's prestige.

The French novels which feature the main character as a writer are not only fewer but are also stories of serious writers rather than romance writers. In Catherine Rihoit's *La Favorite* (The Favorite) (1982), the heroine Stella writes about the impact her sister's death has had on her. Her novel becomes an instant bestseller, and when Stella is offered a movie contract for the book, she's drawn into the cinema world, the main subject of the novel. The narrator of Madeline Chapsal's bestselling *La maison de jade* (The House of Jade) (1986) is also a writer, but her profession is secondary to her misery over the unhappy ending of a love affair which dominates the novel. At one point she gives up her professional journalist activities to please the man she's living with in an attempt to keep him from leaving. Annie, of Nicole de Buron's *Vas-y maman* (Do it Mamma) (1978), comes to novel writing as a form of escape from her boredom and writes a bestseller about women who are fed up with being only housewives. It is her success as a novelist which forces her husband to reassess her worth as "more" than a housekeeper and cook. He must learn to deal with the fact that his wife is capable of doing something outside the home. At no point in any of these three French novels are women assumed to be the heroine's readers.

Fiction written for a broadly based female audience has never ceased to be an important cultural and economic force. The number of readers of series romance fiction alone has currently been estimated at over 20 million in countries all over the world, and millions of novels are published yearly in all possible languages. Romances, most of which are written by and for women, who purchase the bulk of the fiction sold in the United States, account for at least 25 per cent of all paperback sales in the United States. Victor Temkin, president of Berkeley Publishing Corp, comments on the significant rate of growth of romantic fiction: "It's the only category of paperbacks where there's a growth in units in the last 10 years." (quoted in McDowell 1982: 7)

The case of Harlequin

Any discussion of women's popular fiction must also take into account Harlequin Books. One of the largest series romance publishing houses, Harlequin's success illustrates the profound effect mass-marketing strategies have had on the way in which books are produced and distributed, and the radical changes which have occurred in the book market in general. In both the United States and France, the success of the Harlequin imprint has brought about a total re-evaluation of the ways in which books, especially women's books, are perceived and marketed. Harlequin's appearance on the publishing scene in the early 1950s marks the creation of a group of anonymous authors and a completely standardized form of romance writing. Most importantly, Harlequin Books represents a turning point in the kind of fiction produced for female consumption; with the creation of the standardized serial romance, the possibilities for any change in content reflecting changes in the exterior world is slowed down.

Harlequin Books, the largest publisher of romantic fiction, is owned by Torstar Corporation of Toronto, Canada, and was founded in 1949 as a reprint house. By the late 1950's it was printing novels which had originally been released as hardcovers by the British romance publisher Mills and Boon. Harlequin, which publishes exclusively romances, sells 215 million copies in ten languages and covers 45 per cent of the North American market and 25 per cent of the French-speaking paperback market. (Alliot 1984: 18) Launched in France in 1978, Harlequin had become one of the major paperback imprints in the country by 1980. (Julien 1979: 79) In 1982 Harlequin's total sales in France were 30 million volumes, making it the second best-selling publisher after Livre de Poche. Today, Harlequin France sells 40–130,000 copies of each of the eight series it publishes.

Through its association with the other major European publishers, Harlequin now has the possibility of creating a vaster distribution network for its product than any one of the companies can on its own.

The consequences of such a consolidation of resources are twofold. On the one hand, as publishers pay more attention to profitability, the literary venture inescapably becomes a commercial one: the promotion of books as soap packet give-aways, for example, remains a standard Harlequin strategy in all the countries where its books are published. A significant proportion of the company's resources are channeled into promotion schemes and advertising. The success of Harlequin, in fact, is attributed to their innovative application of marketing techniques to publishing. Book advertising in France had been relatively uncommon until the successful campaigns launched by Harlequin produced such positive results. The cost of advertising campaigns for new Harlequin series run to millions of francs and are no longer restricted to those traditional advertising spots such as women's magazines or, in the United States, daytime television. In Paris, huge billboards frequently appear in the subway and on the sides of buses to promote the latest new series, and well-known film celebrities promote the series on the radio. The advertisements are now geared to a much larger public than was previously the case.

In France, one immediate consequence of the successful launching of the Harlequin series was the creation of several French romance series. Livre de Poche came out with "Toison d'or" (Golden Fleece) in 1979, and Presses de la Cité published a series entitled, "Turquoise." Jean-Pierre Duflot, of Presses de la Cité, justified the venture on the basis of the new readers the books would attract:

> Feminine literature corresponds to a need. We wanted to take it out of the framework of Livre de Poche and make it into a separate collection with its own brand, appealing to women readers not familiar with Livre de Poche books.
>
> (quoted in Favier 1979: 80)

The crucial point here is that women who would not normally read the more literary selections offered by Livre de Poche have now become avid romance readers.

Mass fiction of this sort has always operated on the assumption that books like any other product must sell, and when one market is saturated, then another must be found. For the romance industry this has meant reaching out to other segments of the female population which have resisted so far, either on a national or international level. The implications behind this kind of penetration go beyond the financial. Romance fiction, like other manifestations of popular culture, promotes visions of reality which are thought to correspond to what is known and recognized by the particular group of consumers. Up until only recently the world of romance fiction has rigidly held to the view that the world is white and middle-class and heterosexual, or if not middle-class then striving to move up the social hierarchy. Doubleday, in an attempt to reach more readers has begun to experiment with ethnic novels: the company recently published a novel with an American Indian heroine, and was planning another with a black heroine. (Frank 1981: 56) In France, however, Harlequin has remained faithful to the strictly white middle-class love story format, and I have yet to see any of the other romance novels treat contemporary social issues. It is unimaginable, for example, to find a romance centering around the problems of an Algerian family. One practical reason is that the older female members of the immigrant community in France do not yet prominently figure in the publisher's marketing strategies.

If, as has been said, the nineteenth-century domestic novel perpetuated the cult of domesticity, the formula romances of the 1960s and 1970s similarly evoked a social mythology which corresponded to a certain set of values prevalent at the time. Women remained at home, and the few who did have careers gave them up to devote themselves fully to their families. And, above all, women were expected to remain virgins before marriage. The Harlequin novels, for example, when first popularized in North America, rigidly held to these values and the majority of the heroines found in the novels were virgins and passively waiting for their Prince Charming.

For the greater part of their existence Harlequins, and this is true of the other romance publishers as well, have remained faithful to a strictly prescribed formula. The narratives are simple and linear; there is only one major action in each novel, and a minimum of secondary characters. The story revolves around the romantic involvement of a man and a woman who marry when the various conflicts impeding their union are satisfactorily resolved. The heroine, although young and sexually inexperienced, is intelligent and lively. There are never any explicit sexual scenes and intercourse, when it does happen, is only implied, and explicit sexual details are never given.[1]

Over the last forty years, the romances have attempted to respond to women's demands for greater sexual expression with more realistic characterization and plots. One new series introduced by Harlequin, according to Leslee Borger of Harlequin's public relations agency, is designed "to appeal to a broader reader base – not only to readers in the romance genres, but also to paperback consumers who read mainstream fiction." (Maryles and Symons 1983: 53) The novels are beginning to feature more realistic types of female characters. Avon Books has brought out a new line entitled "Finding Mr Right," which shows women who have achieved some level of success and who are definitely not Cinderella types:

> Each of these women faces a crisis in life and reaches the stage where she believes that the idea of finding a "perfect" man is just a myth. But in the spirit of happy endings, each heroine does find a man who is perfect just for her.
>
> (Maryles and Symons 1983: 56)

Likewise, the French have brought out series written by French authors and in French settings. Tatiana Tolstoi, director of Presses de la Cité's romance collection, emphasizes that French authors are being told to develop "feminine psychology and to use realistic settings. It must all be perfectly documented." (quoted in Favier 1979: 80) But the French series have failed to produce serious competition to either Harlequin or Silhouette, the romance series published in the USA by Simon and Schuster.

In spite of these so-called innovations in the novels' contents, the reader is still anchored within the emotional sphere of the heroine's life. The primary narrative goal of the novels, based as they are on the myth of the perfect man, may no longer be current, but marriage continues to be the modern romantic heroine's principal objective in life and her primary means of social identity. External problems such as divorce, managing a single-parent household, or unemployment do not – and according to the fictional conventions cannot – enter the romantic fictional world. Anything approaching the real day-to-day problems women encounter, apart from their relationships with men, remains off limits, or if such problems do enter the narrative they are resolved by the end of the narrative in a non-problematic fashion.

Rita Hubbard, in her examination of Harlequin novels over the last twenty years, concludes that although the Cinderella myth has undergone a transformation, the novels

> stop short of recognizing many real changes in society or integrating them into their formulaic plotlines. They reflect cultural shifts by their recognition of greater militancy in female attitudes, but they take a stand against changes in social mores and social institutions.　　　(Hubbard 1983: 177)

Harlequin characters may have now become active participants in the external world and may conduct themselves in a lively and intelligent manner, but they still stop short of presenting role models other than one which supports traditional female roles. The myth of woman as wife and mother is such an integral part of the narrative structure that without it the fiction would become something quite different, and unpredictable.

Harlequin Books, a remarkable example of the international-ization of book production, is of relevance to the discussion of bestsellers for the lesson it has taught publishers about the efficacy of marketing techniques applied to the literary product. Critics have attacked Harlequins and the series romances both for their detrimental effect on the publishing industry and for the reactionary message they convey to and about women. Yet, in spite of this, millions of women all over the world continue to buy them because they provide them with a relatively innocuous form of escape. Can one blame women's continued inferior status on the existence of cultural products such as Harlequins? The problem is complicated in that, on the one hand, the novels do not exist in isolation, and they tend to reinforce the same traditional views of women perpetuated by television, cinema, and other forms of popular culture. But, on the other hand, it is not possible to dismiss their importance in shaping women's attitudes towards the world. Modleski, in her study of Harlequins, concludes that women would continue to experience the contradictions they experience in the "real" world without the influence of the novels:

> Even though the novels can be said to intensify female tensions and conflicts, on balance the contradictions in women's lives are more responsible for the existence of Harlequins than Harlequins are for contradictions.   (Modleski 1984: 57-58)

Harlequins may not be to blame, but they also do little to resolve the more pressing contradictions in women's lives. While I, too would not directly place the blame for women's inferior position on the Harlequin-type novels, it is also true that they perpetuate and sanction a way of life which diametrically opposes any kind of radical change to the existing structures of society.

The historical novel

Harlequins of course are not the only form of popular feminine fiction which have experienced such phenomenal growth. Erotic historical romances – what have come to be known as the "bodice rippers" – have attracted a wide audience and are often paperback bestsellers. Like the series romances, the so-called bodice ripper erotic historical novels focus on the romantic involvement of the heroine. They differ however, in scope and complexity from the series romances in that they are considerably longer, and contain a much broader group of characters. They are more explicit sexually and often contain scenes in which the heroine is raped or seduced.

Some critics have praised the erotic historical romances as furthering strong independent female characters. In her study of the genre, Carol Thurston writes that "rather than the abductions, rapes and betrayals common to the subgenre, it is the overcoming of these misadventures that is the central focus of the stories." She concludes with:

> A mass medium that is constantly being changed and shaped by consumers, as these books have been by volunteered reader feedback and market research for a decade or more, *at the same time* reflects and acts as an agent of social change. Whether knowingly and intentionally or not, many of the

assumptions and messages found in these romance novels match those advocated by the women's movement.

(Thurston 1985: 43-44)

It is difficult for me to conclude, as Thurston does, that the novels actually act as an agent of social change; there is too great a reliance on conventionalized modes of female behavior. But it is also true that the erotic historical novels she discusses present the strongest image of women available in mass-market romances. Radway comments that the women she interviewed concerning their romance reading habits mentioned an article which had appeared in *Romance Report*, the newsletter of the Romance Writers of America, approving of the conclusion in Thurston's article that the historical romances provide readers with "new suggestions about female possibilities." (Radway 1984: 219) The heroines who appear in the historical romances are consistently strong, independent, and intelligent female characters. The majority of the novels, however, end, as do the traditional formula romances, with either the marriage of the heroine or the resolution of the love conflict. And it is here that the greatest contradiction emerges. The role model presented to women hints at the possibility of revolt against traditional modes of behavior, and the passive accepting female is shown to be a weak derisible character. But in the end she is rewarded for her rejection of this unconventional behavior with the man of her choice. Despite her stronger approach to the world, her sense of identity is still tied to the love of a man and within if not a total, then a quasi-domestic setting.

The bestselling historical novel in the form of the family saga, biography or period history comprises one of the largest categories of contemporary feminine bestsellers and falls in the shadowy area between the erotic historical romances and the contemporary mainstream bestsellers. Unlike those novels which purport to retell history, the feminine historical novels rewrite history to offer a feminine vision of the past condition of women. Women's fiction has always centered around female experiences with external social or historical events subordinate to domestic or emotional concerns. The bestselling historical novel has not suddenly reversed this trend, nor are the historical novels factual accounts of actual events. But many of the novels today integrate the exterior world into the day-to-day lives of the female characters. The romances, in contrast to the bestsellers, are notoriously ahistorical and external events function uniquely in relation to the domestic sphere and the life of the heroine. Lillian Robinson rightly points out that the so-called historical romances emphasize personal rather than public events, whereas in the real world

> sexual events take place in the margins of the larger movements of history, which are motivated and enacted by men, those transfers of kingdoms and affairs of nations whose details are state quarrels, wars and pestilences. (1978: 200-201)

History functions in the romance novel as a setting or a vehicle which removes the reader from the everyday. In the bestseller, by contrast, novels which are set in another period than the present weave historical circumstances and political struggles into the narrative in such a way as to redefine women's roles. Personal experiences in the form of marriage, childbirth, and love affairs co-exists alongside those larger movements of history yet assume greater significance when women's concerns are, for example, shown to affect the course of public events.

American and British novelists have rewritten the role women played in historical events or record their attempts to achieve professional recognition within a system that was previously closed to them. The reader is given a detailed description of the period and the prejudices women have had to overcome. Barbara Wood's *Domina* (1983), a story loosely based on a fictional contemporary of Elisabeth Blackwell, one of the first women physicans in the United States, and Gay Courter's *The Midwife* (1982), a detailed rendering of the obstacles women had to overcome in order to enter the medical professions at the beginning of the twentieth century, fall into this category. *Silver Wings, Santiago Blue* (1984) by Janet Dailey narrates the prejudices women pilots had to overcome and their invaluable assistance to the war effort during the first and second world wars. Judith Rossner's *Emmeline* (1981) tells of the oppression young girls suffered in the New England textile mills at the turn of the century, in the tradition of Rebecca Harding Davis's *Life in the Iron Mills* (1861). *Spring Moon* (1981) by Bette Bao Lord spans five generations of change in China from the days of

Mandarin rule to the death of Mao Tse-tung; told from the perspective of the young Spring Moon, the novel also presents a critical view of foot-binding and female oppression. *The Mists of Avalon* (1984) by Marion Zimmer Bradley retells the Arthurian saga from a feminist point of view.

In each of these novels, history functions not to record actual events but to demythify previous accounts and deny the traditional inferiority of women. Desires of the present are placed within the context of the past. In *The Mists of Avalon* Igraine justifies her rebellion against the priests when she says, "She would not have her daughter brought up to feel shame at her womanhood." (91) The "new woman" of the 1980s reappears through her counterpart in other times or countries. In *The Midwife*, the young revolutionary Lazar, Hannah's husband, speaks admiringly of the "'new women' who freely choose their own paths, refusing to subjugate themselves to the old traditions." (125)

The family saga

The publication in 1977 of Colleen McCullough's *The Thorn Birds* turned the family saga into one of the most popular and varied forms of the historical novel today. McCullough's novel, according to John Sutherland, combines elements of the Michener/Haley/Uris

> "birth of the nation" theme as well as these authors' massive spread of narrative. But in other ways it is closer to the family saga or "dynasty" style or epic.   (Sutherland 1981: 77)

The immediate and almost overwhelming success of the novel – which still periodically appears on the bestseller list after a television rerun of the mini-series – set a pattern which many writers continue to imitate. Sutherland identifies four main elements which contributed to the appeal of *The Thorn Birds* and which can also be found in the other novels of this type: 1) The "sweeping panorama of an 'epic moment' in the formation of a nation;" 2) high life and gracious living; 3) the forbidden loves of the female members of the family; and 4) a preoccupation with women's emancipation. (Sutherland 1981: 78)

If the fourth item Sutherland identifies is slightly altered to include preoccupation with women's success then we have a fairly accurate description of the family saga novels of the 1980s. In addition to the customary story of several generations, which forms the bulk of the family saga corpus, the phenomenal climb to the top by the family's female members is added. The narration of the changes which occur in the lives of one family's female members over several generations equally document the growth and development of the country in which the family members are born or to which they emigrate. Strong female characters begin with nothing and by sheer force build up an enormous empire after having survived a multitude of adversities and misfortunes. Barbara Taylor Bradford's *A Woman of Substance* (1983) and the sequels *Hold the Dream* (1985) and *To Be the Best* (1988) tell of a department store magnate who began as a maid. Judith Gould's *The Love-Makers* (1986) is the tale of a young mother with three small children who fulfills her dream of owning a hotel. By the end of the novel she is the head of a chain of luxury hotels. In each case, the heroine starts out with nothing and, through hard work and her fiercely independent spirit, emerges victoriously as the matriarch of the family. Moreover, her rise to power parallels that of the nation, thus giving her story a more than privileged significance by suggesting that female success has contributed to the nation's development and greatness.

The case of the Jewish family saga novels

A significant number of American bestselling family saga novelists have structured their novels around Jewish topics. These are not, by any means, the only novels of this type being published, nor is the myth of superwoman specific to them. But in view of their consistent popularity in the United States, and to a limited extent in France, I have decided to use them as an example of the family saga/historical novel form. Although structured around Jewish themes, the following novels also all contain the elements Sutherland alluded to in his discussion of the family saga. Only, in these examples, the epic moment recounted concerns a group of people united by a common religion rather than place of birth. Cynthia Freeman, Belva Plain, and Gay Courter have each written several novels which treat

115

non-Jewish as well as Jewish topics.

Cynthia Freeman in her first novel *A World Full of Strangers* (1975), examined the question of anti-semitism and assimilation in the second generation of Eastern Europe Jewish immigrant families. She returns to this issue in *Portraits* (1979), the story of the rise of a family from the poverty of the Lower East Side to riches in California, in *Come Pour the Wine* (1980) and in *No Time for Tears* (1981).

No Time for Tears (1981) remained, as do most of Freeman's books, over six months on the *New York Times Book Review* lists. Chavala Landau, its heroine, combines, unlike Freeman's earlier heroines, in true superwoman style both the strength to overcome any obstacles which threaten the well-being of her family with the ability to excel in the business world. *No Time for Tears* follows Chavala's journey from Odessa after the pogram of 1905 which killed a large part of the Jewish population to Israel and then to New York. The novel spans three generations and through the adventures and ordeals her family undergoes depicts the struggle for a Jewish state.

The novel opens with poverty and despair: Chavala, 16 years old and the oldest of five children, is helping deliver her mother's child. With the birth of the child and the death of her mother, Chavala assumes the role of mother for the new-born child and protector for her family, and this remains her principal role throughout the novel. At the moment when she takes on the responsiblity for her family she swears never to lose control of her life: "she was going to *direct*, she was going to *plan* her life. Somehow she would do the impossible." (14) Everything she does after this point is done in order to hold together her family: she proposes to her childhood friend Dovid and arranges to marry without her father's consent and during the period of mourning for her mother; she kills two men, once during a pogrom and once when she is attacked by a Bedouin outside Jerusalem; and she leaves her husband to go off to the United States to make her fortune. In none of these cases is she punished for her acts. In fact, her non-traditional actions, done for the good of her family, yield positive results. After she kills the Bedouin she finds a bag of gem stones on his body which is what enables her to lcave Palestine and go to the United States where she makes her fortune through a chain of jewelry stores.

The men in the novel are either ineffective and unable to protect their families or dreamers. Chavala, after the death of her mother, dismisses the possibility of her father's functioning as the head of the family:

> She had to be the strong one. So much and so many depended upon her. Let her father have the blessed release of grief. It was the only solace left for him. All the failures of his life were descending upon him. (4)

Her disregard of her father's role as "man of the house" is made clear a few pages later when Chavala announces that she is going to marry without his consent:

> my father's no longer the head of the family. He stopped caring about anything when he lost my mother, seemed to give up on life. (15)

Chavala initially marries because she feels that the children need a man in the house, but there is little doubt that her husband's presence is superfluous. At a later point in the novel, Dovid also becomes aware of this:

> Dovid thought bitterly to himself that he hadn't really protected her at all by sending her away. A woman like Chavala one never protected. (196)

The affirmation that the modern woman can control her own life at the same time that she retains her feminine qualities and values runs throughout the novel. After Chavala and her family flee to Palestine from Odessa, she and Dovid leave her sisters and brother behind in the city with their father to join a kibbutz. Chavala experiences loneliness for the family she has left behind, but when she admits to longing for them, she is mocked by the other women, who tell her:

> She hadn't really escaped the *shtetl* . . . her problem wasn't her longing and love of the old place but her Jewish guilt . . . "Wake up to today," one said, "we've been so conditioned by family obligations, it's become a kind of Jewish disease." (77)

By encouraging the reader to suffer Chavala's rejection by the other women, the text not only refutes the modern rejection of the family advocated by the women, but also defines the "new woman," in this case the kibbutz woman, in a negative way. Furthermore, Chavala also quite vehemently refuses to understand how the kibbutz women can accept doing the same work as the men and refuse being "treated as women." This opposition between the portrayal of dogmatic feminists who are thought by the heroine to want to be like men and the heroine who, despite her unconventional behavior, retains traditional values, can be found throughout the entire corpus of contemporary women's bestsellers. The implied rejection is not so much of feminism but the extremes to which it is too often carried. Chavala assumes what could be considered men's work throughout the novel but since she always demands to be "treated like a woman," she sees no contradiction between herself and the kibbutz women.

When, in order to provide for her family, Chavala leaves her husband and goes off to the United States, her family is hurt but they do not criticize her defiance of traditional roles. Rather, the reader is told that her decision enables her to become the equal of her husband. In 1929 Dovid comes to the United States in order to raise money for the Haganah, the secret Jewish self-defense army. Chavala is proud that he has come to her for help, and in an amusing episode she cajoles the Jewish mafia into contributing $2 million dollars to the cause. Dovid realizes her power at that moment, and also forgives her abandonment:

> She was the giver, and he, in fact, was somehow the taker. Her love of Eretz Yisroel was just as great as his. It had only taken a different direction. Come from a different direction, source . . . love of her family. . . (370)

The unique aspect of the Jewish novels is that throughout the corpus of family saga novels the love of Israel is equated with the love of family. Both become within the contexts of the novels equally unassailable concepts.

Chavala's pragmatism is constantly contrasted to Dovid's idealism, which becomes identified as a male trait throughout the novel. For Dovid, the only solution for the Jews is Zionism and the state of Israel:

> we live as the oppressed, the downtrodden, but one day Eretz Yisroel will rise up, and on that day we will have our revenge for all the tyranny and injustice perpetrated against us. (27)

Chavala, however, dismisses his dreams as idealism and wants only to go to America. She doesn't reject the Zionist dream but since her objective is her family she opts for the more practical choice of the United States:

> If there was any chance to change their lives, it was, she was convinced, in America. That was a new land. There was real equality and freedom there. And people lived decently, not in squalor. She'd literally dreamed about America, about arriving there and seeing the famous golden land of opportunity. *That* was where hope had reality. . . . Let papa have his dreams and Dovid his hopes. . . . (27)

The notion that politics is an affair of men is repeated throughout the novel by the women:

> For Chavala, politics was what men constantly, boringly talked about. If a rebellion had occurred, it hadn't touched her life here in Zichron. For her there was one small sacred place that seemed impenetrable . . . her home, and her family. (102)

The title of the novel, however, belies the problematic contradictions facing the contemporary heroine. If women are to succeed in a male world, they must shed female signs of weakness; there is, as the title implies, no time for tears. This sentence appears after Chavala's mother dies when Chavala must assume the responsibility of the family, and later in the novel, when Dovid leaves her and the family to join the fight against the Turks in Palestine. Women's strength, like that of the Jewish people, is shown to be derived not from signs of weakness, but through an adherence to power and loyalty to the family. Early on in the novel, Chavala reflects on and then rejects what she sees as having been the fate of her people: "Jews for centuries had accepted their fates with passive resignation. Not Chavala." (11) Chavala, typical of the superwoman myth which permeates the bestselling family sagas, not only combines the responsibilities of family and career but also manages to overcome any doubts she may have as to the likelihood of her success.

Belva Plain is another major Jewish family saga novelist whose novels are consistent bestsellers. From her early novel *Evergreen* (1978), the story of a Jewish immigrant woman's rise from the Lower East Side, to her latest three *Crescent City*

(1984), *The Golden Cup* (1986), and *Tapestry* (1988), she follows the lives and fate of one Jewish family from the time they leave Germany up until the end of the Second World War. *Crescent City*, Plain's fourth bestseller, was on the *New York Times Book Review* list for twelve weeks and reappeared on the longest-running paperback list.

Crescent City, the story of Miriam, the daughter of a wealthy Jewish merchant in nineteenth-century New Orleans, explores Jewish participation in the abolitionist movement during the Civil War as well as treating the themes of anti-semitism and Jewish assimilation in the United States, racism, and women's emancipation. The novel follows the story of Miriam Raphael from the moment her father returns from the United States to Germany to rescue her and her brother from the ghetto where they had been living with their grandfather, through her childhood in New Orleans, her marriage, and her survival throughout the Civil War. But above all, the novel examines the question of power and the powerless position of women in a patriarchal society. Unlike the portrayal of Chavala in *No Time for Tears*, Miriam's solution is not in becoming a superwoman in the world of business, but rather in developing and eventually counteracting an awareness of her inferior position in society.

Miriam's awareness of her powerlessness comes when she is forced into a marriage with a man she neither knows very well nor likes but of whom her family approves. For Miriam, marriage is seen as the only course of action open to someone of her class and social standing. The following excerpts from her journal explicitly make clear her unhappiness, and the dilemma in which she finds herself:

> What is there left? To be married, of course. Everyone knows that's what life is for a woman. Even the old-maid teachers at school know that. They are supposed to teach us how to be better wives and mothers. But how can an old maid possibly know? (98)

The issue of women's emancipation is linked to this consistently negative representation of marriage and the limits placed on female participation outside the home. Miriam's unhappy situation is placed within the context of female emancipation when her brother David raises the question of female education:

Eager little Miriam, curious, quick, and fanciful! Surely that mind was the equal of David's one? It occurred to him that a girl's mind might be wasted just as much by idle luxury as by the meager poverty of their European village. (68)

Miriam, who understands she has no other choice open to her, enters into her marriage as a prison and compares her situation to that of the slave boy Blaise: "it occurred to her how odd it was that Blaise had some possibility of freedom, whereas she had none." (179) Within the confines of her social group, however, Miriam has no way of revolting other than an unsatisfying affair which she mistakes for love.

As for Chavala in *No Time for Tears*, the motivating force behind Miriam's attaining independence is her family. Her true strength emerges during the bombing of Atlanta when she, in the style of Scarlett O'Hara, becomes the mainstay around which the family gathers. After she has been tested through all possible tribulations and, more importantly, has discovered her own sense of self-identity and worth outside the traditional role of wife, she finds love with a man she has known and trusted since childhood.

Another variation among the Jewish-oriented novels is the semi-historical semi-family saga novel. *Rivington Street* (1982) by Meredith Tax, *The Markoff Women* (1985) by June Flaum Singer, or *The Midwife* (1981) by Gay Courter are a few of the mainstream hardcover women's novels which integrate Jewish topics into the text. *The Midwife*, a 1981 bestseller, recounts the life of a young Jewish woman and her struggle to succeed professionally as a midwife. The novel traces the career of Hannah Blau from the Imperial College of Midwifery in czarist Russia to her practice on New York's Lower East Side. The reader closely follows Hannah through her training at the Imperial College to her struggle against the hypocrisy of a misogynous male medical world in New York.

Like so many of the female characters present in women's novels, the heroine studies on her own while the father teaches the less gifted son. Hannah recognizes from an early age the differences between her prospects and those of her younger brother, who is not her equal intellectually. Even though Hannah may be educated, she is reminded by the rabbi that the priority in her life must remain being a good Jewish woman, and fulfilling the accompanying responsibilities. When Hannah expresses the desire to continue her education, she is told:

> And you, little Hannah, you will be a woman, and your area will be the home, where you will be the absolute ruler, like your mother. (44)

He points out her mother as an example to follow:

> Sarah Blau, you are a pious woman. . . . You keep a kosher home, you follow all the prescribed mitzvahs. You make a happy family. Would you rather have a man's head on a woman's body? (45)

As in the other Jewish historical novels, and the family sagas in general, the role of the mother as keeper of the family attains nearly mythic dimensions. In *The Midwife*, it is Hannah, like Chavala and Miriam, who holds the family together: her father dies early in the novel, and while her husband Lazar satisfies her sexually and provides her with the social position of wife and mother, he is ineffective when it comes to supporting the family financially. At one point in the novel, Hannah, pregnant and hungry, fights a rat for a discarded piece of meat while Lazar sits drinking tea and discussing politics in a cafe. This absence of the father, either through his actual death or his inability to support the family, is by no means unique to the Jewish novels but as was seen in the discussion of the nineteenth-century novel it is a common theme which reappears throughout women's popular fiction. Women are initially propelled out into the world because they have lost their primary means of financial support.

The characterization of Hannah Blau, like that of Chavala, Miriam, and the other Jewish heroines, depends upon a number of contemporary myths which compete with and contradict one another. The myth of the mother – in all three cases, the Jewish mother – who is the nurturing support of her family contrasts with the modern independent woman who aggressively attains her goals in spite of tremendous obstacles. Chavala, for example, succeeds because what she does is in the interest of her family. In all the novels, as is the case in other feminine bestsellers of the 1980s, the roles are shown to be not only compatible but complementary. Furthermore, in the Jewish novels, the idea that women are inferior beings is also contested. Eve in Singer's *The*

Markoff Women links the oppression of Jewish males and the humiliation they have suffered with their insistence on keeping women in an inferior position.

In these novels, historical events not only have a direct consequence on the lives of the characters but often assume an importance in themselves. In *No Time for Tears*, the reader is given enough information to understand and sympathize with the Zionist cause. And in *Crescent City* the anti-racist discourse is connected to the issue of female inferiority. In *The Midwife* the narrative focuses on the professional discrimination of women, and the reader follows a well-documented account of anti-woman practices rampant in the male medical community at the beginning of the twentieth century. The separation of historical events from political ones – politics become an affair of the men – effectively gives women a role in the development of events. The women react to historical events in so far as they threaten or touch upon the lives of their family, and through the extended metaphor of family and country, the participation of women is revalorized. Whereas the men in so many of the novels are directly involved in public affairs (Dovid in *No Time for Tears* is a Zionist and an active leader in the Haganah, Lazar in *The Midwife* a Socialist, and David in *Crescent City* an abolitionist during the Civil War), the women are more pragmatic and impatient with the ideologies which fascinate their men. In *The Markoff Women* when Eva's husband reproaches her for ignoring the revolutionary ferment taking place in Russia she tells him that the young girl who had once thought freedom was the major thing in her life

> was grown-up to realize that there is no Utopia. That's what Marxism is all about, really. . . . Now that I'm a mother I know one thing. You have to fill your children's stomachs first so that they can live. . . . (293)

Thus, the women are not completely outside the currents of history, but their concerns are personal and practical first rather than political or ideological. The inability of the men in Freeman's or Plain's novels to survive without constant female attentiveness further devalorizes their activities. The women are constantly saving the lives of the male members of their families: Chavala saves Dovid's life on at least three occasions, and he is never around when her life is threatened. Miriam finds and saves her brother David from a prisoner-of-war camp and nurses him back to health. She also assumes charge of the family after her husband Eugene is blinded. The implication is that although these men are involved in major activities without the women, outside the context of the family, their activities are meaningless. As Chavala says in *No Time for Tears*,

> It was what she *did*. Some people fought for big causes . . . like Dovid. . . . Well, her life was her family, and whatever and wherever she had to pursue its survival, health and yes, someday prosperity. (327)

The Jewish family sagas and historical novels use historical events, and in particular, past oppression of the Jewish people, to create a Jewish identity which emphasizes the role of women in a world which has been traditionally suspicious of female participation outside of the confines of the home. Furthermore, in the light of a resurgence of anti-semitism the novels while asserting a Jewish identity also document progressive moments in Jewish history to which the reader can refer. The history lessons proffered in the novels, however, are not the sort which tend towards a transformation of the future: stories of the Holocaust and National Socialism teach that Jews must always be on the alert to attacks from the outside, and not the danger fascist ideologies present to minority groups as a whole. The world of the Jewish novels is an insular one. And rather than the novels saying "it happened to us, we must prevent it from happening to others," the message which comes most strongly across is "we must protect our own."

French historical novels

Few of the American family saga novels which appeal to the multi-ethnic population of the United States become bestsellers in France although they are systematically translated. One possible reason for their lack of success is that they bear no relation to French life. The historical novel by French authors, however, has always enjoyed a wide audience in France and is by no means limited to women writers. French readers with whom I've spoken tend to favor a homogeneous image of history and view the historical novel as an educational experience as well as pleasant reading. Therefore they insist on factual and documented accounts rather than on a purely fictional version of history.

Unlike the family sagas or historical novels published in the United States many of the French bestsellers are fictionalized biographies of great men or women, especially queens or, frequently, the mistresses of kings. Françoise Chandernagor, author of the 1981 bestseller *L'allée du Roi* (The King's Way), the story of Madame de Maintenon, mistress of Louis XIV and uncrowned Queen of France, uses her correspondence and diaries. Geneviève Dorman's 1982 bestseller *Le roman de Sophie Trébuchet* (The Novel of Sophie Trébuchet), the story of Victor Hugo's mother, mixes historical documents with passages of fictionalized dialogue. Sophie's story, according to Dorman, has been left untold because

she didn't have a life compatible with the traditional morals required in the nineteenth century and the first half of ours. Sophie, in effect, had a lover whom she loved passionately.

(373)

It is more probable that Sophie Trébuchet's story has, up until now, been left undocumented because of her political involvement during Napoleon's Directory, and her status as a "great man's" mother. Kenzié Mourad's *De la part de la Princesse morte* (On Behalf of the Dead Princess) (1987) is a fictionalized account of life of the author's mother who was wife of the last Sultan of the Ottoman Empire. Mourad's story, told in novel form, was an immediate success when it came out, and reappeared on bestseller lists one year later when Laffont relaunched the novel through articles and interviews. In these sophisticated biographical novels, it is the choice of personage rather than the manner of presentation which is important. Although the heroines are usually historic figures, these strong female characters have been either largely or completely neglected in historical accounts of the period being treated.

In addition to the biographical novels, historical romances similar in content and form to those published in the United States are also popular. In fact, Carol Thurston credits the eleven-volume series of Angelique novels by the wife and husband team Anne and Serge Golan with being the model for the current wave of historical romances. (Thurston 1987: 36) Juliette Benzoni and Jeanne Bourin, to cite two of the more popular women historical novelists, write primarily about the French Middle Ages. Their novels are consistent bestsellers and are particularly popular with the bookclubs. Fanny Deschamps, a newcomer to the historical novel scene, depicts the adventures of a high-spirited young girl during the period of Louis XV in her novel *La Bougainvillée* (1982), translated into English as *The King's Garden* (1985).

Deschamps' *The King's Garden*, which combines elements of the historical novel and the romance, moves between accounts of the intellectual, scientific, and artistocratic personages who lived in and around the court of Louis XV and the loves and adventures of Jeanne Beauchamps. Befriended by Diderot, Buffon, and Jussieu, Jeanne, a highly intelligent, spirited young woman, is in love with two very different men: Dr Philibert Aubriot, the King's botanist, and Vincent de Cotignac, pirate and Knight of Malta. In fact, the novel opens with Jeanne's daydreaming about the first and ends with her in the arms of the second. Jeanne is very much the liberated woman who refuses to be manipulated. When she feels hindered by the fact that she is a woman she assumes the dress of a young boy. She is open about what she thinks and is rarely hesitant to defend what she believes. At one point, the image of the "modern" woman emerges when Jeanne reacts in anger to a letter sent by Vincent:

> How dare he! . . . He wills, decides, commands, and lays down the law. He thinks that after God he is master of our love boat. Do you think he knows that Louis XIV is dead and we now live in an era when women are allowed to speak and act for themselves? (613)

The contradiction which surfaces is that the motivating factor behind Jeanne's actions is her love for the two men. It is within the conflict of her love affairs that she demands equality.

Régine Deforges, Irène Frain, Paul-Loup Sulitzer, and Maurice Denuzière have all written bestsellers which, similar to the American novels, present a romanticized version of a past moment in French history. Historical details assume a greater importance than in the American novels, and the point of view is not exclusively, except in the case of Sulitzer's *Hannah* (1985), from a woman's point of view. In Denuzière's *Louisiana* (1977), for example, unlike several of the American novels on the city, detailed information about the history of New Orleans is an integral part of the narrative and long passages read as if taken from history books.

Régine Deforges' trilogy, comprising *The Blue Bicycle* (1983), *101 Avenue Henri-Martin* (1983), and *The Devil Is Still Laughing* (1984), was a record-breaking bestseller. *Gone with the Wind* transposed to France during the Second World War, the trilogy spans the war years from 1939 until the signing of the Armistice in Berlin in 1945 and takes place in a similar rural setting – a vineyard in the south of France.

In the tradition of the historical novel, *The Blue Bicycle* is about love, intrigue, and a significant historical moment. The story of Léa Delmas, the narrative traces her maturing from being the spoiled teenage daughter of a wealthy family through her war experiences and participation in the Resistance until the liberation of the Bergen-Belsen concentration camp and her return to Montillac, the family home. Léa Delmas, the French Scarlett O'Hara, is in love with Laurent d'Argilat who is married to Camille. The triangular relationship between Léa, Laurent, and François Tavernier reflects that of Rhett, Scarlett, and Ashley. A major difference between *The Blue Bicycle* and *Gone with the Wind* – and it is difficult to discuss Deforges' novel without making the comparison – lies in the two authors' different conception of the modern woman. For Deforges, feminine independence translates into sexual freedom; Léa is neither prudish nor reluctant to express her sexual desires:

> In her neighborhood she never felt the constraints of her sex, but rather an exaltation of her femininity as a value in and of itself and not as an object of submission or calculation.
>
> (*Henri-Martin*: 332)

The importance of sexual freedom as a vital component of the modern woman is made clear in this reflection of François Tavernier's on Léa as a true woman:

> she was a real woman, just as he liked them, both free and submissive, coquettish and natural, brave and weak, happy and

wistful, sensual and modest. Modest? . . . not really, if anything, she was provocative. (*The Devil is still laughing*: 280)

He goes on to reflect that she does not act like a well raised young French girl, but rather is like the heroines seen in American films:

> She did not behave like a well brought-up young French-woman, but more like the heroines of American films, enticing and prim but capable of sitting on a chair with their skirts hitched up to reveal the tops of their stockings, or leaning over to let you glimpse their cleavage. Léa was one of those. He knew how she liked to arouse men's desire. She blossomed under their gaze. (*Devil* 280)

The reader is led to believe that although Léa is unaware of François' description of her as the "new woman," she approves of his vision of her and his way of behaving:

> She would like to have protested, to have been shocked by his offhandedness and tell him that she did not want to be treated like a whore, but none of that would have been true. He behaved exactly as she would have wished. (*Devil* 280)

Unlike Scarlett O'Hara, Léa Delmas is provocative and sensual. She neither marries François during the course of the three novels, although she does make love with him, nor does she assume or even consider assuming responsibility for the family home. Her independence derives from the power she has over men rather than from self-sufficiency. She moves through a series of events which cause her to mature, but unlike the American heroines, she rarely takes control of the situations in which she finds herself. At the end of the novel she returns to her home not to take charge of its rebuilding but to find the site of her childhood.

The Blue Bicycle is also the story of a country torn by war and divided in its loyalties. Deforges examines the conflicting loyalties of the French during the war and attempts to understand the reasons why certain of her countrymen opted for Pétain and why so many young men went off to fight on the side of the Germans against the Russians. The most interesting aspects of the novel are those which deal with the mechanisms of collaboration and betrayal.

Irène Frain's bestselling *Le Nabab* (1982) is the story of French involvement in eighteenth-century India and spans a period of twenty-four years from June 1754 until 1778 when the French finally left India. The novel also centers on the love between Sarasvati, an Indian princess, and René Madec, a European and the principal male character. Contrary to the American or British historical novels which retain a consistent feminine perspective, the narrative vacillates between the exploits of Madec and the Princess Sarasvati, with a significant portion of the text given over to Madec's war-time activities. Furthermore, the purpose of the novel's epilogue is to inform the reader of Madec's fate and his final return to France from India.

The initial description of the Princess Sarasvati emphasizes her feminine characteristics and her lack of independence: "Love and beauty: those were her two sole worries." (36) Yet the reader learns through the course of the narrative that she is unlike other women, rather she is what the priest calls "a woman of war":

> It wouldn't take much for sweet Sarasvati who still believed in love to become what she had always been in the eyes of the stars: a woman of war. (I, 185)

At the time that these words are spoken by the Brahman, Sarasvati is still unaware of her destiny. It is only later, when she begins to contemplate a life spent in the woman's part of the palace, the *zenana*, living out what is considered to be the proper role for a woman, that thoughts of revolt form in her mind:

> Her destiny was elsewhere. Outside of the zenana! Far from the women's prison, a place of mirrors and births, a cloistered life, waiting for love. (I, 420)

It is not, however, until the violent death of her husband and her subsequent refusal of *sati* that she is liberated from her position as wife and free to assume a male role:

> Such a voice sweet, its inflexions still sensual, to pronounce sentences spoken by a man, syllables of force, words of authority. (I, 453)

Madec, on whom the dying prince had conferred the power of regent, is hopelessly in love with Sarasvati and initially believes in the possibility of an equal yet sexual relationship between them. However, once Sarasvati assumes the power formerly held by her husband and rejects her traditional feminine role, she ceases to be considered a woman despite her beauty. Unlike the situation in the American novels in which femininity and power are redefined so as to compliment each other, in Frain's novel they are deemed incompatible. Sombre, a French adventurer who fights the English and has come to know Sarasvati, tells her, "You are not a woman. . . . There is a man in you." (II, 138) It's impossible for Sarasvati to combine the role of the "modern" independent woman with that of being the ruler of her country. From the moment that she takes command, she relinquishes all her feminine characteristics. The choice for her lies in either fighting like a man, which she does, or retreating to the traditional submissiveness of a woman, which she rejects. *Le Nabab* attests to the incompatibility of public strength and femininity.

Reminiscent of Freeman's novel and the historical rendition of a woman's rise to power found in other American novels are the French Paul Sulitzer's 1985 bestseller *Hannah* and its sequel *L'Impératrice* (1986). Although I have until here limited my discussion to novels written by women, it is important to look briefly at Sulitzer's bestsellers which, in terms of characterization and plot, resemble more closely the American family saga novels than they do the French novels. Hannah's independence and power, rather than being defined in terms of her sexuality, derive from her forceful character and intelligence.

Hannah, which is roughly based on the life of Helena Rubinstein and the creation of her cosmetics empire, is one of the few novels which uses as its model a woman who succeeds in the world of business and finance. Whereas the novels by Dorman, Chandernagor, and Mourad integrate actual historical documents into the text and pretend to be true stories, *Hannah* is a completely romanticized version of a woman's life. The novel begins in Poland in 1882, follows Hannah's initial entry into the cosmetics world and the eventual launching of her empire in Paris, and ends with her foray into the American market in 1900 at the age of 25. At 7 years old, in the company of her best friend Taddeuz, a young Polish Catholic boy, Hannah watches as her village is attacked by a unit of Russian soldiers. The initial description of Hannah as a child already foreshadows the strength she will later acquire:

> She is not at all just a very young girl . . . in her sleeps a sharp intelligence, cold, sometimes cruel, that the years to come will wake. . . (10)

Hannah is neither very large nor pretty and is compared to the unlikely image of an owl. Hannah's outstanding characteristic, like that of the American heroines, is her intelligence. Mendel, her life-long friend, reflects on the words of her father when Hannah was still a child:

> I have a daughter who is not at all ordinary, Mendel. She reads like someone drinks water and understands even better. It wouldn't take much for her to make me afraid of her precocity. (38)

Her intelligence is alluded to on a number of occasions: her brother goes off to school, "even though he doesn't know his books as well as I do. But he's a boy and I am a girl although I am as flat as a board." (46) It is also Hannah who runs the house after her father's death because her mother, with whom she has practically nothing to do, is insignifcant and predisposed to submission.

Hannah's lack of relationship to and complete disregard for her mother is one point on which this novel written by a man differs from those by women. Although the mothers in most of the other novels are also left behind by their daughters, they are never reduced to the non-entity Hannah's mother becomes in this novel. Furthermore, maternity and the nuclear family occupy a minimal place in the narrative. Once Hannah finds and marries Taddeuz, her childhood sweetheart, she expresses the desire to have children and start a family. But for Hannah children are part of her overall life plan and not the expression of a particularly maternal desire. Hannah's two aims in life are the acquisition of wealth and power and marriage with Taddeuz both of which she accomplishes.

The French women who write historical novels which succeed as bestsellers appear to continue to be influenced by the warning given a hundred years ago to Josephine Maldague to avoid writing books which only treat feminine topics. Neither *Adieu Volodia*, the story of a Jewish working-class family in the 1920s by Simone Signoret nor *Le Nabab* restrict the narrative to a woman's perspective, nor do they treat issues which are considered to be women's topics. *The Blue Bicycle* remains the story of a painful period in a nation's history, rather than the development of one woman's life.

Two major differences exist between the French and the American novels of this type. First, the American emphasis on the family and the attempt to reconcile the role of woman as mother and as a person active in the outside world is virtually absent in the French novels. Perhaps this is because the American myth of the land of opportunity encourages this kind of historical rewriting. The many American novels treating the immigrant's rise to fame and fortune attest to a certain pride each group experiences in their ethnicity. Whereas, in the French novels either the narrative ends with the marriage of the heroine, as is the case in Deschamps' or Deforges' novels, or the family is simply relegated to a position of secondary importance.

Second, men in the French novels are accorded a more active role in the women's lives. Unlike the ineffective dreamers found in the American novels, the men in these novels never recede into the background. Although Taddeuz in *Hannah* is a writer and never actively contributes to the household, he is never dismissed in the way Hannah of *The Midwife* dismisses her husband. *Le Nabab* ends on the fate of Madec and his triumphant return to France. In *The Blue Bicycle*, François Tavernier, unlike the men found in either Freeman's or Plain's novels, rescues and provides emotional support, not only for Léa, but for the other women in the novel. As will be seen in the novels which treat the contemporary woman, the active participation of men in the French novels also points to a more positive, or at least a more dependent, relationship with men than is presented in the American novels.

Finally, the contradictions between woman as an object of desire and the need to assume new modes of behavior in order to enter into the public sphere still remain unresolved in the French novels. Other than Sulitzer's *Hannah* the combination of power and femininity appears rarely and when it does, it's judged to be impossible. Women who seek to empower their positions in a male world give up their claims to being women.

Notes

1. For more on Harlequins, see Rabine (1985), Modleski (1984), and Mussell (1984) for a detailed analysis of Harlequin romances and the changes which they have undergone.

Chapter five

The dilemma of marriage

"What were your hopes and dreams when you graduated from college..?" Ken was her hopes and dreams. Marriage was, and a romantic, harmonious life.
Question Two: "Did you achieve them?" Of course. Oh yes. I was given the wrong dream to want and I got it.
Rona Jaffe, After the Reunion (1985)

Mass-produced fiction for women, Kay Mussell writes in her book on women's romance fiction, always ends with the marriage of the heroine. Once the conflicts around which the narrative are organized have been resolved, the novel must terminate because with marriage a woman's story effectively ceases:

> Once a woman's love story has been told, repetition of the experience for her is inappropriate – repetition would, in fact, undermine the entire premise of her story – and her life is, for dramatic purposes, over. Romances suggest that the greatest adventure for a woman occurs when she finds the one man with whom she will share the rest of her life.   (Mussell 1984: 6)

The modern romance formula essentially affirms the ideals of monogamous marriage and feminine domesticity. Even in the longer "contemporary romances," marriage, despite the novels' more complex structure, closes the narrative. For example, Vera Cowie's *Fortunes* (1985), a 600-page novel whose cover proclaims it to be an "international bestseller" is little more than a very long romance. Set in the world of art and auction houses, the love intrigue dominates the narrative. The workings of the auction house, with the emphasis on its more glamorous aspects, provide the impetus which moves the narrative along until the heroine and the hero are able to straighten out their misunderstandings and come together at the end. Characters fall into the category of good or bad, and are identified according to supposed national characteristics: so and so is either very French, or American, or Latin. Once the good characters are clearly recognized as such and find each other, the narrative concludes with their coming together in a reaffirmation of monogamy and gentle yet strong femininity.

"Marriage," Carolyn Heilbrun writes, "in fiction even more than life, has been the woman's adventure, the object of her quest, her journey's end." (1978: 309) In contemporary fiction, she continues, the abandonment of marriage has replaced its achievement. This is as much the case in today's bestsellers as it is with other forms of contemporary women's fiction, the difference being that in the bestsellers, the contemporary heroine seriously reflects upon her marriage; frequently she rejects it when it no longer fits her but in spite of her reservations, only rarely does she walk away at the end of a novel single. The fictionalization of marriage has dramatically changed along with the actual social position of women. Marriage may figure high on a woman's list of priorities, but she no longer assumes it to be either the only option open to her or the end point of her life. The high divorce rate and an increasing disillusionment with marriage as a stable social institution, which has meant that more and more women are looking for fulfillment outside the home, has also produced a fiction which, by the 1980s, has become less oriented towards marriage. The evolution of the treatment of marriage in the bestselling women's novels of the sixties, seventies, and eighties corresponds to the financial and social gains women have acquired, at least in the United States. The myth that woman's unique place is in the home has not only lost its credibility but also comes under attack in the texts. The heroine of the bestselling novels of the 1980s places much less emphasis on marriage as a means of social identification than was the case in the novels published ten or fifteen years previously. In France, the problem is articulated somewhat differently. Although marriage still remains an important means of social identification, it is also less problematic. Love or being desired have become the crucial issues rather than acquiring a wedding ring.

Marriage in the majority of bestsellers is by no means simple, although many novels still end with the heroine's marriage. Often, as in the nineteenth-century novels, marriage is an affair of desertions, beatings, and unhappiness. An increasing number of contemporary novels now end on what is considered, according to romance conventions, an ambiguous note: in some cases, the heroine considers living with a man to whom she is not married, or there may be a reaffirmation of a shaky marriage. Frequently, the resolution of a love relationship occurs simultaneously with the heroine's career decisions or advancement. It is not uncommon to find a heroine who decides in favor of her career or her need to find herself. In Spellman's *So Many Partings* (1984), Megan tells the man she loves:

> If I stayed now – without knowing for certain who I am, and what I have to offer . . . and without your having had a chance to think it through – it wouldn't last for us, either. . . . If you sensed that you had absolute power over me, or that I was unsure of my own worth, sooner or later you'd want to discard me as you've done with so many others. . . . I must be a whole person, my love, or we'd be doomed. (492)

Although she does decide to marry him at the end of the novel, it is only after she has gone away, as she says, to discover what her own worth is independent of their relationship. Self-identity is more important than love. Megan rejects the traditional husband –wife relationship for a relationship which redefines the power roles.

Mussell's comment that life for women in fiction ends with marriage also ignores the gamut of contemporary bestselling family sagas and historical novels which now carry the heroine through a series of adventures. To show that life for women does not stop with marriage, some authors have gone on to write successive volumes about those heroines who proved to be popular. The three Barbara Taylor Bradford novels, for example, form the saga of the Harte women's struggles to amass and retain control of a financial empire. Although the second volume does end with the (second) marriage of the younger Harte woman, this occurs only after Paula has proven her individual power as head of the family corporation and established that her marriage is one between equals. Jean Auel, author of *Clan of the Cave Bear*

(1980) has given her readers three volumes of the story of the prehistoric character Ayla. The romance here is balanced by a detailed rendering of the author's vision of prehistoric life.

In many of the American novels of the sixties, the heroine, either forced to earn her living because of economic reasons or desirous of escaping a confining small town situation, entered the public sphere of work and career. Yet marriage remained her primary role and goal in life. Many of the texts, such as Jacqueline Susann's *Valley of the Dolls* (1971), or Rona Jaffe's early novels including *Class Reunion* (1979) or *Family Secrets* (1974), are either handbooks on how to find a man or stories of unhappy marriages chillingly similar to those of the nineteenth century. Similarly, the French novels of the 1960s by such bestselling women writers as Françoise Sagan or Françoise Mallet-Joris either depict women searching for love, or, as in Flora Groûlt's *Maxime ou la déchirure* (1972), unhappy women caught in unsatisfying marriages against which little alternative is imagined.

Yet, if the dominant myth of the sixties implied that what all women want is to find a man and get married, many of the bestselling novels of the period also undercut this notion. Some, like Jacqueline Susann's novels, were mass circulation bestsellers. Others belong to what has come to be known as the "raised consciousness" school: Bel Kaufman's *Up the Down Staircase* (1965), Allison Lurie's *The War Between the Tates* (1974), or Sue Kaufman's *Diary of a Mad Housewife* (1968), to name only a few, all center around the disillusionment of middle-class housewives. These novels, which were translated and as widely read in France as they were in the United States, represented a new direction in women's fiction. According to Kathryn Weibel,

> Not since the last liberation period of the 1920s have the heroines of so many bestsellers been so eager to question and discard traditional female roles and behavior. But echoing the outcome of such 1920s novels. . . endings of the modern novels suggest no new or satisfying alternatives for liberated women.
>
> (Weibel 1977: 1)

Weibel, however, contends that the content of women's fiction has not significantly changed over the last two and a half centuries and that the values communicated to women have remained unaffected:

> Although the prescriptions for achieving it have altered somewhat over the years, novels continue to portray marriage as a good woman's Great Reward and courtship as her Great Adventure. (9)

There is no denying that women's popular fiction has remained centered around marriage, but Weibel dismisses too easily the frequent attempts in fiction to subvert marriage. Much of women's fiction, serious or escapist, has dealt with experiences uniquely feminine of which courtship and marriage constitute major elements. Perhaps the most important thing happening in the novels is that, in addition to an expansion of the definition of women's arena outside the home, authors are now situating women's concerns in relationship to the outside world and not only in competition with it. A look at some of the major bestsellers of the 1960s and the 1970s shows the process of evolution which is occurring in women's popular fiction.

Bestsellers of the 1960s

Madonne Miner in her recent book on bestselling American women's fiction writes that Jacqueline Susann, unlike earlier bestselling novelists and, in particular, unlike Grace Metalious, author of *Peyton Place* (1956), "does not encourage defiance on the part of her heroines or her readers." (1984: 80) Susann, according to Miner, rather than suggesting that "the origins of female woe lie in an oppressive patriarchal culture," lays the blame for women's oppression on mothers who fail to nourish their daughters properly. (79) In many of the novels, mothers represent traditional behavior and, when placed in opposition to their daughters, assume the brunt of the blame for their daughters' initial passive acceptance of what they have been taught. But in the case of Susann, it is through her negative portrayal of marriage that she dispels the romantic illusion of women which is the cornerstone of female socialization. Although Susann fails to offer any constructive alternatives for her heroines, who never manage to achieve either emotional or financial independence, by dispelling the myth of marriage as the one true road to happiness, she anticipates the feminist writers of the seventies.

Susann's *Valley of the Dolls* was an immediate success when it was published in 1966 and became one of the year's top sellers. The novel follows a twenty-year period in the lives of three young women, Anne Welles, Neely O'Hara, and Jennifer North, who come to New York in the fall of 1945 to find careers and husbands.

Anne Welles, the novel's heroine, leaves her small hometown for the big city to escape from the life pattern common to the women of her family: marriage, children, and growing old without having experienced anything outside the everyday routine of a small town. For her, marriage means imprisonment in a restrictive kind of life, and she makes the distinction between a married life such as her mother has lived and an exciting life as a "career girl."

Anne's initial image and rejection of marriage is indeed linked to the life her mother leads:

> She would never go back to Lawrenceville! She hadn't just left Lawrenceville – she had escaped. Escaped from marriage to some solid Lawrenceville boy. The same orderly life her mother had lived. And her mother's mother. In the same orderly kind of house. (3)

Anne, however, never really rejects the possibility of marriage completely. Rather, she idealizes it and believes completely in the myth of "the right man" who will one day come along. Her particular insistence upon the one right man contrasts with the other female characters' uncritical desire for marriage; for them the status of being a married woman outweighs the choice of partner. This is made clear from the start of the novel. Upon arriving in New York Anne goes to an employment agency and when she explains to the young woman that she left her hometown to escape marriage to a childhood sweetheart the woman is incredulous:

> "And you left such a place? Here everyone is looking for a husband. Including me! Maybe you could send me to this Lawrenceville with a letter of introduction."
> "You mean you'd marry just anyone?" Anne was curious.

"Not anyone. Just anyone who'd give me a nice beaver coat, a part-time maid, and let me sleep till noon each day." (2)

Anne's naivete, her beauty and her innocence are contrasted throughout the novel with the other young women's materialism. She is looking for neither the status nor the material security normally attached to marriage, but for the ideal love relationship.

Neely O'Hara, the young girl Anne meets in the house she lives in when first arriving in New York, yearns to be a famous singer. She succeeds, but at the cost of her youth and innocence. Having barely survived a drug overdose, by the end of the novel Neely has become completely disillusioned. Furthermore, she cuts herself off from her most important support, namely Anne, when she enters into an affair with Lyon, Anne's husband. Neely is as much destroyed by her progression through the career world of Hollywood as she is by her personal isolation.

Jennifer North, the third heroine, is a beautiful model and movie star who also comes to New York to find fame and fortune. Of the three, she is the most practical and regards marriage more as a business proposition than anything else. This view of life and marriage prove to be equally destructive. Jennifer marries three times: first to a penniless prince, second to a mentally retarded country music singer, and finally to a politican with whom she finally hopes to find happiness. But marriage and happiness are incompatible within the novel's narrative scheme. One week before her marriage, Jennifer goes into the hospital for a simple surgical procedure and the doctor discovers she has breast cancer. She is unable to tell her fiancé the true nature of her illness, so when she informs him that she needs an operation which might prevent her from having children, he thinks that he is reassuring her when he says that he doesn't want children:

> He caressed her breasts. "These are my babies," he said softly.
> "These are the only children I want, to lay my face against
> their perfection each night. . ." (372)

His reduction of her humanity to one aspect of her physical appearance and his insistence on her perfect breasts prevents her from telling him the real reason for her surgery and drives her to commit suicide. She leaves him a note saying, "Dear

Win – I had to leave – to save your babies. Thanks for making it all almost come true." (376) Despite Jennifer's desire to be something more than "a body," she sacrifices her own life because of her conviction that her happiness depends upon the absence of any physical disfigurement.

The text undercuts the myth of marital happiness through its discouraging end and its note of disillusionment. Whenever happiness appears to be possible, death or illness intervenes. None of the characters, including Anne, achieves any semblance of happiness or fulfillment. Anne quits a job she enjoys with a publishing firm to work as a model and then when she manages to build up a a promising career, she leaves it in order to marry. She never considers the possibility of fulfillment from a career. Neely and Jennifer do their utmost to succeed in their chosen professions, but their career aspirations ultimately cause their ruin rather than bringing them any degree of satisfaction. Neely burns out on drugs and alcohol and Jennifer, before committing suicide, finds herself driven to making pornographic films.

The novel closes with Anne's marriage to Lyon, the man she has desired and who lives up to her ideal image of a husband. She discovers rather quickly, however, that not only does he continue to have affairs, he also has a well publicized relationship with her friend Neely. At this point, Anne is resigned to her life and completely without illusion:

> She had Lyon, the beautiful apartment, the beautiful child, the nice career of her own, New York – everything she had ever wanted. And from now on, she could never be hurt badly. She could always keep busy during the day, and at night – the lonely ones – there were always the beautiful dolls for company. (500)

Either the beautiful dolls, as she euphemistically calls the pills, or keeping busy are the only solutions women find to living with marriages which are unsatisfactory.

Valley of the Dolls is, as Miner suggests, a revealing portrait of women engaged in a consumption-oriented society and in selling themselves as representatives of a particular look or image: Anne, until she falls from grace with the modeling agency she works for and becomes pregnant, represents a cosmetics company, and Jennifer and Neely are media stars whose appeal depend upon their physical appearance. Ultimately the three women find themselves trapped in a system which offers them little alternative to the route of self-destruction upon which they are embarked. The myth of the happy housewife in the suburbs has been dispelled and the only career possibilities open to them lead to their individual destruction. Unlike the myth of the right man which structures the traditional romance, love, in fact, does not triumph at the end because it is proven insufficient to overcome the obstacles.

If Susann's novels show the dilemma of women caught in a consumer system in which they unwittingly participate and out of which there is no escape, the feminist version of the sixties novel is no less encouraging. Sue Kaufman's bestselling *Diary of a Mad Housewife* (1968), coming four years after the publication of Betty Friedan's *The Feminine Mystique* (1963), is, as Fishburn points out, the "modern revolt against the cult of domesticity," (1982: 21) and marks the beginning of the wave of "raised consciousness" novels which were so popular in the late sixties and early seventies.

Bettina Balser, the 36-year-old housewife heroine of Sue Kaufman's *Diary of a Mad Housewife*, is married to a rising young lawyer and is the mother of two daughters. Through her diary, Tina's means of coping with the unpleasant reality of her life, the reader learns that after a prolonged session of analysis at the age of 20, Tina has become resigned to the fact that there is no point in fighting:

> I finally learned to accept the fact that I was a bright but quite ordinary young woman, somewhat passive and shy, who was equipped with powerful Feminine Drives – which simply means I badly wanted a husband and children and a Happy Home.
>
> (25)

First her family and then her analyst persuade her that wanting anything other than a husband and home is abnormal. Written in the confessional form of a diary, the novel traces Tina's unhappiness and discontent, which ultimately center on her husband Jonathan, an ambitious lawyer who treats his wife as a child, a situation which she unconsciously rebels against through a series of ailments and fears.

At no point, however, does Tina accept the thought of divorce or a different kind of life:

> the very idea of my divorcing Jonathan or of Jonathan divorcing me fills me with terror, puts me on the brink of the abyss. Why? I've asked myself a thousand times. Why, when life with Jonathan has been such hell, should the idea of losing him or that life throw me into such a panic? (269)

In spite of her ambivalent feelings about being married, she rationalizes that the problem lies in Jonathan and the ways in which he has changed during the course of the marriage. Nor does she ever question the actual institution of marriage. If the old Jonathan can be found, hope for the survival of their marriage persists:

> I've finally begun to perceive that the life I've been living is right for me, that I'm in the right niche. That if I divorce Jonathan or Jonathan divorces me, I'll never find the right niche again. (269)

Scared into this introspection because she fears that she might be pregnant as the result of a once-a-week affair, Tina – once she is reassured that she is not pregnant – tells herself that she is now free to resume her life,

> Now . . . I know at last what I'm going to settle for and who I'm going to be. Who? Who is that? Why Tabitha-Twitchit Danvers, of course. The lady with the apron. And checklists. And keys. It's me. Oh it's very me, and I can't for the life of me see why I didn't realize that before. I suppose for one thing, Jonathan wouldn't let me. It hardly fits his image of what the wife of a Renaissance man should be. (281)

The dilemma in the end is not whether to be or not to be a wife, but how to find the style which best fits. In that regard she consciously makes the decision to be where and what she is. Her identity, however, remains one which has been imposed upon her from outside and one which she only questions when the pain becomes too much to bear.

The novel ends on an ambiguous and disappointing note. After having listened to Jonathan confess to having had an affair of his own and admitting to his own role in their troubled marriage,

Tina sits contemplating a cockroach caught under the hands of the kitchen wall clock. She removes the clock from the wall and with a hammer breaks the glass cover, thereby freeing the captured insect to escape his prison, run across the counter, and vanish "down a hole in the plaster between the tiles – damaged but undaunted – home to wifey and the kids." (293) The cockroach, at best an ambivalent image, encompasses both Jonathan, the straying but repentant husband, and marriage in general. Jonathan, like the insect, escapes virtually unharmed thanks to the person he was initially fleeing from. Caught in a no-escape situation, wifey has little choice but to sigh and welcome him home. It is Tina who, in the end, has the power to free him to return to his domestic situation. The final assumption of the novel is that if he has really now changed, then she can continue living her life. The need to question the premise on which her life is based is thereby avoided.

The 1970s

The 1970s, in contrast to the 1960s, marshall in a period of liberation, and traces of the women's movement can be seen in many of the bestsellers of the period. There is a proliferation of novels which interpret the discourses of the women's movement in terms of sexual liberation. Women begin to declare their independence from house and family. Alix Kates Shulman's *Memoirs of an Ex-Prom Queen* (1973) opens on such a promising note. Sasha Davis divorces her husband, declares her independence from men, but winds up at the end of the novel the mother of two children without any clear direction. Men still define her world. Erica Jong in *Fear of Flying* (1973) was one of the first novelists to write about women's sexual fantasies and pleasure. Men and sex, however, remain, throughout the adventures of Isadora, which span a ten year period, the main focus in her life.

The major suggestion of these novels is that one of the ways of living with marriage is through extra-marital affairs. Judy Blume's *Wifey* (1978), for example, depicts the middle-class American housewife as living in a prison of suburbia and marriage, the principal goals of the American middle class of the sixties. As in Kaufman's *Diary of a Mad Housewife*, the main character of Blume's novel is identified by her domestic role as wife. In Kaufman's novel, the narrator qualified herself as mad, and in Blume's, she is diminished through the title's use of the diminutive. In both cases, the authors' preoccupation remains firmly rooted in the domestic sphere.

Sandy, the 30-year-old heroine of *Wifey*, could very well be a cousin or sister of Bettina Basler of Kaufman's *Diary of a Mad Housewife*. A white middle-class American housewife with two children transported to the suburbs, she is married to a man who is upwardly mobile and preoccupied with the acquisition of the appropriate symbols of his new wealth. Pleasing her husband rather than seeking her own self-fulfillment is her principal goal:

> She would please Norman in every way. If she made him happier, if she concentrated on his every wish, then she would be rewarded. She would become a happier person. A better person. (59)

Yet, in spite of her family's comfortable middle-class situation, she is dissatisfied with her suburban life and with her uncommunicative husband. Like Tina of *Diary of a Mad Housewife*, and a long succession of other female protagonists, she finds that her married life has become a series of physical ailments and renewed promises to improve herself and make her husband happy. In *Wifey*, as in so many of the novels, the illnesses and ailments she suffers from function metaphorically to represent the unhappiness she suffers in her marriage. The symptoms however, rather than the cause of the distress, are what is treated.

Sandy considers divorce as a viable solution only when it leads to another marriage. Her sister tells her: "The only way to a decent divorce is through another man. So get busy and find one if you're so unhappy." (240) The way out for Sandy, however, is not a new marriage but rather a series of sexual fantasies and unsatisfactory affairs. At one point in the novel Sandy is lying on the beach thinking of her old boyfriend,

> She opened her legs a bit more, letting the hot sun warm her there, warming her all over . . . on her nipples . . , erect now . . . fuck me, sunshine . . . so delicious, as it crept up her legs, to her thighs, to her cunt . . . kiss me there . . . lick me . . . oh, please . . . oh hurry . . . (53)

Her erotic fantasy is interrupted and made to appear ridiculous, however, when she opens her eyes she finds a middle-aged man standing in front of her insisting that he loves her. She runs back to the house and takes up her briefly rejected role of wife and mother. Reality, when measured against her fantasies, is recurringly disappointing.

The final confrontation between Sandy and her husband Norman, who promises to work on improving their marriage, rings a false note. The reader knows that Norman does not really understand what the problem is, and that things can only continue in their old way. It is clear that he has no basis on which to form any real change. For Sandy, the solution to her unhappiness is her acquiescence to the status quo. The novel ends with a line which recalls the ending of *Valley of the Dolls*. Sandy reflects upon the fact that her children will soon be home from summer camp, and "She'll be busy again. Much too busy to think about him or anyone else." (259) In both *Valley of the Dolls* and *Wifey*, the unhappiness of married life is seen as inevitable, and the heroine must find some way to cope with it rather than seek an alternative. The way out of Sandy's situation is to follow the advice her sister gives her, fill her days with activities so as not to think too much about her unhappiness. The fact that she admits to the problem suggests a coming to awareness on her part, but any independence this new consciousness may bring her remains quite ambiguous.

The 1980s

Blume's 1983 bestseller *Smart Women* provides an interesting contrast to *Wifey* and indicates the direction in which current novelists are rewriting the old myth of wife and mother. Marriage has been proved to be an unreliable institution and women have discovered that they can actually survive on their own as divorcées. *Smart Women* follows the lives of three divorced mothers, their conflicts with their daughters, and their ways of coping with career, family, and lovers. Margo, the principal female character, is a recently divorced ex-New Yorker solar design architect who, having moved to Colorado has managed to rebuild her life. The novel opens with Margo resting in her jacuzzi after a hard day:

Margo slid open the glass door leading to the patio outside her bedroom. She set the Jacuzzi pump for twenty minutes, tested the temperature of the water with her left foot, tossed her robe onto the redwood platform, then slowly lowered herself into the hot tub, allowing the swirling water to surround her body. (3)

Just as she begins to relax, Andrew, her new next door neighbor and the former husband of one of her friends, arrives. The scene, situated as it is outside Margo's bedroom, is intimate and sensual and hints at future involvement between the two. But any hint of sexuality is cut short: Andrew cannot tolerate the tub's heat, and it is up to Margo to help him out before he faints. From this inauspicious beginning the reader is lead to expect a reversal of traditional behavior. Andrew quickly reveals that he is not a traditional male: he may have forced his way into the tub, but no sooner there he immediately finds himself in Margo's power. He is a man who laughs and talks with his daughter, does his own shopping, and wears bikini underpants which Margo sees when he insists upon joining her in the hot tub: "Margo was suspicious of men who wore boxer shorts, Freddy had worn boxer shorts, had insisted that they be ironed." (7) Freddy, Margo's former husband, embodies the traditional expectations women are now rejecting. One day after an especially bitter argument with him, Margo reflects on what her marriage with Freddy was like and the reasons for its failure:

He still blamed her for having had her own needs and he was still able to make her feel guilty. Freddy had wanted a Stepford wife. . . . "A plastic princess who doesn't think!", . . . A plastic princess who'll give elegant little dinner parties and fuck whenever you feel like it. (187)

The surburban dream which had previously structured so much of women's fiction has been found wanting and women are no longer content to stay at home and be treated like princesses. Successful in her profession, Margo discovered once she separated from Freddy that she was capable of surviving both financially and emotionally. Given her past marital experience and those of her friends who have been equally hurt, Margo has become wary of marriage and it is only after Andrew has proven himself to be capable of understanding her needs that she consents to marry him. The novel ends not with their marriage but rather when it becomes clear that it will work.

The message of the fiction of the beginning of the 1980s is that women have now managed to acquire economic independence, that they have "gotten smart" and, unlike their counterparts in the 1970s, are no longer afraid to leave unhappy and unsatisfying marriages. This assertion of independence also makes a happy ending possible. The ambiguous ending of *Wifey* disappears from *Smart Women*. Unlike Sandy or Bettina, Margo is less fearful of what the future may bring. She has gained enough power to control the direction of the changes in her life. *Smart Women* moves full circle to end in the same setting in which the the novel began. Margo reflects on her relationship with Andrew which has managed to survive through a series of family crises:

> For once, everything was turning out right, she thought. Not that she'd ever doubted, seriously doubted, that he would come back. After all, they loved each other. He wasn't going to just throw it all away. But having everything turn out right was a scary idea, even for an optimist. *Look*, she told herself, *you deserve it. You've paid your dues and so has he. Besides, this is real life. Just because it's all going your way tonight doesn't mean that tomorrow won't bring surprises. So count your blessings and be happy.* Isn't that what her mother had told her when she was a little girl? *It's okay to count your blessings, darling, so long as you remember to knock, after.*
>
> (375)

Almost Paradise (1984), Susan Isaacs's third bestseller, is a novel about different kinds of marriages and in particular the story of a modern-day marriage threatened by the disproportionate career success and fame of its members. Nicolas, the handsome son of one of the East Coast's oldest families, has parents who end up barely tolerating each other, and Jane is the result of a union between a fading burlesque queen and the dreary Cincinnati bank clerk she dupes into marriage. Despite their both being products both of unhappy marriages and from completely different backgrounds, their marriage comes close to being "almost paradise" until the demands of career intrude. The novel opens quite simply with a prologue:

Jane Cobleigh was on a British Airways Concorde, flying faster than sound to try and reclaim her husband. At the end of the flight she managed to look out of her window. Grey London was opalescent under the haze of a summer heat wave.   (7)

Jane's arrival at the hotel in London, her anxieties over her trip, and her desire to be reconciled with her husband set the tone for the novel. The reader quickly learns who she is and why she has overcome her fears to fly to London:

The estranged wife of the world's most famous actor should not be popping up in London. Hi! My affair is over. It never really meant anything. How about yours? Ready to ditch her? What does a forty year-old man need a twenty-four-year-old for anyway – someone people describe as having shining, cascading red hair and a figure like a very expensive, extremely delicate porcelain doll?   (8)

Jane, the reader is told a few paragraphs later, is definitely not a delicate porcelain doll, nor has she been the faithful wife. But she does expect her husband to feel similarly to how she does about their relationship and their life together. To counter Jane's negative thoughts about herself, Jane is then presented to the reader through her husband Nicolas's eyes as an attractive, insecure woman.

The prologue, in addition to informing the reader of how the two actually feel towards one another, also injects a sense of futility into the novel. Jane's attempt to assume control of her life ends tragically. After she arrives in London, she rushes to the site where Nicolas is shooting a film. Thinking that the passenger in a passing car is Nicolas, she steps out of her limousine into the oncoming traffic and is hit by a car. Fate, the reader is told, prevents their reunion. The driver of the car, normally drunk and dangerous, was quite sober at the time of the accident.

The conflict in their marriage arises when, as is described midway through the novel, Jane becomes a television personality as a result of publicly speaking about her successful struggle with the agoraphobia which has kept her a prisoner in the house. Using both her own earlier drama training and the fact that she is the wife of a well known actor Jane rapidly advances in her new career. Nicolas, however, is unable to cope with either his wife's success or her friendship with the analyst who helps her through the painful process of overcoming her phobia, and embarks upons an affair with a young drama student and leaves Jane when she refuses to give up her new found fame and independence.

Almost Paradise ends, as it must, on an unhappy note with Jane's death. Paradise, or that world in which true and lasting love is attainable, only occurs in fictions, not real life. In actuality, we, the readers, like Nicholas in his belated realization that Jane is his true love, are always endlessly searching for love which just escapes us.

French bestsellers

Some of the major French women writers of the sixties included Christiane Rochefort and Françoise Mallet-Joris, whose novels appear on the bestseller lists in the late seventies when these lists come into usage. In *Les petits enfants du siècle* (Children of the Century) (1961) Christiane Rochefort treats the problems faced by families living in low-income housing blocks through the life of a working-class family in the Parisian suburb of Sarcelles. Josyanne, the novel's 16-year-old heroine, enters adulthood through a series of sexual adventures. Try as she may to escape the dreary life she sees around her, at the end of the novel she is pregnant and must marry, thereby continuing in the same path as that of her mother and neighbors.

The politically aware novels of the 1960s, however, give way in the 1970s to novels in which the heroine looks to the male regard for her self-identity. Although the French heroine is not caught up like the American woman in the limitations suburban life imposes, she also struggles with the unequal balance of power upon which marriage depends. In *Le jeu du souterrain* (The Underground Game) (1975) Françoise Mallet-Joris examines the life of a married couple, the husband's infidelities, their temporary estrangement, and their eventual reconciliation. The reader follows the detailed rendering of the game the couple and their family members play with one another. Robert Guibal, the main protagonist, is a man in his fifties who has had a minor success as a writer. His wife Catherine, who has stopped hoping for any satisfaction out of her marriage, works as a high-school literature teacher. The perfect wife, Catherine encourages her husband's work, shields him from outside demands and tolerates in silence his affair with a singer named Reine. When she initially finds out about Robert's affair with Reine, she is more disturbed by the fact that Robert is not truly in love with Reine than by his betrayal:

> At least love the woman! As if that love could push back upon all women and upon herself their share of love – Yes, she reflected, I would feel closer to him if he were capable of loving as I love, even capable of loving another woman. . .
>
> (215)

Carol, a secondary female character in the novel, also attempts to fill the void in her life through her love for Gerry, a friend of Robert's:

> She had violet eyelids and blue lips. She looked at her reflection in the mirror opposite her and was utterly satisfied. Her eyes reflected the mirror that reflected her eyes. If she shut her eyes, if the mirror was taken away, what would remain? Nothing. The nothing that Gerry passionately loves.
>
> (132)

For Catherine and Carol any meaning in life is conveyed through their love relationships with men.

Initially, Robert reproaches Catherine for being an anachronism; women in love are, in his view, a thing of the past. By the end of novel, however, after the couple has tentatively been reconciled, Robert comes to understand that her fidelity to him throughout his meanderings is the love she feels for him:

> That stubborn fidelity was nothing more than love – a vocation. The only man in her life. The idea was as marvelous as those picture-book stories he had brooded over as a boy, stories of explorers coming upon deserted cities in the jungle. (249)

The theme of love and the identification of self through this all-encompassing love runs through Mallet-Joris's work and, as will be seen, undergoes only minor changes in her later novels published in the 1980's.

In her 1981 bestseller *Un chagrin d'amour et d'ailleurs* (Deceived by love and more) Françoise Mallet-Joris continues to examine the lives of women caught in the trap of marriage, a theme more reminiscent of the American novels of the sixties than it is of the novels being published today. Covering the events of one afternoon, the novel is a study of the thoughts and interactions of a husband, his wife, and his mistress. Jeannette Lefèvre, 43 years old, is neither a professional woman nor a mother but rather a woman in search of her own identity within the confines of an unhappy marriage.

The novel opens with Jeanette, who as the reader quickly learns has been in a rehabilitation clinic for the third time because of a drinking problem, having just left it in order to attend the opening ceremonies of the cultural center over which her husband, the mayor of the town, is to preside. The importance of appearance quickly becomes obvious as the reader follows Jeannette's movements upon leaving the clinic to the center of town where she must buy presentable clothing for the ceremony: "It was a question of dressing the deputy mayor's wife as the deputy mayor's wife." (17) Jeannette's lack of self-identity is further emphasized by her awareness that her choice of clothing is decided for her in advance by the role her marital status imposes upon her:

> Because I am Mrs Lefèvre, the wife of the deputy mayor, and everything that I am going to do or say and even the way in which I'm going to dress is codified in advance and pro-grammed by this invisible computer which has made of me this Mrs Lefèvre. . . . The only thing that the computer doesn't anticipate is despair, love, alcohol. . . (18)

Jeannette is caught in her unreasonable love for her husband, the butcher's son who married this rebel child of good family because of her large breasts and the escape she promised from his own working-class environment:

> These breasts with which he could converse were the promise of a harmonious world in which instead of wrapping the steak in newspaper he could finally eat it while reading the newspaper. (32)

Marie-Christine, the mistress and third member of the triangle and the most pragmatic of the three, holds on to Gilbert not because she loves him but because she wants to become the wife of a powerful man. She sees herself and her pragmatic approach to life as indispensable to the success of a man like Gilbert.

The confrontation between the three characters at the end of the novel occurs when Jeanette finally realizes her own self-identity. Rather than pursuing her original plan to get her husband back, Jeannette capitulates to Marie-Christine's arguments and decides to leave her husband because she realizes that her love for Gilbert is self-destructive. Yet none of the three really win. Jeannette understands that she is leaving of her volition and that she, and not Marie-Christine, has managed to free herself from an ultimately oppressive relationship but she has nowhere to go nor any idea of what kind of alternative life she might lead. Furthermore, Marie-Christine's ambitions to be the partner of a politican are no longer feasible. Gilbert, caught as he is between the two women, effectively ends his political career in a disastrous interview he gives to the television. When asked by the interviewer why he invited a popular singer of love songs to the inauguration of a cultural center, Gilbert loses control and condemns love and private life as destructive of society's values. By denying the force of his love for Jeannette Gilbert is ultimately entrapped by that love. The ending of the novel, however, remains ambiguous, and although Marie-Christine loses her politican she appears to be the only real survivor of the three. Because she has no illusions about Gilbert's feelings towards her – she knows that he still loves his wife – she is able to plan her life in a seemingly cold-hearted fashion.

Françoise Dorin, a consistently bestselling novelist and playwright, offers a more contemporary view of marriage. Her 1980 bestseller *Les lits à une place* (Single Beds), examines the reasons people marry and remain married as well as offering alternatives to married life. The novel opens with a description of a table setting:

White table cloth embellished with silver threads.
Silver paper flowers in a silver vase.
Silver table runner and angel's hair.
Silver candlesticks holding silvered candles.
Individual menus written in silver letters.   (5)

and an introduction to the event being celebrated:

Doctor and Mrs François-Achille Buisson, in the company of eight of their friends, are celebrating their silver wedding anniversary. Well named given the circumstances: twenty-five years of a union which owes everything to money. Its beginning and its non-end. (5)

The silver wedding anniversary being celebrated represents the close tie money and marriage mean for the Buisson couple, and by extension, the hypocrisy of their union. The narrator's disgust with the celebration is made explicit with the introduction of Antoinette Audricourt, who answers the hostess's toast of "To twenty-five years of happiness," with "To twenty-five years of lies!" Antoinette clarifies her position. She doesn't oppose marriage because of love, but rather when it is done for social reasons and is used as a form of social identification. The women at the dinner, according to Antoinette, are "legal prostitutes" who remain married for the sole purpose of retaining their husbands' illustrious names on their calling cards despite the known infidelities of their husbands:

Four women who accept all the compromises, all the humiliations, all the cowardliness rather than relinquish the advantages inherent in their title of wife. (9)

The novel also tells the story of a house called "the Eight" and the four friends, all recently divorced or separated from their mates, who live there. The narrative follows their attempts to find a satisfactory solution either to marriage, which, for the most part, is revealed as being based on hypocrisy, or to the loneliness of living alone, the major problem faced by big-city inhabitants today. The title of the novel reveals one possible solution: single beds – each person with his or her own bed, supportive of one another, yet living an independent life. In other words, celibacy and a redefinition of love which excludes materialistic motives are proposed as an alternative to marriage. Antoinette, a recently divorced woman of 43 who earns her living by creating and selling hand-painted silk items, converted the mansion she inherited from her father into the four-apartment house called "the Eight" as a solution to her own loneliness. Her work is important to her but she is neither an aggressive businesswoman nor particularly ambitious. In food, dress, and general behavior Antoinette is neither a feminist nor a radical and her conservative nature is made quite clear from the start. When she dines with her lawyer, we are told, he marvels at "the way she respects the hierarchy of flavors." (33) Her respect for the proper combinations of food and wine in a culture which places a high value on the correct way to dine immediately characterizes Antoinette as a reasonable person who adheres to traditional values.

Antoinette and each of her friends experience events and sexual adventures which not only leave them disillusioned but reconfirm their belief in the rightness of their choice of life-style. Michel, the occupant of the third floor apartment, falls in love with a woman considerably younger than himself, attempts to live with her during the vacation period and, after suffering the inconveniences of a shared bed, returns to the Eight. Catherine, Antoinette's close friend and the tenant of the second floor apartment, is a press agent for a publishing house who originally came to the Eight after her husband left her. Catherine similarly goes off on her own to the south of France and experiences the loss of her close friend Antoinette. She eventually renounces her plans to resettle in the south where she had been offered a job and returns to the Paris house.

The women characters in the novel can be divided according to those who agree with Antoinette – Pauline, Catherine, and Florence – and those who disagree – the original four women who were present at the anniversary dinner. Pauline, the wife of the editor for whom Catherine works, is Antoinette's doctor and friend. Her husband has just left her for a younger woman who has become pregnant. Florence, the mistress of François-Achille Buisson, the man whose anniversary was being celebrated in the novel's opening scene, comes to understand through the course of events the injustices she has tolerated in her position as mistress. By the end of the novel, she has left François-Achille, found a new male friend (who conveniently lives in Holland), and become a convert to Antoinette's way of celibacy. The four women are independent and self-sufficient. Their careers and children are important to them but they do not take priority as they do for the women in the American novels. The novel, however, ends on a positive note. The scattered members of the "Eight" return home from their various adventures with a renewed commitment to their chosen independent life-style. Having recovered from her husband's desertion, Pauline renovates her house and opens a second "Eight" with new converts to Antoinette's philosophy of celibacy. Antoinette's lawyer, Vanneau, Florence, and Antoinette's former young lover Christophe move into Pauline's "Eight bis:"

> Two men, two women. Ties of friendship. Four solitary people reunited. Four new followers of single beds. What counts is that they are happy. (442)

Female independence is not singled out as an isolated concern in the novel. Rather independence in general, be it for male or female, is arrived at as a consequence of a person's choice of life-style – in this case, celibacy – and the resistance to an institution which is too frequently entered into for the wrong reasons.

Chapter six

Superwoman: The "new woman" of the 1980s

You can have a men's novel with no
  women
in it except possibly the
  landlady
or the horse, but you can't have
a women's novel with no men in it.
Sometimes men put women in
  men's novels
but they leave out some of the
  parts:
the heads, for instance. . .
Margaret Atwood, Women's Novels, (1986)

A woman is given to a man in order to have children. She is
therefore his property like a fruit tree belongs to a gardener.
Napoleonic Code, quoted in Sarde (1983)

**The Eighties: Social and political condition of women in the United
States and France**

The tendency towards the end of the 1980s in both the United
States and France has been a return to traditional values with an
increasing emphasis on family, work and country. Any residual
radicalism left over from the early 1970s has been channeled into
assuring job security in face of a continued economic crisis. When
it comes to the improvements women have gained, both the
French and American media claim that the situation of the
contemporary woman couldn't be better. In the United States,

newspaper and magazine articles announce that American women have (at least on the surface) won their battle for job equity. In 1981, the percentage of working women in the United States was 51 per cent as compared with 74.7 per cent male labor force participation (Blau and Ferber 1986: 311), and rose to 54 per cent in 1985. United States Bureau of Labor Statistics data shows that the percentage of the total number of women in the work force will have grown from 33.9 per cent in 1950 to an estimated 57.5 per cent in 1990. William Greer cites a United States Labor Department report which claims that women have entered the majority of professional occupations in the USA:

> Now the barriers have fallen or at least have come down so that there is a significant and substantial movement of women into traditional male occupations. The 1980s mark an accelera-
> tion of that shift.   (Greer 1986: 1)

But, as Greer goes on to point out, two troubling areas remain that reveal the contradictory position in which women currently find themselves. One, the professional occupations covered by the statistics omit executive, managerial, or administrative positions, of which women account for only 36 per cent, although considering that ten years earlier, the percentage was only 20 per cent significant progress has been made. Little actual change has occurred in women's entry into fields traditionally dominated by men such as law, medicine, and engineering. Julie Bailey, in a July 1988 *Ms.* Special Report on jobs for women, states that "one out of every three law associates in the country's largest law firms is a woman, but only one in every 13 partners." (77) Furthermore, as women replace men as the majority in traditionally male occupations, there is concern, according to University of Illinois sociologist Barbara Reskin, that as an occupation's prestige declines there is a corresponding drop in wages. Women's earnings still significantly lag behind those of men. Blau and Ferber place the ratio of women's to men's earnings in the United States, as of 1982, at 71 per cent. They emphasize in their study that "women are always paid less than men." (1986: 325) Thus, although American women may have made some gains in the last years in the area of work, they are still excluded from certain prestigious occupations, and continue to earn lower salaries than men for comparable work.

Countering the hard-won gains women have acquired in the workplace, the 1980s also mark a period of retrenchment. If women have succeeded in entering previouly closed fields, they have also suffered from the growing conservatism of the United States and the pro-family agenda of the Right. The defeat of the Equal Rights Amendment and the dangerous growth of the anti-abortion movement threaten to deprive women in the United States of the rights they have fought many years to acquire. Furthermore, American women continue to be penalized if they need time off from their jobs to care for new borns or seriously ill members of their families. In 1988 legislation proposing ten weeks of unpaid leave every two years to care for a newborn, adopted, or seriously ill child or a sick parent was defeated in Congress, but is up again in 1989. In a survey of 127 nations, the United States is, according to Women at Work, International Labor Office Global Survey, the only country which does not require some form of parental or maternal leave. Women, while demanding and fighting for more equality in the public sphere, are, despite the fact that by 1985 one third of American households were headed by a woman, seeing a move towards a repressive return of the old myth of "a woman's place is in the home."

Up to the eve of the Second World War, French women lived completely under the domination of their husbands. The Civil Code, a relic of the Napoleonic code, stipulated the total legal incapacity of a married woman, who not only carried her husband's name but received his nationality as well. Adultery was illegal, "marital duty" was an obligation, and rape between a married couple did not exist. Although the law abolished a wife's obedience to her husband in 1938, he still had the right to choose where a couple lived, had complete authority over their children, and could refuse his wife the right to work. (Hamon 1988: 46) Since the 1970s a series of new laws have significantly improved the situation of French women. In 1970 the term "parental authority" used in the Family Code replaced "father's authority." In 1975, divorce by mutual consent was initiated, and job discrimination laws and the right to an abortion passed. It was only in 1985, however, that the notion of a male head of the family disappeared from fiscal law.

On paper, French women have won a number of benefits in the

last fifteen years which women in the United States or England are still fighting for. A sixteen-week maternity leave with 70 per cent pay is available to all working women, and women classified as "cadres" (executives and management) receive 100 per cent of their pay. Fathers or mothers can take unpaid leave from their work for up to two years to raise their children, with the guarantee that when they return they will have a job equivalent in salary and responsibility to the one they left. Families with more than three children benefit from special privileges such as reduced transportation costs, special health benefits, and special prices for cultural activities, and all families, regardless of their income, receive a monthly supplement, "allocation familial," which increases in proportion to household expenses and income. Relatively low-cost municipal day care facilities further help mothers who want to combine career and motherhood.

When it comes to salaries and career advancement possibilities, French women lag significantly behind women in the United States, as does the percentage of women in top management positions. French women may not have yet reached the positions of financial and professional responsibility held by American women, but the same picture emerges. Significant numbers of French women continue to leave their homes to enter the labor force: whereas in 1968, only 45 per cent of the female population was active outside the home, this number rose in 1985 to 71 per cent for the age group 25–39 years and to 65 per cent for the group 40–54 years. The French National Institute of Statistics and Economic Studies (INSEE) 1985 projection for the year 2000 is over 80 per cent. In 1986 women occupied only 20 per cent of executive positions in contrast to the figure of 36 per cent for American women. (Sacase 1986: 113) Although the definitions of what constitutes an executive position differ in the two countries, other reports corroborate the low participation of women in upper level jobs. A 1986 *Nouvel Economiste* article stated that only 3.9 per cent of the 20,840 top executives of France's major businesses are women. Women's salaries also remain less than their male counterparts'. A General Commission of Scientific Organization (Cégos) study carried out in 1985 showed that in the last thirty-four years, the gap between male and female salaries has only narrowed by 10 per cent – from a difference for women of 36 per cent in 1950 to 26 per cent in 1984. (Valence and Lhaïk 1985: 53) In 1987, while the salary differences for women in non-management positions had narrowed to 15.5 per cent, women executives had only gained 1 per cent in the battle for equal salaries.

Inequalities also exist in the area of job advancement. In the area of education, like in the majority of French businesses or administrative offices, women have a hard time attaining positions of responsibility. The Ministry of National Education found that whereas 78 per cent of school teachers are women, only 24 per cent of the Principal or Director positions are held by females. (*Liberation* 31 August 1988) Despite an increase in the level of education for women, four out of five humanities baccalaureates are female and the prestigious schools of higher learning which train future presidents of the Republic, the "grandes écoles," still resist female candidates: at ENA (National School of Administration) only 21 per cent of the student body is female and 6 per cent at the Polytechnic. (Hamon 1988: 59)

French women also strongly feel this discrimination, and in my four years of teaching adults English in Paris, I've heard a number of women in business emphasize the reality these figures represent. The vast majority of my women students have been secretaries who complain of the discrimination they experience in terms of advancement possibilities. Prejudices against hiring women still exist, and certain employers, according to the head-hunter Isabelle Levielle, "systematically refuse to hire a woman for a position which requires a firm hand or authority." (Brizard 1988: 14–16)

Today, despite the phenomenal progress French women have made in terms of career and salary advances, for the majority of French working women, their salaries are still viewed as secondary income used to pay for "little extras." Furthermore, working women are accused of contributing to the high level of unemployment. Parallel to the optimistic reports published in the national press on the progress women have made, the women's press regularly presents articles extolling the values of home and family. In the summer of 1985 a national campaign was launched reminding women that their place is in the home with a hoard of children. Billboards appeared all over France depicting pregnant women and children. On one, a pregnant woman was shown with her head missing, and her hand on her stomach. The caption read

"France loves babies." On another there was a smiling infant and underneath the slogan, "It appears that I am a socio-cultural phenomenon. France needs babies." In both cases the mother and the baby are white. The decrease in the number of births of non-immigrant children is blamed on the high number of women entering the work force. So is the current economic crisis. French sociologist Margaret Maruani cites this revealing statement of Jacques Henriet, a senator from the Doubs region, on the current attitudes felt about women and work:

> No one contests either the legitimacy or legality of women's work which is, nonetheless, a factor behind unemployment and decreasing birth rate. Rather than sending women to work, it would be more worth while to send them to bed.
>
> (quoted in Valence and Lhaïk 1985: 53)

Jean Dutourd of the French Academy seconded the idea that women could contribute more to the family budget as an occasional prostitute than as a career woman. He suggested quite seriously in a *France-Soir* article of March 1985, that if women need some extra money at the end of the month, why not resort to the "custom" of sending housewives out onto the streets:

> strolling down certain streets with a pretty dress, high heel shoes and a beckoning smile. . . . One or two days should be enough for the honest woman or mother to earn the three or four thousand francs she needs to keep the family pot boiling.

This image of the housewife who moonlights as a prostitute to earn some extra money, even if it is meant somewhat ironically, is not all that unusual and occasionally appears on the cinema screen. As unlikely as it seems, it is more acceptable for women to walk the streets than to have a career.

One positive consequence of the large number of working women in both the United States and France has been increased economic and domestic independence for women. A greater number of women in both countries are living alone, marrying at a later age, if at all, and are not having as many children. Although the number of women not marrying is not about to put bridal offices out of commission, the number is significant enough to warrant magazine articles and television specials questioning the "new" way of life of modern women. An article in *Le Monde*

(14 March 1986) reporting on the rise in unmarried couples living together stated that the number of legal marriages has been steadily declining since 1972 – only 273,000 in 1986 – and the one major reason is that more women are working: "women's work makes women more independent and permits them to remain unmarried or to divorce." (Solé 1986: 24) Today, fewer women marry because of economic reasons: many earn both an income and social status through their own labor. In addition, the availability of contraception and abortion has further decreased the number of marriages for the purpose of legitimizing childbirth.

In the final analysis, however, despite the supposed advances, women in both the United States and France continue to earn lower salaries than their male counterparts, advance in their careers at a slower rate, and encounter resistance when they place the demands of a career over those of the home. One strategy women in both countries have used to circumvent discrimination and deadend jobs has been the creation of their own work conditions. Over the last few years there has been a significant increase in the number of women opening their own businesses. Françoise Giroud, bestselling author and the first French woman to become a Cabinet member, admits that the only way for a woman to become Number One is to create her own business. The US National Association of Women Business Owners estimates that two out of every three new businesses employing less than 100 employees are opened by women. In France, the figure is slightly lower – one out of five new businesses are created by women – but this figure has doubled in only four years, and in 1986 15,000 women opened their own businesses.

Career-woman novels: Superwoman in the United States

In response to this movement of women into positions of responsibility in the work force, from the mid 1970s through the early 1980s books with such intriguing titles as *Superwoman* (1978) or *Superwoman in Action* (1979) by Shirley Conran or *The Superwoman Syndrome* (1985) by Marjorie Hansen Shaevitz began appearing on the *New York Times Book Review* non-fiction bestseller lists. If the novels of the 1960s and 1970s treated the contemporary woman as victim but sexually liberated, then those of the 1980s sought to counter this image with that of the woman who is capable of doing everything. The issue is no longer how to choose between work and family, but rather how to manage them. The "new woman" of these very popular 1980s version of the raised consciousness novel is superwoman in all her glory. Anatole Broyard in a 1982 *New York Times Book Review* article remarked that a new kind of woman has appeared in fiction over the last decade:

> not the feminist's woman, with whom she has some qualities in common, but something more idiosyncratic, more a product of the literary than the political imagination. One might say that in the new woman's politics, she herself is the candidate.
>
> (Broyard 1982: 40)

This new woman, he continues, is no longer sentimental nor is she "the repository for tradition and nostalgia." Her "traditional reticence" has disappeared and is replaced by "articulateness . . . her favorite form of attack or defense." Broyard's comments reflect the general direction in which women's popular fiction has been moving since the mid-seventies and into the eighties. The social mythology of woman as wife and mother which previously structured women's fiction has given way to a stronger female image which not only challenges the myth of female weakness but also denies the too familiar woman-as-victim syndrome. If today's fiction still insists upon motherhood as the quintessential female role and the most rewarding experience for a woman, it also offers her other ways to live.

The female fictional characters now so popular in contemporary women's bestsellers do, as Broyard points out, share certain qualities with the feminists, even though their creators choose to have them deny it. For one, their lives no longer conform to traditional mores, and, increasingly, authors are treating topics which at one time were considered taboo in escapist fiction. Today it is not unusual to read of women characters who have suffered sexual abuse as children, who have been raped and publicly deal with the trauma, who have had abortions or face the possibility of breast cancer. In Iris Dart's bestseller *Beaches* (1985), one of the two main female characters dies of breast cancer, a topic which has only very recently made its way into popular fiction. And in Dorin's novel, *Les lits à une place* (Single Beds) the main character puts off a mamography until forced to go by her physican friend. The reader follows her fears and relief when she is given a clean bill of health by the doctor. Women align themselves, if indirectly, with the women's movement or support the Equal Rights Amendment, women's suffrage, job discrimination, or anti-racism.

Women have stepped out of the kitchen and, in more and more cases, out of the domestic space in general. Fewer stories of housewives who remain housewives throughout the narrative are appearing on the bestseller lists. Alongside this devalorization of domestic work, women's professional activities are being given a new importance. Many of the current American or British female characters create financial empires, achieve international success as writers or actresses, or climb to lofty executive positions. Whereas at one time the heroine's work situation functioned in the text as a kind of window dressing, the bestsellers of the 1980s focus on her active participation in a particular industry such as clothing or perfume, or even the stock market and Wall Street, and provide a certain amount of insight into the workings of areas in which women have traditionally and non-traditionally worked. Meredith Rich's *Bare Essence* (1981) and Johanna Kingsley's *Scents* (1984) treat the perfume industry and in both cases the heroine works to develop or market the product. Fashion in all its different aspects, be it the designing, the marketing, or the modeling of it, fills the pages of countless bestsellers. In addition to these female-oriented areas, women executives are now increasingly common: in Susan Rautbord and Elizabeth Nickles' *Girls in High Places* (1986), heroine Catherine McBride is the assistant to the chief executive officer of a mineral corporation. Catherine Bourton of Celia Brayfield's *Pearls* (1988), who starts her career out as a minerals trader, then moves on to become a financial advisor. The boardroom has replaced the kitchen as the prime narrative site in the contemporary bestsellers published in the United States.

If *Gone with the Wind* and *The Thorn Birds* are often cited as engendering spin-off copies, the same thing can be equally said for Barbara Taylor Bradford's novels. One of the earliest versions of the superwoman story, Bradford's internationally bestselling rags to riches novels *A Woman of Substance* (1983), and its sequels *Hold the Dream* (1985) and *To Be the Best* (1988), have since been imitated many times over. Bradford who was born in Great Britain and now lives in the United States, originally published her novel in the United States in 1979. A resounding success in the United States, England and France, *A Woman of Substance*, which has sold over 5 million copies worldwide, contains all the elements found in so many of the superwoman bestsellers. A poor young girl goes to work for the local wealthy family, falls in love with the younger son, becomes pregnant by him, and after he refuses to marry her sets out to revenge the wrong that was done to her. Motivated by her need for revenge, she ends up the head of a colossal financial empire. Revenge for some wrong committed by a man, be it rape or abandonment, motivates most of the earlier superwomen characters: the woman who sets out to acquire wealth and power in and of itself is rare. Wealth and power are the means a woman needs to revenge the wrongs done done to her by a man, or to ensure her children's security, for which she has the sole responsibility. In an increasing number of novels, however, women have become more comfortable with the idea of power and feel less and less need to justify its acquisition.

Bradford's Emma Harte is a superwoman because she succeeds in all areas of her life. In the following passage the description of Emma by David Kallinski, one of Emma's future partners, reiterated in various forms throughout the three volumes, sums up both her character and the characteristics of the fictional superwoman found throughout women's fiction of the last decade:

Emma possessed *natural genius*. There was no other term appropriate to describe her *incredible talent* and coupled with her *prodigious energy*, it made her formidable. Apart from her *brilliance* as a designer, she had an *innate understanding* of the public's whims, an *uncanny knack* of discerning ahead of time what they wanted and, more importantly, what they would buy. It was as if she had a daemon telling her things, and all of her ventures were *instantaneous* successes. David suspected that Emma Harte would make money at whatever she decided to turn her hand to, for *her touch was golden*. Both he and his father had been staggered at her *total grasp of financial matters* and her capacity for structuring complex monetary schemes, all of which stood up to thheir accountant's scruntiny and won his astonished approval. She read a balance sheet the same way other people read a newspaper and she could pinpoint its flaws and its virtues in a matter of minutes. She was only just twenty-one and already *she was scaling ambition's ladder with the swiftest and most determined of steps*. It seemed to David that nothing could hold her back – it would have been like trying to harness lightning, he had long ago decided. She continually managed to amaze him and he dare not speculate where she would be in ten years' time. At the top of that ladder, he conjectured, and *the prospects were dizzying*.

(*A Woman of Substance*: 547) (italics mine)

Putting aside the improbability of finding all these qualities in one person, Emma's abilities cut cross sexual stereotypes, and like the many superwoman characters who follow in her steps, the personage of Emma Harte combines feminine qualities with male-identified achievements. Her grasp of financial matters, her understanding of a balance sheet, and her ability to structure monetary schemes are identified in the text as being far from traditional feminine qualities, as is her swift movement up "ambition's ladder."

Not all superwomen, however, can cope with the confusion this sort of life style creates. Caro Harmsworth, the heroine of Freda Bright's 1983 novel *Futures*, and another type of superwoman character, is a successful young lawyer, but she has difficulty managing the contradictory qualities needed to succeed in the two worlds:

she felt like she was leading a Jekyll–Hyde existence; two sides of her, constantly alternating and mutually exclusive, waged a perpetual war. All the qualities needed at the office – toughness, suspicion, aggressiveness, the never-ending quest for personal aggrandizement – fought with those nurturing qualities called upon at home. There she must be tender, soft, pliant. And unlike Jekyll, she had no magic potion, one sip of which would effect instant transformation. Bits and pieces from one life kept dribbling into the other. (215)

Success in the male world, as Caro painfully learns and Emma knows, implies not only professional achievement but also "success in woman's role." (Janeway 1971: 110) Within the fictional framework, women who enter the male world of ambition and either forget or ignore the female quality of nurturing fail or are inevitably punished. Emma, the reader is repeatedly told, succeeds because she never forgets how important people are and how vital it is to care about others. Not long after her arrival in Leeds, Emma comes upon a man who has been knocked down by a group of boys, she chases them off, and when she sees to the man, she asks him why the boys had attacked him. When Emma learns that the act was motivated by racial hatred and she admits to not knowing what a Jew is, the man goes on to explain to her who the Jews are. She understands racial hatred in terms of class differences:

> instantly comparing the rabid class differences in England that also bred cruelty and terrible inequities.
>
> (*A Woman of Substance*: 429)

But later, during the Sabbath dinner to which Mr Kallinski invites her, she reflects:

> Why are the Jews hated? They are loving and gentle people and kind and considerate. It is despicable the way they are treated. And this was the way Emma Harte was to feel all of her life, staunchly defending her Jewish friends, constantly shocked and grieved by the excesses of naked racism that infected Leeds like the blight for many years. (440)

Her analysis of racism, anti-semitism, and class differences is, without a doubt, simplistic and presented in personal rather than political terms:

> Because people are always afraid of what they do not know, what they do not understand, the unfamiliar or the different, and that fear invariably turns to hate. Unreasoned hatred that makes no sense. In these parts the Jews are hated and defiled. . . . Ah, the human condition is strange, is it not? There are some people who hate for no reason at all. They just simply hate. They do no realize that their unjustified hatred inevitably turns inward to destroy them. Yes, it is self-destructive in the long run. (427)

The exceedingly liberal message that good triumphs over evil structures the entire narrative and, to a large extent, the superwoman character. Emma is, as the reader quickly learns, rewarded for her "goodness." The friendship that subsequently develops with the Kallinski family sets her on the way to becoming a woman of substance.

Success, however, is only one aspect of superwoman. The flipside is her ability to love and be loved. Emma Harte's failed marriages show how superwoman must work to find the rare man capable of living with and understanding the modern woman who has different needs than previously imagined. Not all men are capable of living with a superwoman. Arthur Ainsley, Emma's second husband, becomes sexually impotent in his relationship with his wife because of the unequal balance of power:

> He frequently desired her, yet his constant fear of sexual failure isolated him from her; he needed her strength and her wisdom, whilst resenting these attributes; he boasted of her achievements but was envious and insecure because he did not measure up in his own career. In his way, Arthur loved Emma. Unhappily, he also harboured many grudges against her, at the root of which was his terrible sense of powerlessness. This manifested itself in repressed rage, and sometimes he actually experienced a real hatred for her. (716)

Female powerlessness once so characteristic of women's popular fiction has now become a male attribute of many of the male characters in the superwoman novels. In Freda Bright's novel *Decisions* (1985) the heroine's husband, Jordan Croy, typifies the male character who, while he struggles against male chauvinism, is, because of his sense of powerlessness, unable to accept his wife's success:

> "I'm not much of anything, am I? I'm nobody in the world except the guy who has the privilege of being married to Super-woman Dasha Croy. Well, I don't need you to tell me that I'm strictly minor league." (220)

Whereas at one time men like Arthur or Jordan, once standard fare in women's fiction, represented the type of man women married, they are now considered as the major obstacle to a woman's fulfillment, an obstacle which can be surmounted.

Emma Harte, like the many superwomen to come, despite the odds eventually finds a man who understands and sympathizes with her abilities. When she meets Paul McGill the reader immediately knows that Emma has found the man who will turn out to be her one true love and that the balance of power lacking in her relationship with Arthur is present:

> He was taller and broader than she had realized at the Ritz, and he seemed to overpower her. He exuded a sheathed strength, an earthy and domineering masculinity that disturbed her. (*A Woman of Substance*: 651)

Only a stronger and more powerful man is able to meet with her expectations. The obvious contradiction is that Emma, like the other heroines, still finds herself in a position of, if not inferiority, lesser power. The myth of the strong, protective male has not lost any of its importance. If women are still being presented as wanting a man stronger than themselves, the desired characteristics have none the less undergone some change. The ideal hero must, in addition to being strong, understand and support a woman's non-traditional behavior. When Dasha Croy thinks about the ideal partner, her version of superman resembles that of Emma:

> Someone to whom she could entrust every thought, confide every anxiety. A partner with whom she could share her work, her deepest aspirations. Strong, Unjudgemental. Loving, Yes, loving. Ardent. Someone who would bury her with the act of physical love. Possess her totally in mind and body.
> (*Decisions*: 263)

Both texts, however, blur over the contradiction between a woman having an equal relationship with a man and being "possessed" by him. Within the context of liberation within the public sphere, the fictional heroine remains tied to the myth of man as protector. Despite the portrayal of women in positions of greater power the unresolved contradiction lies in the fact that although many of these women have achieved financial independence, they still remain emotionally dependent on men. In Aviva Hellman's 1984 novel *Somebody Please Love Me*, Cat Willingham, a top fashion model, reflects upon her husband from whom she is about to separate:

he could never have taken over the financial responsibilities for their lives. He was the dreamer, the artist, and she was convinced that he had no idea about what their expenses really were. Besides, that had been the bargain she had made with herself. She was to be the bread-winner. (60)

This same woman, who has complete financial responsibility for her family, is emotionally dependent on the man who threatens to desert her. Financial independence, which is the first step to autonomy for women, remains secondary to emotional stability and a secure sense of identity.

Superwoman, having entered the business world and found the man of her heart, must still straighten out the mess this has all created in her family circle. Bright's *Decisions* (1984) introduces the conflict a wife's career exerts on a marriage in one of the most common and familiar situations: a husband asking his wife where to find his belongings:

> In the bedroom a dresser drawer snapped shut. Then another. And another.
>
> "Hey, honey" – Jordan's voice drifted in to where she stood before the bathroom mirror putting on eye shadow – "You wouldn't happen to know where my gold cuff-links are, would you?"
>
> "No." Dasha Croy responded with an impatient shrug. No, she hadn't the foggiest notion where they were and she was half inclined to answer "Be reasonable." Honestly, she couldn't be expected to keep track of every bitsy item in his life. But her second reaction was a tweak of conscience. (7)

The next statement alerts the reader to the importance of this opening: Dasha Croy knew where her husband's things were to be found until her life changed:

> For Jordan was being reasonable, and once upon a time (not so very long ago, for that matter), she could have laid her hands on the missing cufflinks without a second's hesitation. Why, when they were first married, when the kids were small, she was the world's greatest living expert on Jordan Croy: the state of his wardrobe, the state of his mind, and what he'd had for Monday's lunch.
>
> But that was before.

Before. Before. Before.
Before her life divided so sharply into Now and Then.
Into Before and After. (7)

The path which led up to this scene is familiar. A good student at Smith College, Dasha had followed her husband to a mediocre law school, and then dropped out midway because she was afraid she would make a better lawyer than he. Out of boredom with her life as a housewife, she resumed her studies after her children were in school, did very well and obtained a law position superior to that of her husband's. The conflict arises when her work becomes more demanding and better paid than his. Unlike earlier fictional heroines however, Dasha refuses to give up her new-found freedom in order to smooth her husband's pride. The message is quite clear, if a man is unable to cope with his wife's success than the relationship must end. Guilt because of a husband's supposed loss of status is no longer tolerated.

The same thing is true when family conflicts arise out of either a woman's career preoccupations or her status as divorced women. Dasha articulates the dilemma her working poses for the family in a rather straightforward way. When trying to explain the problem she has communicating with her 13-year-old son Geoff, Dasha lays the blame on her work:

"He resents my going out to work. . . . It's as simple as that. For some reason, Geoff still expects me to be there with milk and cookies when he gets home from school." (189)

Although neither her husband's objections nor her son's unhappiness prevent her from continuing with her career plans, Dasha, as is with the case with almost all the superwomen characters, must come to terms with motherhood. In a majority of the superwoman novels the heroine is either looking for her mother, wanting to be a mother, or fleeing from her status as a mother. Shirley Conran's bestselling *Lace* (1982) begins with an abortion, a failed attempt at motherhood. After the initial introduction of the main characters, four good friends, and Lily, the young woman who had invited them together, Lily asks them "All right, which one of you bitches is my mother?" (29). Despite her successful career, Lily is obsessed with finding the woman who she believed abandoned her. Her self-image is intimately tied to the discovery of her mother. *Pearls* (Brayfield 1988) is also a story about the two heroines' discovery of their "real" mother. Bright's *Infidelities* (1986) opens with Annie's thirtieth birthday and her husband's Seth's words: "Make a wish." She mentally reviews what she might wish for, sees that she already has health, sufficient wealth, beauty, marriage. What she wishes for is a child.

Deceptions, the 1982 long-running bestseller by Judith Michael, a husband-and-wife writing team, neatly resolves the conflicts of career and family. It is the story of identical twin sisters who, having decided to switch lives for one week, suddenly find themselves drawn into unfamilar situations and emotions. Stephanie Anderson, the quieter, less secure of the two, is married to a prominent scientist and university professor she no longer understands and is the mother of two children with whom she can't cope. She attempts to escape from the problems of her marriage by exchanging places with her sister Sabrina Long-worth, the more vivacious twin, who, formerly married to an English viscount, and the owner of a hugely successful London antique and interior decorating shop, epitomizes the contemporary superwoman. Sabrina, feeling that something is missing in her life, agrees to the switch in order to escape some problems and to see how the other half lives.

The novel combines the world of children and dishes that is familiar to most of its readers, and that fantasy world of British nobility and yachts that most women supposedly dream about. The novel, the ideal fictional fantasy, allows its readers to escape the conventionality of their lives to experience a world which they know only from the television and its incessant parade of Royalty or from other equally generic novels. The reader, however, remains reassured that her life has its instrinsic value through an ending which simultaneously re-enforces the values of home, family, and female independence. Stephanie, having left her family behind to live the forbidden life of her sister, is punished for her rejection. Caught up in a story of greed and art counterfeiters she doesn't really understand, she loses her life when the luxury cruiser she is on explodes. By choosing to prolong the charade long enough to have that final dream experience on the yacht with a man she finds irresistible yet has been shown to be evil, Stephanie loses the possibility of returning to her husband and family. Sabrina, in contrast to her sister, learns the value of family. After having disclosed the deception to Garth, Stephanie's husband, she then leaves him to return to London and her former life. The message of the novel lies in the discovery Garth makes after Sabrina's departure; he understands that Sabrina is neither his wife nor his wife's sister, but an individual who combines what is best in the two: "a woman with the caring and loving of Stephanie and the independence and strength of Sabrina." (482) A marriage, the novel says, can only succeed if it incorporates change. Sabrina, representative of the new independent woman, only finds happiness when she recognizes the value of what she thought had to be rejected in order to succeed.

The separation between the home and the domestic sphere and the outside world which has always played such an important role in women's fiction continues to dominate the lives of even the most modern superwomen. Outside social or political events assume only an ambivalent or peripheral position in the narratives, and when they do appear they serve as a basis for a character's actions and to reveal aspects of her character: Dasha of *Decisions* (Bright 1985) tries a case which deals with the issue of freedom of speech and the press. Outside of a few comments on the importance of the issue of free speech, the emphasis of the narrative remains on her personal involvement and the effect this has on her life rather than on the social implications of the case.

The same thing is true when it comes to feminism or job discrimination. In *Pearls* (Brayfield 1988) the heroine, Catherine Bourton, is told by the man she works for:

> "You'll find it doesn't pay to get clever with me, young lady. What are you, one of those women's libbers? Burned your bra, have you?" (434)

The superwoman of the bestsellers acts against her inferior job status, but for the most part her inequality is linked to her personal relationships with the men in power rather than to general social attitudes and policies. Rather than attack the system, she creates parallel institutions which replicate in form those of her male counterparts. In Bradford's novels, where women compete against men in a man's world to attain the same power as men, at no point do the women question the system which engendered the inequalities nor do they question their elevated status as superwomen. This is changing however, and in recent novels explicit statements which challenge sexist behavior in the work place occur. In *Pearls*, when Catherine is finally admitted into the "Ring" as a metal trader, a job which is usually closed to women, she realizes after the customary celebrations that her acceptance is only on the surface:

> The cat-calls, the hunting horns and the football rattles – it had seemed like innocent horseplay, but underneath she sensed real hostility to a stranger who had dared to penetrate the group. (446)

Catherine not only understands that as a woman she will always be judged more harshly but also that she must not only be good in order to gain the respect of her male co-workers, but she must be better.

Since the publication of Bradford's novels important changes have occurred in the American and British superwoman novels. Not only have the characters descended into the realm of the possible but a woman's advancement and career are now being taken more for granted. Furthermore, the conflict between the female character and a man has become secondary to the problem of "finding one's self." Rather than the typical romantic conflict which is resolved by the happy union of the couple, the resolution of these women's lives only comes when self-awareness has been realized. In *Decisions* Dasha, having decided that her marriage to Jordan cannot work because he has not grown in the ways she has, replies to her lover's desire to live together with a statement which summarizes the dilemma each heroine faces and resolves:

> I expect it sounds funny, darling, but I have never in my life been truly on my own. And I think I owe myself this time to see what it's like. At least for a while. I want to see how I manage. From the day I was born I've been dependent on men. I've lived in their shadows. First my father, then Alex, then Jordan. Then after a while, Jordan began living in my shadow which wasn't much good either. But then I became dependent on you.
>
> What I'm trying to say is . . . I'd like to reach some

arrangement that's . . . oh, I don't know – more honest, more equitable . . . I think something better is possible between men and women. At least I hope so. A real partnership, a genuine balance. I want your love. . . . But I want my independence, too, if that's not a contradiction in terms.   (413)

Love and lasting relationships are not the question, but rather women's demand for understanding from the men they live with that they too have needs which extend beyond the domestic sphere. *Decisions* ends with Frank agreeing with what Dasha says, and the words "The Beginning." Throughout the corpus of superwoman bestsellers, the message is that women are no longer content to define their worth uniquely through their marital status.

The relationship women have to each other has also changed. Margaret Atwood in a May 1986 article "That Certain Thing called the Girlfriend," discusses the number of novels being published today which show women in a more positive supportive relationship to one another. In the majority of the current bestsellers being published today, women look to one another in friendship rather than competition. Whereas female friendship in the earlier novels is either virtually non-existent or else quickly turns to betrayal, today although it may still be a source of conflict it is also the salvation of the principal characters. When Lindsay in Elizabeth Forsythe Hailey's bestseller *Life Sentences* (1982) decides to attempt a pregnancy against the advice of her doctor, she calls upon her former college roommate for help. Meg is unable to meet up to her expectations, but Cissy, the outsider who had always wanted to be close to Meg and Lindsay, assumes the care of Lindsay. The three women must come to terms with what female friendship means during the course of the nine-month period. The issue of female friendship is also raised in Blume's *Smart Women* (1983). Margo, in response to her friend Clare's assumption that once one of them found a male friend their relationship would suffer says: "That's bullshit. . . . Why should we have to choose between a man and a friend?" (77) Women turn to their female friends, and not their husbands or lovers, in times of crisis to help see them through the crisis. In Conran's *Lace* (1982) the friendship between the four women is what sustains them and in Rona Jaffe's *After the Reunion*, her

1985 bestselling sequel to *Class Reunion*, Daphne, one of the four friends, comments on their continued, and in fact strengthened, friendships:

"I still think how strange and lovely it is that we're all here together, good friends, after all the things that happened to us in our lives, and not even seeing each other for so long. The first time we met, at Radcliffe, we liked or didn't like each other for such silly reasons." (420)

The French novels

Benoîte Groult, in the preface to *Les Nouvelles Femmes*, a study of the changes in the life styles of French women published by *F* magazine in 1979, writes:

"New Women" do not always lead a "new life." But they wish to, they prepare for it, they dream of it. They may not yet resemble the ideal type they imagine . . . but they no longer resemble the stereotypes of the Virgin, the admirable Mother, the Wife-Servant or the Woman who Inspires (Groult 1979; 12)

Women have begun to change their life style, she concludes, but they have not yet succeeded in changing their environment. Since Groult wrote these words, the situation of French women has changed and the conflict women experience between their desires to lead different lives and their actual day-to-day situation emerges in some of the current bestsellers written by women in France today. Unlike the positive and very pragmatic approach taken by the American heroines, however, the lives of the French women in many of the novels flounder in traditional roles that they contest but for which they find no real replacement. The French bestsellers offer only a perfunctory appearance of the "new woman." This is not to say that the French novelists deny the existence of the new woman, nor that the myth of superwoman is absent, but its appearance manifests itself primarily on the level of male–female relationships. The absence of a larger social structure which encourages or at least tolerates such "super" women is immediately apparent when one looks at the types of heroines who populate the current French best-sellers.

Other than Paul-Loup Sulitzer's *Hannah* (1985) or Françoise Dorin's female characters, few bestselling heroines have much to do with the business world or the public sphere in general. Women are either actresses or socialites, as is frequently the case in Françoise Sagan's novels, or, if they do have a professional life, it is often incidental to the narrative. In Nicole Avril's *Jeanne* (1984), Jeanne's career as a heart surgeon functions principally on the metaphorical level: a modern-day Don Juan, Jeanne captures, as much as she repairs, men's hearts. In Katherine Pancol's *Scarlett, si possible* (1985), one of the characters passes her law exams and secures a position in a prestigious law firm, but her studies and profession remain secondary to her emotional life. Unlike the American novels which feature, for the most part, adult women with children as main characters, many of the principal characters in French novels are either adolescent girls as in Marie-France Pisier's *Le Bal du Gouverneur* (1984), mothers whose children have left home and who are trying to deal with turning 40, or men as in Irène Frain's 1986 bestseller *Desirs* (1986). In Nicole de Buron's 1978 novel *Vas-y maman* (Go on Mama) (1978), the heroine Annie rebels after fifteen years of marriage. Having given up her career as a journalist when she married, she attempts to go back to it but finds that she has been absent too long. In a way not unreminiscent of the stories Tillie Olsen recounts in *Silences* (1979) Annie sets to writing a novel because it is the only thing she can do which doesn't disrupt her family life: she can still be there when the children come home, have dinner, etc. The problem arises when her novel is a success and her husband must deal with living with a bestselling author.

In her 1984 bestseller *Les jupes-culottes* (Divided Skirt), Françoise Dorin examines the changing definitions of masculinity and femininity, the effect this has had on relationships between men and women, and the problems the contemporary man faces when caught between his own traditional notions of how a woman should be and how she has changed. In contrast to the American fiction with which it shares its theme, this novel introduces the problem of male–female relationships from a man's perspective:

Hello! Enter! Please come into my life! My name is Philippe
Larcher. Yes, I know that we don't know one another, but
come in anyway! I'm alone and I want to talk. I need to talk.
(5)

The narrator, a young man in his thirties and recently divorced,
immediately introduces his problem – his recent divorce and his
subsequent inability to find a woman who is neither a "guy,"
someone who makes love and attaches no importance to the act,
or a "whore," a woman who makes love with a man out of her
own self-interest. Rather Philippe is looking for a woman who
will "permit me to be or to believe that I am a Hero." (8)

Philippe's continued insistence on the myth of the hero and his
confrontation with the independent woman provide the novel's
narrative tension. At the same time that Philippe tries to come to
terms with the modern businesswoman who demands to be
viewed as an equal, he must also re-evaluate his traditional
notions of what constitutes a male–female relationship. Initially,
he is searching for the woman he can protect and through whom
he can define his masculinity. In one episode, Lauranne's display
of her fear of flying while they are on a small airplane gives
Philippe the occasion he has been looking for to play the role of
the male protector. He expresses his satisfaction at her need of
him:

Lauranne timid and vulnerable, Lauranne a small fragile
sparrow. Me, confident. Me, calm. Me a large invisible eagle.
Things are, at least temporarily, sorted out. (232)

Her fear, however, is generalized when the airplane flies into
turbulent weather and everyone aboard is equally afraid. Order,
as Philippe perceives it, is as quickly reversed as it had
manifested itself.

The reader initially views Lauranne through Philippe's eyes.
He is drawn to her because, among a group of women invited by
his sister to their apartment, she is the only one in a skirt: "It was
her legs that I noticed first. I couldn't be mistaken. She was the
only one wearing a skirt." (16) Everything about her is elegant
and classic; her shoes are "classically elegant," her ankles,
"purebred." Moderately pretty, her face is healthy-looking
without any trace of make-up. The item, however, which

completely weakens his defenses is the glimpse he has of her lingerie:

> through the opening of her blouse what I saw was none other than that disappearing symbol of femininity: a bra . . . ravishingly honest, manifestly useless and, moreover, in gray silk. It was this last detail which moved me the most.   (17)

This aspect of his perception of the still unknown young woman emphasizes her femininity, a quality the narrator feels is rapidly disappearing. After he has gotten to know her and sees her bedroom, he sighs in relief at its feminine decor: "her room. Marvelous! It's blue and romantic beyond all hope. Ah! the satin trimmed with frills and flounces is reassuring!" (100) Philippe repeatedly allows his perception of Lauranne's femininity to guide him in his often mistaken moves. He assumes that because Lauranne looks so feminine she must conform to his male ideas of female behavior.

Lauranne, however, despite disclaiming any relationship to feminism, is neither a traditional woman, nor does she live what can be called a traditional life style. Professionally, she owns and manages a group of beauty institutes. The orbit of finance coincides with a business which caters to the particular needs of women: beauty and weight reduction. Furthermore, she lives in a household in which traditional roles have been completely reversed. Divorced and the owner of a large apartment, Lauranne shares her home with three homosexuals, each of whom contributes to the smooth functioning of their home. Doudou, the owner of the neighborhood bistro Lauranne frequents, moves into the apartment when he falls ill and is no longer able to keep up with the hectic restaurant schedule. He does the cooking, the general housekeeping and is "the woman, the soul of the household." Louis, a retired gentleman and friend of Doudou, plays the part of grandfather who tells wise stories of his past to the younger generation. Olivier, Lauranne's former husband's godson and the youngest member of household, works for Doudou and plays the role of the child in a home ruled by Lauranne:

> who is in charge, who takes responsibility, who works outside the house, who hates to do housework, but loves to come

home evenings and sit down at the table to be fêted, to find flowers in the vases and her slippers in their place.   (88)

Unlike what occurs in the American or British novels however, despite what may seem to be a complete reversal, roles are still defined in terms of traditional norms. Although Lauranne works outside the home, expects to find dinner on the table when she returns home and dislikes housework, this is simply a change of gender and presents little deviation from traditional male–female roles.

Lauranne clarifies her independent position to Philippe the moment he reveals his intentions to pursue her. She tells him that she is content with her life as it is, and that any relationship between them would be impossible: "I am unbearable for a man, being that I am one." (91) Despite such a statement, however, in a way quite reminiscent of the American or British superwoman, she goes on to tell Philippe that she prefers traditional men: "like they were imagined in the past: strong, protective, and dominating." (92) The problem as she sees it is that she is also strong, protective, and dominating, and that what Philippe is looking for is a "real" woman, something she denies being. For Lauranne a real woman is someone who manages to combine feminine and masculine qualities: the woman who has "her heart in a skirt and her head in pants." (176) Lauranne believes that to succeed professionally she must "become" a man because as a woman entry into the male world of business is closed to her. Yet, like the heroines of the British and American novels, she's also looking for what she terms a "real" man. Dorin, in an attempt to break down traditional roles, only re-enforces them by leaving the contradictory aspects of Lauranne's character unresolved.

The novel ends with Philippe and Lauranne's marriage and their resolution to redefine traditional male and female roles. They acknowledge that the myth of the independent woman and of the male Hero are not as clear-cut as might be assumed and they agree to make concessions in order to live harmoniously. Although Philippe doesn't totally reject his cowboy self-image, he quits his job as an insurance agent and opens an art gallery as his way of coping with Lauranne's business success so as not to feel that he must compete with her and the continuing expansion of her business concerns. Since Lauranne views traditional male behavior as the obstacle to a meaningful relationship between a working woman and a man, her decision to marry Philippe implies that such equality can exist. Furthermore they understand their pledge not to compete with the other as the basis for establishing an equal relationship. The novel, however, ignores the issue raised in the American novels of juggling home and career. Lauranne's family bears little resemblance to any kind of real life situation, and the couple's wealth – someone is hired to do unpleasant household tasks – and the absence of children facilitates the reassesment of their roles.

Jeanne, Nicole Avril's 1984 bestseller, defines superwoman in terms of sexual liberation, and examines the consequences of a reversal of the traditional balance of power. A slightly more human and less cruel version of Don Juan, who hunted women without consideration of either love or pleasure, Jeanne Marsilly, according to Avril, experiences his insatiable thirst for sexual conquest:

> Jeanne desired the bodies and souls of all men. Like a XVIIIth century lord she held the power of life or death that she exercised in the operating room. She plunges her hands deep into their hearts. (iv)

The modern woman in Avril's novel is defined by the God-like hold she has over men. Jeanne, an attractive 40-year-old heart surgeon, holds the lives of the men she encounters literally in her hands:

> Every day these hands plunge deep into the heart and cut the flesh. These hands which have life and death at their fingertips. (20)

Before introducing either her name or her identity, the narrator reveals Jeanne through the sexual power she exerts over men. The opening scene of the novel takes place in the bedroom of her most recent conquest. On her way out the door, she glances briefly at the man whose bed she has just shared:

> He had that fragile look of a man whom she was about to leave. Jeanne slipped out of bed and drew the sheet over the body which would soon rest in her memory. He had exhausted

in her one instant of life and his features had already disappeared into the pillow. (9)

Sex roles have been reversed, and here it is the man who is presented as fragile and the one who is being left behind. For Jeanne, in keeping with the myth of the seductress, men belong to the night and are either objects to be conquered or asexual beings. As Jeanne walks home one night she senses someone following her and thinks, "Only a man out hunting walks on your trail . . . to rob you of the joy of a walk at night." (13) A few lines later, she expands on her distrust and dislike of men: "Whoever dares to disturb her air, her water or her walk is an enemy." (14)

The reader initially discovers Jeanne through the perceptions other people have of her. Men, however, both admire and fear her. In a cafe, a drunk comes up to her and, although he doesn't know her, he immediately perceives her as a man-hunter. At a dinner party to which Jeanne is invited but doesn't attend, the guests when discussing her allude to her profession "What an idea for a supposedly seductive woman to have chosen a man's job!" (29) But for the most part, her work as a heart surgeon functions metaphorically in the text: "Jeanne Marsilly seemed to have consecrated her entire life to men. She knew how to seduce and care for them." (33) In even further contrast to the family and community orientated lives found in the American bestseller, Jeanne lives outside the limits of conventional female behavior. A young homosexual friend of Jeanne's reassures his partner that he need not be jealous of Jeanne, who is, after all, only a woman! Whereas his friend replies, "Of a woman no, I couldn't be jealous of a woman. But isn't Jeanne more than a woman?" (34).

Jeanne's defeat, however, is caused not by a man but rather by Viva, her godchild and the daughter of her best friend. Mathieu, the 18-year-old son of one of Jeanne's patients, falls hopelessly in love with her and commits suicide because he realizes the futility of his passion. Viva, in love with Mathieu and grief-stricken by his death, turns on Jeanne and blames her for Mathieu's suicide. In an attempt to regain Viva's lost affection, Jeanne accompanies her home and, outside the apartment entry, tries to discuss their differences. However, Viva refuses to be comforted and as

Jeanne reaches out to caress her cheek, she pushes her and Jeanne falls from the landing to her death. Despite her attempt to achieve independence through her sexual powers, Jeanne's inability to love ultimately brings about her demise. Thus feminine power and sexual independence can only lead to one's own self-destruction.

A third and still different view of superwoman in the French bestseller is that found in Françoise Xenakis' *La vie exemplaire de Rita Capuchon* (The Exemplary Life of Rita Capuchon) (1988). Funny yet ironic, the novel traces the life of Bernadette Gaudron, a.k.a. Rita Capuchon, who starts out as an orphan, works first as a prostitute and then as a top level fashion model, ends up as one of the richest women in the world, Nobel Peace and Literature prize winner, and the candidate chosen by both the Right and the Left to be the next president of the Republic. Rita's fabulous career begins when the woman she believes to be her mother dies exhorting her to revenge her having been raped and abandoned by Adonis Libourakis Cooper, a wealthy businessman she had led Rita to believe is her father (but who as it turns out is not). Rita marries Cooper's son after having paid a friend to stand-in as her bridegroom (a procedure which, according to Xenakis, is not only plausible but has actually occurred), plots to kill her new husband but is too late, and then presents herself to her father-in-law as his widow.

Unlike either Dorin's Lauranne who can't decide whether she's male or female, or Avril's Jeanne who is destroyed by her sexual ambivalence, Rita succeeds, in contrast to the American superwomen, in a way which is unquestionably feminine. Despite her sordid childhood – after her mother's death, she goes from orphanage to youth detention centers to prison – Rita still manages to achieve a quite spectacular life. She acquires her fortune not through her prowess in the business world but first through her manipulation of Adonis – he must accept her claim to be his daughter-in-law – and then through capturing his heart. Adonis leaves her his fortune not because he believes her story but because he is impressed with her courage and tenderness.

Love, sexual independence, and male–female relationships, rather than financial success and power or marital happiness, emerge as major concerns in the French bestsellers. Only one of the novels ends with a marriage, *Les jupes-culottes* (Dorin 1983), whereas *Un chagrin d'amour et d'ailleurs* (Mallet-Joris 1981) ends with a woman's decision to leave her husband and *Les lits à une place* (Dorin 1980) renounces marriage completely. The death of Jeanne at the end of *Jeanne* (Avril 1984) places in question the possibility of female power in sexual relationships, and by extension, over her life. And in Dorin's most recent bestseller *Les corbeaux et les renardes* (Crows and Vixens) (1988), she once again attacks marriage. The narrative follows the consequences of a mother's admonition to her two daughters that the only way to succeed in life is to marry a rich husband. Of the two daughters, only Nadège, the oldest, follows her mother's advice and ends up a wealthy but unhappily married woman. Agathe, the younger sister, soundly rejects their mother's advice, and goes out on her own to succeed as a film director.

Why is it that the superwoman image that has become so widespread in contemporary bestselling fiction in the USA was so easily exported to France in the form of women's magazines and advertising? And why, in view of the financial success of American and British superwoman novels, haven't French women writers either copied the US writers' models or produced French versions of this super modern woman? The low status accorded to fiction produced for mass consumption is one major deterrent to French women writers. Unlike journalists who write for women's publications and who have a clearly delineated audience, the novelists, in order to succeed professionally, must write fiction which will appeal to a sexually mixed audience, a problem American authors do not have to contend with. So, to a certain extent, the absence of a specifically French version of the superwoman myth in fiction has as much to do with a literary tradition which places a greater value on "universal" literature than on "women's topics" as it does with the position women occupy in society.

Literary tradition alone, however, is only one explanation. The actual social circumstances of French women also contribute to the absence of the high-powered Emma Harte type superwoman in French novels. French women, still in the process of acquiring the kind of power American heroines take for granted, continue to view superwoman in terms of actual female celebrities. Once women begin to take public success for granted, superwoman will begin to infiltrate the fictional world. Views on the subject, however, are divided. When I questioned Hortense Chabier, former publisher of Acropol Press in Paris, about the relative absence of superwomen characters in fiction in 1986 she said that although the novels which succeed are those which permit women to dream, definite boundaries must not be exceeded. Novels which depict women successfully maneuvering in the business world do not work in France: "The French public does not like a woman's success." The appearance of superwoman in the women's magazines, the consistent popularity of Françoise Dorin's novels, the exceptional success of Barbara Taylor Bradford's novels which always appear on the French bestseller lists, and the popularity of other American bestsellers not only contradict Chabier's contention but also indicate a growing desire on the part of the French feminine readership to read about a woman's success. The absence of this successful career-woman image in the fiction currently being written, interestingly enough, is remarked upon by Martine, in *Scarlett, si possible* (Pancol 1985). One of the three young women of the novel, Martine sees the United States and not France as the country where she can fulfill her professional ambitions. She reads American novels because they offer her an image of women not found in French culture:

> Lately, she has been devouring especially women's books. Translations from the American. It's not quite the thing in Pithiviers. She recognized herself in these books. She wasn't any longer the only one who wanted to see that things changed. (56)

The myth of superwoman functions so effectively in the American bestsellers, and has not yet really entered French popular fiction, because American women have been led to believe that they have achieved equality in the workplace. The representation of superwoman in France, however, is still tied to the achievements of real women in a real world. The French media, and this includes the women's press, still regards women who achieve in the business world as having done something unusual. In other words, the models of French self-made women are still being created, and once such achievement becomes more commonplace, superwoman may well become as current in French bestsellers as she is in the United States.

Conclusion

By way of conclusion, I want to try to bring together what might at times have seem like two separate discussions. In the earlier chapters I looked at the contrasting ways in which two different countries define and view a bestseller. I found that, despite almost opposing literary traditions, the movement in both French and American publishing has been, and will continue to be, towards greater control of decision-making by financial powers rather than literary along with the concentration of publishing in the hands of large multi-national companies. Despite claims to the contrary by some of the publishers with whom I spoke, the change in ownership of previously independent houses can only threaten the publishing of new and exciting literature. I also looked at the long history of women writers producing bestsellers in both France and the United States, some of the texts, and one of the major myths which structures that fiction. It became obvious that throughout the long tradition of women writing popular fiction, the texts have evolved and changed according to the ideal women have of their own liberation. Rather than now attempt a reductive type of conclusion which would force me to assign a value judgement to either the bestseller or women's popular fiction, I would like to suggest some tentative propositions as a starting point for future work.

My original project when I first began this study was to examine the ideological messages offered to women in the bestselling fiction since the mid-seventies. But it soon became obvious to me that any discussion of the fiction isolated from the context in which it is produced only gives half the picture. The bestseller, I discovered, operates on several levels, and as such is neither monolithic nor generic. Sometimes the most successful "formula" fails to produce a bestselling book; sometimes luck or events bring to the public's eye a book which might have been read by thousands rather than millions. The Thatcher government's initial ban on the publication of *Spycatcher* in England or Khomeini's condemnation and death threat to Salman Rushdie for his *Satanic Verses* are only two examples of books being catapulted to bestseller status which might otherwise have done well but not broken any records. Conversely, poor judgement or timing of the launching of a book, author–publisher dislike or simply the loss of a book in the shuffle of a publishing house's restructuring sometimes account for a book's "failure" rather than its poor writing. On the other hand, accidents aside, the bestseller also most certainly functions within the popular culture of a particular society as a reflection of contemporary concerns and provides an important understanding of the dominant ideologies of that society. The absence of the superwoman novel in France, for example, is as much a reflection of the inferior position French women still experience within both the literary world and the workplace as it is of the French tradition which marginalizes popular or mass expression. Furthermore, as I have tried to point out, written cultural products are neither static nor impervious to change, and, in fact, tend to evolve to a greater extent than economic or social structures. Gina Marchetti, in her analysis of the action-adventure film points out that particular genres

> tend to be popular at certain points in time because they somehow embody and work through those social contradictions the culture needs to come to grips with and may not be able to deal with except in the realm of fantasy. As such, popular genres often function in a way similar to the way myth functions – to work through social contradictions in the form of a narrative so that the very problems can be transposed to the realm of fantasy and apparently solved there.   (1989: 187)

The bestseller is not reducible to one particular genre in and of itself but rather functions as one of the most obvious carriers of "genre" found in popular culture. In other words, those popular fictions which touch a large part of the reading population contain within their pages contradictions which would otherwise explode into demands for radical change. The history of bestselling fiction, for example, shows a parallel between the genres the public favors and uncertain political climates.

It is at this point that the discussion of the bestseller in general meets with that of women's popular fiction. The large corpus of popular bestsellers written by women since the mid-seventies use the language of the women's movement which, watered down in its fictional rendition and devoid of much of its historical specificity and radical import, questions, and then affirms women's identity in relationship to the larger social body and their ability to function as equals. Women's bestsellers, as is the case with bestsellers in general, rarely propose a world vision which necessitates any radical change of existing social structures, yet they have told women that yes, they are capable of achieving greatness outside their traditional roles of wife and mother. But as is also the case with most bestselling fiction, genres, or to be more exact mythical representation lose their appeal or give way to new representations. In the case of the myth of superwoman, fewer and fewer bestsellers with superwomen are appearing on the lists in the United States. The three novels written by women on the 1 January 1989 *New York Times Book Review* bestseller list – Anne Rice's *Queen of the Dammed*, Danielle Steel's *Zoya*, and Rosamunde Pilcher's *The Shellseekers* – contain female heroines who live full lives, if one can call the life of the mother of vampires a normal life. As inevitably occurs when a particular type of novel is over-exploited, readers lose interest in reading the same story. It is not because women are no longer victims and seek revenge, but rather women consider success as their right. Given the almost impossible way of life the superwoman novel proposes to its readers it is not surprising that women readers are beginning to refuse the thinly veiled trap presented in the novels, out of which there is no easy exit. Prisoner of the superwoman game, a woman is expected to be and do better; she becomes her own exploiter.

Yet, as seen, in the Anglo-American novels of the late 1970s and early 1980s, superwoman was not only a normal woman but also a figure which represented the hopes of many and a means of escape from unhappy and unfulfilling lives. Rejection of the superwoman image does not, by any means, imply that women are prepared to return to their homes or give up their careers.

Rather, the awareness that life doesn't have to be so difficult has become a permanent element of current women's popular fiction.

The bestseller is, as John Sutherland (1981) concludes in his study of 1970s bestsellers, not only a potentially powerful instrument for social change which is alas too rarely exploited, it is also an equally important guide for students and critics to understanding contemporary culture. For both these reasons, it is vital for feminist critics of popular women's bestsellers to move away from judging the novels on the existence or absence of progressive messages or insisting, as Michelle Coquillat does in her 1988 study of romantic fiction, that women's popular fiction is a tool used to indoctrinate women to accept their inferior status in society. Rather, the novels must be studied as a response to the cultural hegemony of media practices which continue to depict women as one-dimensional beings – either mother/wife or aggressive businesswoman. By creating a fictional world in which women have stopped apologizing for being both mother and career woman and in fact insist that it is normal, and a world in which the combination woman/money/power is not threatening, women writers use the novel and popular fiction as a subtle but persistent challenge to a society which too often relegates women to secondary status.

Bibliography

Novels

Unless otherwise indicated in the bibliographic citation, all the translations from the French are my own.

Adams, Alice (1984) *Superior Women*, New York: Fawcett Books.
Avril, Nicole (1984) *Jeanne*, Paris: Flammarion.
Blume, Judy (1978) *Wifey*, New York: Pocket Books.
—— (1983) *Smart Women*, New York: Pocket Books.
Bradford, Barbara Taylor (1983) *A Woman of Substance*, New York: Bantam.
—— (1985) *Hold the Dream*, Garden City, NY: Doubleday.
—— (1988) *To Be the Best*, New York: Doubleday.
Bradley, Marion Zimmer (1984) *The Mists of Avalon*, New York: Ballantine.
Brayfield, Celia (1988) *Pearls*, London: Penguin.
Bright, Freda (1985) *Decisions*, London: Fontana.
—— (1983) *Futures*, New York: Poseidon.
—— (1986) *Infidelities*, New York: St Martin's Press.
Buron, Nicole de (1978) *Vas-y maman*, Paris: J'ai Lu. Originally published by Flammarion.
Caldwell, Taylor (1972) *Kings and Captains*, Garden City, NY: Doubleday.
Conran, Shirley (1982) *Lace*, London: Penguin.
Coscarelli, Kate (1987) *Living Color*, New York: New American Library.
Courter, Gay (1982) *The Midwife*, New York: New American Library.
Deforges, Régine (1983) *The Blue Bicycle*, Paris: Ramsay. Translated from the French by Ros Schwartz, London: W.H. Allen 1986.
—— (1983) *101, Avenue Henri-Martin*, Paris: Ramsay. Translated from the French by Ros Schwartz, London: W.H. Allen 1986.
—— (1984) *The Devil is Still Laughing*, Paris: Ramsay. Translated from the French by Ros Schwartz, London: W.H. Allen 1987.
Delly (1985) *Les Ombres*, Paris: Tallandier. Originally published 1925.
Denuzière, Maurice (1985) *Louisiana*, Trans. from the French by June

193

P. Wilson, London: Pan Books.
Deschamps, Fanny (1982) *La Bougainvillée*, Paris: Albin Michel.
Dorin, Françoise (1980) *Les lits à une place*, Paris: Flammarion.
(1984) *Les jupes-culottes*, Paris: Flammarion; Editions, J'ai Lu (pbk).
(1988) *Les corbeaux et les renardes*, Paris: Flammarion.
Ende, Michael (1984) *The Neverending Story*, translated from the German by Ralph Manheim, Harmondsworth: Penguin.
Frain, Irène (1982) *Le Nabab*, Paris: Livre de Poche.
Freeman, Cynthia (1981) *No Time for Tears*, New York: Bantam.
Gréville, Henry (Alice Durand) (1927) *Sonia*, Paris: Nelson. Originally published 1877.
(n.d.) *Suzanne Normis: Roman d'un Père*, Paris: Nelson. Originally published 1877.
Gyp (the Countess of Martel de Janville) (1902) *Le Fée*, Paris: Fayard.
(1905) *Maman*, Paris: Fayard.
(n.d.) *Bijou*, Paris: Nelson.
(n.d.) *Mariage de Chiffon*, Paris: Nelson.
Hailey, Elizabeth Forsythe (1982) *Life Sentences*, New York: Dell.
Hellman, Aviva (1984) *Somebody Please Love Me*, New York: Methuen.
Hull, Edith (n.d.) *The Sheik*, London: George Newness.
Isaacs, Susan (1978) *Compromising Positions*, New York: Ballantine.
(1984) *Almost Paradise*, London: Fontana.
Jaffe, Rona (1985) *After the Reunion*, New York: Dell.
Jong, Erica (1973) *Fear of Flying*, New York: Holt, Rinehart & Winston.
Kaufman, Sue (1968) *Diary of a Mad Housewife*, New York: Bantam.
Lesueur, Daniel (1912) *Gilles de Claircoeur*, Paris: Plon.
Mallet-Joris, Françoise (1975) *The Underground Game*, translated from the French by Herma Briffault, New York: Dutton.
(1981) *Un chagrin d'amour et d'ailleurs*, Paris: Grasset; Edition Livre du Poche (pbk).
Maryan, M. (1882) *Un Mariage de convenance* followed by *Hermine*, Paris: Bray & Retaux.
McCullough, Colleen (1977) *The Thorn Birds*, New York: Harper and Row.
Michael, Judith (1982) *Deceptions*, New York: Poseidon.
Mourad, Kenzié (1987) *De la part de la Princess morte*, Paris: Laffont.
Pancol, Katherine (1981) *La Barbare*, Paris: Seuil.
(1985) *Scarlett, si possible*, Paris: Seuil.
Plain, Belva (1984) *Crescent City*, New York: Dell.
Rochefort, Christiane (1961) *Les petits enfants du siècle*, Paris: Grasset.
Sagan, Françoise (1982) *The Painted Woman*, Paris: Livre de poche.
Sand, George (1987) *Marianne*, edited and translated by Siân Miles, London: Methuen.
Singer, June Flaum (1986) *The Markoff Women*, New York: Bantam.
Southworth, Emma D.E.N (1866) *The Bride of Llewellyn*, Philadelphia: T.B. Peterson & Brothers.

Spellman, Cathy Cash (1986) *An Excess of Love*, New York: Dell.
(1984) *So Many Partings*, New York: Bantam.
Steel, Danielle (1983) *Thurston House*, New York: Dell.
(1985) *Family Album*, New York: Dell.
Sulitzer, Paul-Loup, (1985) *Hannah*, Paris: Stock.
Susann, Jacqueline (1971) *Valley of the Dolls*, New York: Bantam.
Swindells, Madge (1983) *Summer Harvest*, New York: Signet edition.
(1986) *Shadows on the Snow*, London: Fontana.
Tax, Meredith (1982) *Rivington Street*, New York: Jove.
Wallach, Anna Tolstoi (1981) *Women's Work*, New York: New American Library.
Warner, Susan (1987) *Wide, Wide World*, reprinted New York: Feminist Press.
Wood, Barbara (1983) *Domina*, Garden City, NY: Doubleday.
Xenakis, Françoise (1988) *La vie exemplaire de Rita Capuchon*, Paris: J.C. Lattès.

Critical Sources

Alliot, Bernard (1984) "La Saga des 'poche,'" *Le Monde*, 23 March, pp. 17–18. (1985) "Hachette s'associe avec Harlequin," *Le Monde*, 16 February. pp. 17–18.
Alphant, Marianne (1984) "Ma Tasse de Thé avec Barbara Cartland," *Libération*, 18 October, pp. 36–37.
Andrae, Thomas (1987) "From Menace to Messiah: The History and Historicity of Superman" in Lazere, Donald, pp. 124–138.
Angenot, Marc (1984) "Ceci tuera cela, ou: la chose imprimée contre le livre," *Romantisme: revue du dix-neuvième siècle* 44, pp. 83–103.
Anon (1907) "Cinq milles femmes" in *Je Sais Tout* 15 August, pp. 159–166.
Appelbaum, Judith (1983) "The Immutable Meanings Dilemma," Paperback Talk, *New York Times Book Review*, 24 July, pp. 23–24.
Aron, Jean-Paul, ed. (1980) *Misérable et glorieuse la femme du XIXe siècle*, Paris: Fayard.
Assouline, Pierre (1985) "Triomphe pour Deux Dames," *Lire*, January, pp 37–41.
Atwood, Margaret (1976) *Lady Oracle*, New York: Simon and Schuster.
(1986) "That Certain Thing called Girlfriend," *New York Times Book Review*, 11 May, pp. 1, 38–39.
(1986) "Women's Novels" in the periodical *Open Places* cited in "The Best and the Worst", *Parade Magazine, Chicago Sunday Times*, 5 January, p. 14.
Aufderheide, P. (1985) "What are Romances telling us?" In *These Times* 6–12 February, pp. 20–21.
Bailey, Julie (1988) "Jobs for Women in the Nineties", *Ms.*, July.
Barthes, Roland (1957) *Mythologies*, Paris: Seuil.

Baudelaire, Charles (1980) "Aux Bourgeois: Salon de 1846", *Oeuvres Complètes*, Paris: Laffont, pp. 639–640.

Baym, Nina (1978) *Women's Fiction: A Guide to the Novels by and about Women in America, 1820–1870*, Ithaca: Cornell University Press.

—— (1981) "Melodramas of Beset Manhood," *American Quarterly* 33, Summer pp. 123–139.

Beauvoir, Simone de (1970) *The Second Sex*, translated by H.M. Parshley, New York: Bantam. Originally published in 1949 as *Le Deuxième Sexe*, Paris: Gallimard.

Bennet, Catherine (1987) "Conran's Barbarians," *Elle*, UK edn, August, pp. 36–40.

Bichonnier, Henriette (1985) "Les Recettes des Bon 'Mille-Feuilles'," *Marie France* August, pp. 18–21.

Blanc, Anita (1982) "Les hypermarchés confrontés au prix unique du livre," *Livres Hebdo*, 8 February, pp. 87–89.

—— (1984) "Olivier Orban. 10 ans d'edition," *Livres Hebdo*, 6 February, pp. 78–80.

Billington, Rachel (1981) *Guardian*, 5 October.

Blau, Francine D. and Ferber, Marianne F. (1986) *The Economics of Women, Men and Work*, Englewood Cliffs, NJ.: Prentice Hall.

Bolotin, Susan (1981) "Behind the Bestsellers: Janet Dailey," *New York Times Book Review*, 16 August, p. 26.

Brasey, Edouard (1982) "Hypers Leclerc: des librairies modèles?" *Livres Hebdo*, 11 January, p. 114.

Brenner, Jacques (1988) "Le prix des mots," *Le Nouvel Observateur* 5–21 April, pp. 117–19.

Brown, Helen Gurley (1988) "Letters to the Editor," *New York Times Book Review*, 15 June.

Brownmiller, Susan (1984) *Femininity*, New York: Ballatine.

Broyard, Anatole (1982) "The New Woman," *New York Times Book Review*, 10 January.

Cawelti, John G. (1976) *Adventure, Mystery and Romance: Formula Stories as Art and Popular Culture*, Chicago: University of Chicago Press.

Charat, Patrice (1988) *Le livre français a-t-il un avenir?*, Report to the Minister of Culture and Communication, Paris: La Documentation Français.

Chartier, Roger, ed. (1985) *Pratiques de la Lecture*, Paris: Rivages.

Chatman, Seymour (1978) *Story and Discourse: Narrative Structure in Fiction and Film*, Ithaca: Cornell University Press.

Chittendon, Margaret (1984) "My Say," *Publishers Weekly*, 10 February, p. 196.

Cocteau, J. (1985) Quoted in "Triomphe pour Deux Dames," *Lire*, January, pp. 37–41.

Coquillat, Michelle (1988) *Romans d'amour*, Paris: Odile Jacob.

Coward, Rosalind (1984) *Female Desire: Women's Sexuality Today*, London: Paladin Books.

Crubellier, Maurice (1985) "L'élargissement du public," in *Histoire de l'édition française*, Paris: Promodis, pp. 25–45.

Dardigna, Anne-Marie (1978) *La Press "feminine": Fonction idéologique* Paris: Maspero.

—— (1980) *Les châteaux d'Eros ou les infortunes du sexe des femmes*, Paris: Maspero.

de Closets, François (1985) "Existe-t-il un art du best-seller?", *Le Débat*, March, pp. 77–94.

Desanti, Dominique (1980) *Daniel ou le visage secret d'une comtesse romantique, Marie d'Agoult*, Paris: Stock.

Descomps, Pierre (1984) "La librairie et les autres réseaux de vente," *Livres Hebdo*, 19 March, pp. 83–85.

Dong, Stella (1981) "Selling Romances: Often Right Out of the Boxes," *Publishers Weekly*, 13 November, pp. 61–63.

Douglas, Ann (1978) *The Feminization of American Culture*, New York: Avon Books.

Eco, Umberto (1979) *The Role of the Reader*, Bloomington, Ind.: Indiana University Press.

Eribon, Didier (1984) "Des pavés pour les siécles: Un entretien avec Roger Chartier," *Le Nouvel Observateur*, 29 June, pp. 60–61.

Ertel, Rachel (1980) *Le Roman Juif Américain: Une écriture minoritaire*, Paris: Payot.

Ellis, Kate (1979) "Women read romances that fit changing times," *In These Times*, 7–13 February, p. 20.

Escarpit, Robert (1966) *The Book Revolution*, London: George G. Harrap.

—— (1970) *Le Littéraire et le Social: Eléments pour une sociologie de la littérature*, Paris: Flammarion.

Falk, Kathryn (1981) "Who Reads Romances – And Why", *Publishers Weekly*, 13 November, pp. 29–32.

Favero, Jacqueline (1984) "Dix ans de traduction littéraire en France," *Livres Hebdo*, 6 February, pp. 88–95.

Favier, Annie (1979) "Du nouveau dans le roman féminin," *Livres Hebdo*, 2 October, p. 80.

Fiedler, Leslie (1970) *Love and Death in the American Novel*, London: Paladin.

—— (1982) *What was Literature: Class, Culture and Mass Society*, New York: Simon and Schuster.

Fields, Howard (1984) "Survey Finds Eight Million New Readers in Five Years," *Publishers Weekly*, 27 April, pp. 14, 19.

Fishburn, Katherine (1982) *Women in Popular Culture: A Reference Guide*, Westport, Conn.: Greenwood Press.

Fitoussi, Michèle (1987) *Le ras-le-bol des superwomen*, Paris: Calman-Levy.

Follain, Jean (1971) "Le Mélodrame," in Tortel, *Entretiens*, pp. 35–52.

Fox-Genovese, Elizabeth (1980) "The new female literary culture," *The Antioch Review*, 38, Spring, pp. 193–217.

Frank, Jerome P. (1981) "Trade or Mass? Trying to Figure the Odds,"

Publishers Weekly, 13 November, pp. 54–56.

French, Marilyn (1986) *Beyond Power: On Women, Men and Morals*, London: Abacus.

Galumier, Jean (1972) "Sophie et ses malheurs ou le Romantisme du pathétique," *Romantisme* 3, pp. 3–16.

Gaudemar, Antoine (1984) "Vivre avec Régine Deforges," *Lire*, July–August.

Géniès, Bernard (1984) "La Malaise américaine," *Le Monde*, 23 March, p. 19.

Gilbert, Sandra (1986) "From Our Mothers' Libraries – Women Who Created the Novel," *New York Times Book Review*, 4 May, pp. 30, 32.

Greer, Germaine (1971) *The Female Eunuch*, London: Paladin.

Greer, William (1986) "Women Turn 'Professional,'" *International Herald Tribune*, 20 March, p. 1.

Groult, Benoîte (1979) Preface, *Les Nouvelles Femmes*, Paris: Mazarine.

Haedens, Kléber (1976) "Le jeu du Souterrain; La Passion des Profondeurs," in *Françoise Mallet-Joris, Dossier critique et inédit*, Paris: Grasset, pp. 95–98.

Hager, J. Henry (1906) "French Authors and Bestsellers," *The Bookman*, XXIV, September, pp. 30–32.

Hamon, Hervé (1988) "Elles Veulent tout," *L'événement du jeudi*, 14–20 July, pp. 46–71.

Heath, Stephen (1982) *The Sexual Fix*, London: Macmillan.

Heilbrun, Carolyn G. (1978) "Marriage and Contemporary Fiction," *Critical Inquiry*, Winter, pp. 309–322.

Histoire de l'édition française: le temps des éditeurs (1985) Vol. III, under the direction of Henri-Jean Martin and Roger Chartier, Paris: Promodis.

Hubbard, Rita C. (1983) "The Changing-Unchanging Heroines and Heroes of Harlequin Romances 1950–1979," in Ray B. Browne & Marshall W. Fishwick, eds., *The Hero in Transition*, Bowling Green: Bowling Green University Popular Press, 1983.

James, Clive (1980) "Princess Daisy," *London Review of Books*, Reprinted in The Penguin Book of Modern Humour, Harmondsworth: Penguin, 1982.

Janeway, Elizabeth (1971) *Man's World, Woman's Place: A Study in Social Mythology*, New York: Dell.

Julien, Antoine (1979) "Le livre et sa publicité: Un Mariage de raison," *Livres Hebdo*, 11 September, pp. 68–71.

(1979b) "Dossier," *Livres Hebdo*, 2 October, p. 79.

Kayle, Hillary S. (1979) "Booking Authors on the 'Today' Program: An Insider's Account," *Publishers Weekly*, 5 February, pp. 57–58.

Kelley, Mary (1979) "The Sentimentalists: Promise and Betrayal in the Home," *Signs* 4, Spring, pp. 434–446.

Larnac, Jean (1929) *Histoire de la littérature féminine en France*, Paris: Kra.

Lauretis, Teresa de, ed. (1986) *Feminist Studies/Critical Studies*,

Bloomington: University of Indiana Press.

Lazere, Donald, ed. (1987) *American Media and Mass Culture: Left Perspectives*, Berkeley: University of California Press.

Lodge, Sally (1979) "Janet Louise Roberts," *Publishers Weekly*, 5 February, p. 12.

Lottman, Herbert, R. (1979) "Publishing in France," *Publishers Weekly*, 30 April, pp. 53–102.

(1984) "What's New in France's Publishing Capital," *Publishers Weekly*, 9 November, pp. 22–40.

McDowell, Edwin (1982) "The Paperback Evolution," *New York Times Book Review*, 10 January, pp. 7, 27.

McNall, Sally Allen (1981) *Who is in the House? A Psychological Study of Two Centuries of Women's Fiction in America, 1795 to the Present*, New York: Elsevier.

Mann, Peter (1981) "The Romantic Novel and its Readers," *Journal of Popular Culture* 1, Summer pp. 9–18.

Marchetti, Gina (1989) "Action-Adventure as Ideology," in Ian Angus and Sut Jhally (eds) *Cultural Politics in Contemporary America*, London: Routledge, pp. 182–97.

Marin, Minette (1984) "A Bandwagon Named Desire," *The Observer*, 19 February.

Martin-Fugier, Anne (1980) "La Maîtresse de maison" in Jean-Paul Aron, (1980) pp. 117–36.

Maryles, Daisy and Symons, Allene (1983) "Love Springs Eternal," *Publishers Weekly*, 14 January, pp. 53–58.

Maryles, Daisy and Dahlin, Robert, eds. (1981) "Romance Fiction," *Publishers Weekly*, 13 November, pp. 25–64.

Masinton, Martha and Charles G. (1977) "Second-Class Citizenship: The Status of Women in Contemporary American Fiction," in *Essays on English and American Life and Literature*, New York: New York University Press, 1977.

Mattelart, Michèle (n.d.) "Women and the Cultural Industries," UNESCO, Documentary Dossier 23.

Mercier, Michel (1977) *Le Roman Féminin*, Paris: Presses Universitaire de France.

Miles, Rosalind (1987) *The Female Form: Women Writers and the Conquest of the Novel*, London: Routledge & Kegan Paul.

Miles, S. see Sand, George

Miner, Madonne M. (1984) *Insatiable Appetites: Twentieth-Century American Women's Bestsellers*, Westport Conn.: Greenwood Press.

Missoffe, Michel (1932) *Gyp et ses amis*, Paris: Flammarion.

Modleski, Tania (1984) *Loving with a Vengeance: Mass-produced fantasies for women*, New York: Methuen.

Murphy, Brendan (1987) "A Nation of Readers: The best-seller list in France is a serious business," *The Atlantic*, August, pp. 21–25.

Mussell, Kay (1984) *Fantasy and Reconciliation: Contemporary Formulas of Women's Romance Fiction*, Westport, Conn.: Greenwood Press.

Nadeau, Maurice (1985) "Simone Signoret romancière," *La Quinzaine*

Littéraire, 16–28 February, p. 15.

Nagourney, Peter (1982) "Elite, Popular and Mass Literature: What People Really Read," *Journal of Popular Culture 1*, Summer, pp. 99–107.

Nathan, Michel (1985) *Anthology du roman populaire, 1836–1918*, Paris: 10/18.

Noffsinger, Loretta (1982) "Her Romance Novels Popular in 14 Nations," *The Champaign-Urbana News Gazette*, 21 March, B-15.

Olivier-Martin, Yves (1980) *Histoire du Roman Populaire en France*, Paris: Albin Michel.

O'Neale, Sondra (1986) "Inhibiting Midwives, Usurping Creators: The Struggling Emergence of Black Women in American Fiction," in Teresa de Lauretis, *Feminist Studies/Critical Studies*, Bloomington: University of Indiana Press, pp. 139–156.

Ozouf, Mona and Ferney, Frédéric (1985) "Et Dieu Créa le Best-Seller: Un Entretien avec Pierre Nora," *Le Nouvel Observateur*, 22 March pp. 66–68.

Papashvily, Helen Waite (1956) *All the Happy Endings, A Study of the Domestic Novel in America, the Women Who Wrote it, the Women Who Read it, in the Nineteenth Century*, New York: Harper & Brothers.

Pattee, Fred Lewis (1940) *The Feminine Fifties*, New York: D. Appleton-Century Co.

Pawling, Christopher, ed. (1984) *Popular Fiction and Social Change*, New York: St Martin's Press.

Poirot-Delpech, Bertrand (1984) seminar on the best seller, Ecole de Hautes Etudes en science sociales, Paris.

—— (1985) "Dans le maquis des best-sellers," *Le Monde*, 23 March, p. 18.

Poulain, Martine, ed. (1988) *Pour une sociologie de la lecture: Lectures et lecteurs dans la France contemporaine*, Paris: Cercle de la libraire.

Prial, Frank J. (1985) "The World's Most Popular Book Show: Five Million Viewers in Prime Time," *New York Times Book Review*, 29 September, p. 3.

Prudon, Hervé (1984) "Qui a Peur des Best-sellers?" *Le Nouvel Observateur*, 29 June, pp. 60–63.

Rabine, Leslie W. (1985) "Romance in the Age of Electronics: Harlequin Enterprises," *Feminist Studies* 11, 1, Spring, pp. 39–60.

Radford, Jean, ed. (1986) *The Progress of Romance: The Politics of Popular Fiction*, London: Routledge & Kegan Paul.

Radway, Janice A. (1981) "Utopian Impulse in Popular Literature: Gothic Romances and 'Feminist' Protest," *American Quarterly* 33, Summer, pp. 140–162.

—— (1982) "The Aesthetic in Mass Culture: Reading the 'Popular' Literary Text," in *The Structure of the Literary Process*, Amsterdam: Benjamins.

—— (1983) "Women Read the Romance: The Interaction of Text and Context," *Feminist Studies* 9, 1, Spring, pp. 53–78.

—— (1984) *Reading the Romance: Women, Patriarchy, and Popular Liter-*

ature, Chapel Hill: University of North Carolina Press.

Reuter, Madalynne (1984) "Talk with Mitchel Levitas: Can N.Y. Times Book Review and Publishers See Eye to Eye?" *Publishers Weekly*, 2 March, pp. 18, 23.

Rihoit, Catherine (1983) "Les Milliards des Marchandes d'Amour," *Marie Claire*, August, pp. 24–32, 66.

Robine, Nicole (1982) "Les jeunes travailleurs et la lecture," *Livres Hebdo*, 11 January, pp. 56–57.

Robinson, Lillian (1978) *Sex, Class and Culture*, Bloomington: Indiana University Press, 1978.

Rosenberg, Carol Smith (1984) "Their Writing was Suspect," *New York Times Book Review*, 22 January, p. 16.

Rosset, Pierette (1986) "Lire en Vacances," *Elle*, 25 August, p. 20.

Russ, Joanne (1973) "Somebody's Trying to Kill Me and I Think It's My Husband: The Modern Gothic," *Journal of Popular Culture* 6, Spring, pp. 666–689.

Sacase, C. (1986) "Les Femmes aux Avant-Postes," *Biba*, August, pp. 113–115.

Sarde, Michèle (1983) *Regard sur les Françaises*, Paris: Stock.

Sauvy, Anne (1985) "Une littérature pour les femmes," in *Histoire de l'édition française*, Paris: Promodis, pp. 444–453.

Schuwer, Philippe (1987) *Editeurs Aujourd'hui*, Paris: Retz.

Seaver, Jeanette (1984) "Le livre française aux Etats-Unis: un léger mieux," *Livres Hebdo*, 20 February, pp. 56–57.

See, Lisa (1984) "June Flaum Singer," *Publishers Weekly*, 15 June, pp. 84–85.

Shatzkin, Leonard (1982) "La crise de l'édition aux Etats-Unis," *Livres Hebdo*, 29 March, pp. 62–63.

Slama, Béatrice (1980) "Femmes écrivains," in Jean-Paul Aron, *Misérable et glorieuse la femme du XIXe siècle*, Paris: Fayard, pp. 213–248.

Smith, Bonnie G. (1981) *Ladies of the Leisure Class: The Bourgeoises of Northern France in the nineteenth century*, Princeton: Princeton University Press.

Solé, Robert (1986) "Deux millions de concubins," *Le Monde*, 14 March, p. 24.

Spencer, Jane (1986) *The Rise of the Woman Novelist: From Aphra Benn to Jane Austen*, Oxford: Blackwell.

Stern, Madeleine (1985) "Two 19th Century Feminists and their Publishers." unpub. paper given at the 1985 MLA conference, Chicago.

Sutherland, John (1981) *Bestsellers: Popular Fiction of the 1970s*, London: Routledge & Kegan Paul.

Syndicat Nationale de L'Edition (1986) "Données statistique sur l'édition de livres en France," supplement to *Livre Hebdo* 46, 9 November.

Taylor, Helen (1986) "Gone with the Wind: the mammy of them all," in Jean Radford, pp. 113–138.

Thiesse, Anne-Marie (1984) *La Roman du quotidien: Lecteurs et Lectures Populaires à la Belle Epoque*, Paris: le Chemin vert.
(1985) "Les infortunes littérataires," *Actes de recherche en sciences sociales*, November, pp. 31–46.
Thurston, Carol M. (1985) "Popular Historical Romances: Agent for Social Change? An Exploration of Methodologies," *Journal of Popular Culture* 1, Summer, pp. 35–49.
(1987) *The Romance Revolution: Erotic Novels for Women and the Quest for a New Sexual Identity*, Urbana: University of Illinois Press.
Tinayre, Marcelle (1933) *La Femme et son secret*, Paris: Flammarion.
Tompkins, Jane (1985) *Sensational Designs: The Cultural Work of American Fiction 1790–1860*, New York: Oxford University Press.
Tortel, Jean, ed. (1971) *Entretiens sur la paralittérature*, Paris: Plon, 1971.
Valance, Georges and Lhaïk, Connie (1985) "Les Françaises se rebiffent," *Le Nouvel Observateur*, 29 November, pp. 52–55.
Walters, Ray (1982) "Paperback Talk," *New York Times Book Review*, 17 January, p. 35.
(1985) *Paperback Talk*, Chicago: Academy Chicago Publishers.
Weibel, Kathryn (1977) *Mirror, Mirror: Images of Women Reflected in Popular Culture*, Garden City, N.Y.: Doubleday.
Williams, Raymond (1981) *The Sociology of Culture*, New York: Schocken.
Wood, Leonard A. (1983) "Nearly 1 in 5 Adult Americans Bought a Book in Early December," Gallup Poll, *Publishers Weekly*, 28 January, p. 43.
Woodruff, Juliette (1985) "A Spate of Words, Full of Sound and Fury, Signifying Nothing: Or, How to Read in Harlequin," *Journal of Popular Culture* 2, pp. 25–32.

Index